SARATOGA
QUEEN OF SPAS

Island Spouter in Geyser Park

SARATOGA
QUEEN OF SPAS

A History of the Saratoga Spa
and
The Mineral Springs of the Saratoga and Ballston Areas

by

Grace Maguire Swanner, M.D.

Former Medical Consultant to the Saratoga Spa

Published by
North Country Books, Inc.

SARATOGA
QUEEN OF SPAS

ISBN 0-932052-66-5

Library of Congress Cataloging-in-Publication Data

Swanner, Grace Maguire, [date]
    Queen of spas: a history of the Saratoga Spa and the
mineral springs of the Saratoga and Ballston areas / by
Grace Maguire Swanner.
        p.   CM.
    Bibliography: p.
    Includes index.
    ISBN 0-932052-66-5
    1. Health resorts, watering-places, etc.—New York
(State)—Saratoga Springs—History. 2. Health resorts,
watering-places, etc.—New York (State)—Ballston Spa
—History. 3. Saratoga Springs (N.Y.)—History. 4.
Ballston Spa (N.Y.)—History. I. Title.
RA807.N7S85   1988
974.7'48—dc19   88-12441
                                                          CIP

Published by
North Country Books, Inc.
Publisher—Distributor
18 Irving Place
Utica, New York 13501-5618

To my grandchildren,
Timothy, Suzanne and Matthew Swanner,
this book is affectionately dedicated.

Portico, Hall of Springs, looking south

Contents

Acknowledgments

I wish to thank the following people who helped and encouraged me in the preparation of this book.

Mary Ann Lynch, who encouraged me to undertake the task of researching and writing this history of the Saratoga Spa.

New York State Office of Parks, Recreation and Historic Sites, Saratoga State Park Division, for supplying the pictures of the Saratoga Spa reproduced in this book.

George Bolster for his kind permission to use the pictures from his fabulous collection of Saratoga photographs.

George Burns for permission to use pictures he took at the Saratoga Spa.

Beatrice Sweeney, who made available correspondence with the New York State Historian, including some of her personal correspondence on the visit of Sir William Johnson to Saratoga documenting the date of his historic visit.

Carl Edwards, chemist at the Saratoga Spa, who checked for accuracy the chapters "Composition of the Waters" and "Origin of the Waters."

The late Violet Dunn, Saratoga County Historian, who made available to me valuable records on the Kayaderosseras Patent as well as the original patent.

The late Clayton Brown, Historian of the Town of Greenfield, to whom I am indebted for material on the Glass Factory of Mt. Pleasant.

William Kelly, Regional Manager, Saratoga-Capital District, New York State Office of Parks, Recreation and Historical Preservation, Joseph King and the other personnel of the Department, who so generously supplied me with material on the Saratoga Spa and the mineral springs.

Milford Lester, whose knowledge of the springs of Saratoga, especially the Vichy and Quevic springs, was of inestimable value to me.

Jean Stamm and the several fine librarians at the Saratoga Springs library, as well as those of the other libraries where I conducted my research. These included the New York State Library, the Boston Public Library, the Skidmore College Library and others.

Minnie Bolster, past president of the Saratoga Historical Society, for supplying me with valuable information on the springs.

Irene Duval for her interest and her patience and accuracy in typing the manuscript.

Preface

Saratoga Springs has a very rich and interesting history. Its roots are in its springs. Had it not been for these fine mineral springs, there would have been no Saratoga Springs as we know it today with its many-faceted and colorful past. Certainly there would have been no Saratoga Spa.

The Saratoga Spa came into existence through a long, painful process that called for persistent, dedicated hard work against odds on the part of many interested and devoted people. Spencer Trask, George Foster Peabody, Franklin Delano Roosevelt, Walter McClellan, Oskar Baudisch, Bernard Baruch, the many able members of the Saratoga Spa Commission and other capable and talented people all made significant contributions toward making the Saratoga Spa the "Queen of Spas," and to them and the many other devoted and dedicated people who have been a part of this history, we owe a debt of gratitude.

It is my firm conviction that the history of this magnificent and unique spa with its unsurpassed mineral springs is worthy of documentation and recording. Over the years I have discussed this matter with various people who were much better qualified than I for undertaking such a task. Several indicated that this project was on their agenda of things they would like to do before they died. One, Cyrus Elmore, for many years Superintendent of the Saratoga Spa and one of its most loyal supporters, was very serious in his intent to accomplish this. James Benton, one time mayor of Saratoga Springs and an authority on the mineral springs of the area, had actually started work on the project.

However, as the years have passed, one after another of these fine people have all passed on, until, at the present time, the number left who have been associated with or witnessed the history of the Saratoga Spa over these many years is practically nil.

It is for this reason, and none other, that I have undertaken the task of "putting together" the history of the Saratoga Spa and the mineral springs of Saratoga and Ballston: the conviction that it should be done and that I seem to be one of the few people who has lived long enough to have witnessed over half a century of its development.

An Opening Word

In June 1932, I had just finished my third year in medical school and was eagerly looking forward to a summer in Saratoga Springs. The famous Saratoga Spa was being placed under medical supervision for the first time. A large sum of money had been appropriated by the New York State Legislature to make the spa the greatest in the world. The carefully selected Saratoga Springs Commission had made a thorough study of this spa and many other famous spas of the world. They had engaged the world's most knowledgeable people to study the various aspects of the issue and had come up with a well thought out plan for the development of what they believed would be a spa worthy of the fine mineral springs of the Saratoga area. They had plans for constructing magnificent buildings and for developing and landscaping the grounds of the spa reservation to make them functionally and artistically the finest possible.

Interested in the waters as health agents, the Commission provided a sound plan for scientific research on the mineral waters. They were aware from their own experience with European and other spas and from a large amount of research, that these waters were a potential source of health and well-being for the citizens of New York State and the nation.

With their phenomenal vision and foresight, the Commission had provided what was necessary to bring to fruition the dream of a great health spa. A man superbly qualified for the job, Dr. Walter McClellan, was selected as medical director. Graduated from Harvard medical college with honors, experienced in basic research at New York City's New York Medical Center, he had toured Europe's famous mineral springs to study various uses of the waters. He had been impressed by the splendid results the European balneologists were getting in patients being treated for heart disease, arthritis and other conditions. He was anxious to scientifically study the Saratoga mineral waters, firmly believing that they were equal, if not superior, to any of the natural mineral waters of the world. The year 1932 was McClellan's first at the Saratoga spa.

On a June morning in 1932, two medical assistants came to the spa to work with Dr. McClellan in a research program he had devised. The two medical assistants were Eric Joslin, a classmate of mine at medical school, and myself. We were both understandably excited at the prospect of spending the summer vacation away from our books at such a delightful place as the Saratoga Spa working with a man of Dr. McClellan's caliber.

The research program Dr. McClellan had planned for the summer was to determine the effect of the mineral water baths on blood pressure. It was the first of many studies on the mineral waters to be undertaken over the more than twenty years that he would spend at the spa.

Literally hundreds of people were checked by us over the summer. Each day we took blood pressures on selected patients before, during and after the mineral water bath. Various bath temperatures and lengths of time in the bath were studied. The results were later tabulated and published in *The New York State Journal of Medicine*. Like many other studies undertaken at the spa, this study showed that the mineral water baths had a favorable effect on blood pressure.

In the 1930's, the vast majority of the clientele at the Lincoln Bath House were European-born Jews. As a people they understood spa therapy. For many generations their ancestors had included mineral baths in their health programs. These patients appreciated the mineral baths and were absolutely convinced of their value. Actually, they did much to convince others who had had no previous experience with spa therapy of its real value. It is an interesting fact that the majority of spa visitors suffered from high blood pressure and it was gratifying to follow their progress during the summer. As a rule, they were greatly benefited by the course of mineral baths as evidenced by reduced blood pressure and improvement in their general physical condition.

There was one little Russian-born woman who particularly interested me. When I took her blood pressure, the mercury was still pounding as it registered 300 millimeters on the manometer. That was as high as the reading on the manometer scale went. The question was, "How much higher could her blood pressure really be?" In spite of this, she was very happy and tripped about the bath house as spry as could be in her shawl, flat shoes and babushka, a typical European peasant type. One day a very professional looking gentleman came into the medical office and gave me his card. It read: _____, M.D. ____ Park Avenue, New York City. He informed me that he was interested in knowing how his mother was doing with her blood pressure. I informed him that the doctors at the spa were following only "service" cases, and that his mother was probably under the care of a private physician in the city. Just at that moment, my little Russian lady went by the door, and this very affluent-appearing professional gentleman said, "There is my mother now." To say that I was surprised is a great understatement. Where but in the U.S.A. could one go in one generation from the simplest immigrant to a professional with an office on Park Avenue?

In direct contrast to this lady there were at the Washington Bath House (in 1932 the Roosevelt Bath Houses had not yet been built) people at the other end of the social and economic spectrum; industrialists, celebrities, racing people and many others. All came to the spa to enjoy its benefits.

These waters, I thought at the time, are very democratic. They have no favorites. They benefit the rich and the poor, the famous and the unknown, the sick and the well alike. They are lavish with their health giving benefits. What a truly American institution.

1

What Is a Spa?

Queen of Spas is a title indisputably deserved by Saratoga. The Saratoga Spa possesses all of the attributes associated with a great spa: those qualities endowed by nature and those which have resulted from the efforts of man.

The question may reasonably be asked: "What is a spa?" By definition of authorities in the field of spa therapy, a spa is a place where one goes to maintain or restore one's health. It is usually located at the site of a mineral spring or other natural resource which may be used as a therapeutic agent. This latter would include peloids (muds which have been shown to be beneficial in the treatment of various diseases, as, for example, arthritis), plentiful sunshine, salubrious climate and the like. To be located where facilities for desirable living conditions and for recreation are available is an added benefit.

In addition to the qualities bestowed by nature, spas usually have amenities provided by man for utilizing the natural therapeutic agents found in the area. These include drink halls, fountains and bath houses with accommodations for utilizing the waters, muds and other agents used in treatments. Also provided are facilities for physical exercise such as gradual walks, golf courses, tennis courts and the like. A good spa must have provision for recreation and entertainment. In the modern sense a spa is a place where all forms of treatment, spa therapy, rest, exercise, diet and recreation, may be integrated and tailored to the needs of the individual.

The ideal spa is a place away from home where one may go in the interest of health to get away from the routine of modern life with its many pressures and frustrations; where one may relax and renew one's physical vigor and emotional resources; where emphasis is on physical and emotional well-being rather than on anxiety-producing concerns of occupation, business or family problems, and where the atmosphere is cheerful and relaxed.

The Saratoga Spa fulfills all of these criteria and more. In short, Saratoga is rightly considered, by those who are in a position to judge, to be the world's finest spa.

The word "spa" traces its origin to a town near Liege in southeast Belgium in the Ardennes near the German border where a spring of chalybeate (iron) water is found. Its fame dates from the year 1326 when an ironmaster of the town of Collin le Loupe, having heard of a fountain in the woods with health-giving properties, went there in hopes of finding a cure for his ailments. His hopes were rewarded; he was cured. To show his gratitude for this miraculous restoration of health, he founded at the spring or fountain as it was called, a health resort which has since become one of the most fashionable watering places in the world. The place was called Espa, which is the old Walloon word for fountain. From that has come the word spa as we know it in English. The original Espa has since become so popular that the word spa is now used to designate all similar health resorts.

Aerial view of the Saratoga Spa showing the Gideon Putnam Hotel in upper left corner; Administration Building and Hall of Springs in center; Recreation Center, upper right and Roosevelt Baths on the right

Roman Baths,
Aix-les-Bains, France

2

Spas in History

*"Light of heart approach the shrine of health
So shalt thou become with body freed from pain."*
—Old Roman inscription on the Bath of Caracalla.

Spas and mineral waters have an ancient history. They have contributed to the health and well-being of man for thousands of years. The origin of balneo-therapy, the practice of using the waters of various springs, pools, or rivers for the treatment and cure of disease, predates recorded history by many years. The practice developed independently among various and unrelated cultures in different parts of the world. Man has been drinking the waters of the earth and bathing in them with confidence in their therapeutic qualities for as long as he has existed. Archeological findings in areas of Asia substantiate the fact that people there bathed in mineral springs during the Bronze Age, about 3000 B.C. Artifacts have been unearthed in all parts of the world, and especially in those areas where naturally occurring mineral springs are found, that provide evidence that ancient people bathed in the waters and used them internally as well.

There is strong evidence that many of the natural waters of springs were ascribed religious significance and were believed to have mystical powers. This is not strange when one realizes that they appear to have sprung mysteriously from the ground or rock. Man instinctively drank these waters and bathed in them and, finding that they relieved the ailments from which he suffered, quite naturally attributed the miracle to the beneficence of a god. In ancient cultures in every part of the world are found traditions of miraculous healings following the use of the waters of mineral springs either from drinking or bathing or both.

Throughout history mysticism has permeated the atmosphere of spas in legend and folklore. From early records uncovered in Egypt we find accounts of water being used in bathing as a sacred rite. In many of the world's religions are similar accounts. Such use of water for immersion and ablution was to wash away not "metabolic toxins," but spiritual guilt. The Orthodox Jewish rite of bathing is perpetuated in the Christian sacrament of Baptism as a symbol of spiritual cleansing.

Miracles ascribed to springs have continued even to modern times. In 1859 at Lourdes, France, a fourteen-year-old peasant girl reported seeing the Virgin Mary in a grotto and being shown a hidden spring. The Virgin said to the girl, "Go drink at the spring and bathe in its waters." Soon thereafter, miraculous cures were reported from the use of the water. Lourdes has since become a famous shrine and is visited by hundreds of people every year.

In history recorded in the Bible, springs and wells played a very important role. One of the oldest spas in the world is at the hot springs of Tiberius in Israel. There is a reference to them in the Bible (Joshua 19:35) where the Hebrew word for hot springs, *chamat* or *hammath*, is used to describe a settlement at the place. It was beside the well of Haran that Rebecca met Isaac. The gospel of St. John tells of how great multitudes of blind, halt and withered came to the pool of Bethesda in Jerusalem where the first to enter the water after an angel had troubled it, was healed of whatever disease he had. The pool of Siloam was also a shrine of healing. There is the story of Elisha miraculously curing Naaman, captain of the host of the king of Syria, of his leprosy, as recorded in II Kings 5:10. "And Elisha sent a messenger to him saying, Go and wash in Jordan seven times, and thy flesh shall come again to thee, and thou shalt be clean."

In his writings, Josephus mentions the thermal baths of Calirrhea near the Dead Sea. These baths were used by Herod the Great during his illness and were made famous by him. At Ala-Shehr, the Philadelphia of the New Testament, are springs which have been in use since the third century B.C. and are still in use today.

The Greeks had many famous spas, all of which were believed to be presided over by gods. In Greek mythology remarkable healings were attributed to mineral springs. The ancient Greeks believed that their waters had supernatural mystical powers because the springs were the dwelling place of gods. Shrines were erected at the sites, and the springs were dedicated to Hercules, the mythological God of Springs.

At Epidaurus, located in a valley in the mountains of the Peloponnesus on the east coast of Greece on the Aegean Sea, is located a very famous spring. It is here that Asclepius, the God of Health, was said to have been born. A beautiful temple was erected here in his honor and a sanatorium was built where visitors from all over the world came to be treated by famous physicians who used the mineral water both for bathing and drinking. Their regime also included diet, exercise and rest, with a liberal amount of religion. Miracles performed by the gods were given credit for the cures that resulted. The grateful patients left offerings at the spring which were used to enhance the grounds with beautiful structures. In the fourth century A.D. a theater was built seating 14,000 people which may still be seen today. It was built in the form of a large circle with tiers of seats rising from the stage two hundred feet to the top. It is said that the acoustics are so extraordinary that a whisper on the stage can plainly be heard at the highest seat.

Other health centers called *Asclepieia* were built near mineral springs throughout Greece. The Greeks placed great emphasis on physical fitness.

From the Greeks the Romans adopted the concept of the healing power of water along with the worship of Asclepius as the God of Health and Healing. They built a temple for him on the Tiber and translated his name from Greek Asclepius to Roman Aesculapius. They also built temples at their springs, making them health centers. One of the most famous of these was at Bains on the Bay of Naples, a beautiful site between Vesuvius and the sea. Here many celebrities, including Virgil, Horace and other poets and statesmen, came to restore their health.

Water played a very important role in the lives of Romans who developed the cult of the bath to a high degree. They built magnificent bath buildings that were both public and private. Most were controlled by the state and were available to all Roman citizens at a nominal charge.

The Romans made good use of the mineral springs found in the lands of their extensive conquests. At its zenith in the second century A.D., the Roman Empire reached from Scotland to the Sahara, and from westernmost Spain to the Euphrates. The names of many places in Europe are reminiscent of their origin two thousand years ago as Roman spas. Aschem, Aix and similar names are derived from the ,Latin word *aqua*. Aix-en-Provence (d'Aquae Sextiae) in southern France and Aix-les-Bains in Savoie in the French Alps are examples of establishments built by the Romans which are today active, flourishing spas. At Aix-les-Bains one can still see the remains of the original Roman baths which have been carefully preserved by the Division of Antiquities of the French government. These baths are now incorporated in a carefully constructed area of the Marlioz Institute, a modern spa which serves an international clientele.

At mineral springs found throughout the lands of Roman conquest, soldiers drank the waters and bathed in them. Frequently a garrison would be left at the place as a permanent outpost. The waters and the facilities built by the Romans would be used not only by the Roman soldiers but would also be enjoyed by the people of the area.

When the Romans, after invading the continent of Europe, reached Britain in the first century A.D., they found a number of springs. In what is now Wiltshire they found, on the banks of the Avon at the site that is now the city of Bath, some warm springs emerging from a fault in the volcanic structure of the earth's crust. According to legend, these springs had first been discovered in 863 B.C. by Prince Bladud, son of the ancient British king, Lud Hudibras,

*Mohawk Indians
at the High Rock Spring*

Chalybeate Spring near Saratoga (the High Rock) 1787. Taken from the first picture ever made of Saratoga Springs, it appeared in the Columbian Magazine *of March 1787*

the father of Shakespeare's King Lear. The prince, who became afflicted with a skin disease thought to be leprosy, was driven from the court and finally became a swineherd. While watching his swine that had become afflicted with a horrible skin disease, he observed that they wallowed daily in the waters of some warm springs for relief. Finally, when he saw that they were cured of their skin disease, he tried bathing in the waters himself. He was eventually cured of his "leprosy" and was able to return to the court and finally became king. Later he visited the springs which had effected his cure and built a city around them. The Romans believed these springs to be sacred. They named the place Aquae Subis and designated Minerva the patron saint. Over the swamps they built elegant baths, as well as a theater, a temple of Apollo and other structures. The remains, which were uncovered in the eighteenth century, are among the best preserved Roman baths to be found anywhere. These included facilities with all the apparatus for warm and vapor baths and hot air chambers used by the Romans in the heyday of their culture. Aquae Subis was famous thoughout the Roman Empire, and was supported and enjoyed by the Romans until the fall of their empire in 477 A.D.

Many artifacts of Roman origin have been found at the site of springs throughout Europe and as far south as the Sahara. At Baden and other places excavations have revealed evidence of a Roman establishment under the protection of the Goddess Venus. Later, as Christianity replaced paganism, Saint Veronica was substituted for Venus.

The Indians of the Americas were great believers in the miraculous healing powers of mineral waters. Montezuma spent time at Agua Hedionda, a spa just east of Cuantla, where he was carried by the Aztecs in a feather-lined litter across the mountain Popocateptl from Tenochtitlan (today Mexico City). Here he bathed in the spring and sipped its waters, and recuperated from his strenuous existence in Tenochtitlan. In 1605, the Spaniards founded a health-cure settlement at the spring, making it a fashionable spa to later become known to Americans and Europeans alike.

The Iroquois Indians of New York State believed the High Rock spring to be sacred, for they believed that their great god Manitou had stirred the waters, thereby endowing them with health-giving properties. They jealously guarded the spring and kept its existence a secret from the invading white man for as long as possible.

The quest of the Spanish explorer, Ponce de Leon, for the proverbial "Fountain of Youth" has been known to us all since childhood. From time immemorial there have existed legends of such springs and fountains which became the symbol of man's search for youth and eternal life. The Semitic concept of the "Water of Life" was associated in an East Indian legend with an earthly paradise or Garden of Eden. In this garden was to be found the Fountain of Youth which had the power of restoring youth to the aged. The fountain was placed somewhere in India where, traditionally, the Garden of Eden was thought to have been located.

The idea was kept alive over the centuries and was introduced from the

Orient into European folklore and literature. In the twelfth century Alexander de Bernai published an epic poem in which he described the conquests of Alexander the Great in Asia. He gave a detailed account of a Fountain of Youth in whose waters fifty-six aged followers of Alexander were restored to the status of thirty year olds.

Antonio Herrar, in his complete and reliable early history of the West Indies, tells of an early Indian myth of a sacred fountain which had the power to restore youth to the aged. Columbus and his men returned to Europe from the New World with this legend of the Indians. There was circulated a story of an island named Boicuca (Bimini) on which was to be found a spring of water of such amazing power that old men drinking of it were made young again. It is now believed that the legendary Fountain of Youth about which Columbus brought back information to Europe actually existed on the Island of South Bimini in the Bahamas. At the present time it is a small spring lying beside a road leading to the airport.

Incredible as it may seem, all of these legends, both East and West Indian, had an enormous impact on the European mind. The stories gained an astonishing credibility over the years. It is not surprising, therefore, that Ponce de Leon set out on his fateful journey. It was believed at the time that Columbus had visited India, and the tales he brought back confirmed the location of the proverbial Fountain of Youth as actually existing in the Garden of Eden in India. Historians believe that Ponce de Leon had no doubt of the existence of a Fountain of Youth. He felt that he had reliable information and had total confidence in his endeavor as he set out for what he believed to be the Asiatic far east. Such was the power attributed to springs and their miraculous waters.

Mysticism no longer permeates the atmosphere of springs, as it did in legend and folklore. The "miraculous" results experienced by visitors to spas are now being explained on a scientific basis. Such trail blazers as Simon Baruch, Walter McClellan and Oskar Baudisch, to mention only those who have been associated with Saratoga Spa, have done much to explain scientifically the physiological effects of the mineral waters on the human body. According to Licht, "The empirical effectiveness of balneotherapy is best documented by the fact that dozens of European spas have enormously longer continuous histories than any other type of medical institution."

3

Geology of the Saratoga Area

"Mountains are earth's undecaying monuments."
—"The Notch of the White Mountains"

Since the history of the mineral springs at Saratoga is so intimately associated with the history of the rocks from which these springs have their origin, it may be of interest to review the geology of the area.

In order to better understand the changes which the earth's crust has undergone during the years since its beginning, geologists have devised the geologic time table. This table, or scale, divides the known history of the earth into five eras, dating from the Archeozoic, the earliest, to the Cenozoic, the present era. These eras are further subdivided into periods, each of which marks a stage in the growth and development of the earth and its living inhabitants, both plant and animal. The time scale is shown in the accompanying table on the following page.

The very earliest period in the earth's history is usually referred to as the Precambrian. It includes all of the time between the birth of the planet Earth and the beginning of the Cambrian period of the Paleozoic Era, or about 85% of the four and a half billion years since the earth came into existence. Very little is known about this time. It is clouded in mystery. It bore very little resemblance to the earth as we know it today. There was no life, save the most elementary forms that began to appear toward the end. Man did not appear on earth until much later. If the total geologic time scale were to be compared with a calendar year, man would not appear until one hour before midnight on December thirty-first.

GEOLOGIC TIME TABLE

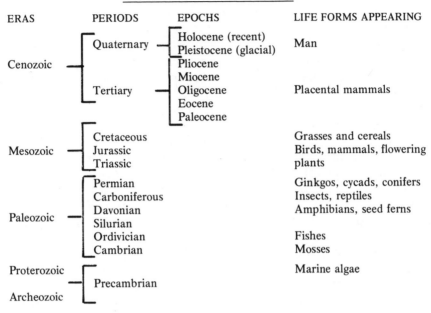

ERAS	PERIODS	EPOCHS	LIFE FORMS APPEARING
Cenozoic	Quaternary	Holocene (recent)	Man
		Pleistocene (glacial)	
	Tertiary	Pliocene	
		Miocene	
		Oligocene	Placental mammals
		Eocene	
		Paleocene	
Mesozoic	Cretaceous		Grasses and cereals
	Jurassic		Birds, mammals, flowering
	Triassic		plants
Paleozoic	Permian		Ginkgos, cycads, conifers
	Carboniferous		Insects, reptiles
	Davonian		Amphibians, seed ferns
	Silurian		
	Ordivician		Fishes
	Cambrian		Mosses
Proterozoic			Marine algae
	Precambrian		
Archeozoic			

During the Precambrian period the whole eastern half of North America lay under a primeval sea. Sediments poured into this shallow sea from land masses, the exact location of which is not certain. As these sediments accumulated they solidified into sedimentary rocks. It was during this period that the most ancient rock formation of New York State, the Grenville, was laid down. The name derived from a town in Canada where the formation was first observed. Grenville strata, piled in layers, in some places up to many thousands of feet, form the basement layer of the area. The thickness testifies to the fact that the era lasted many million years. It does not necessarily follow, however, that the ocean was thousands of feet deep. The sea floor gradually settled as sediments accumulated, which means that there was not necessarily deep water at any time. The character of the sediment indicates that the ocean was for the most part shallow.

After accumulation of the Grenville sediments great masses of molten rock were forced into them from the depths of the earth below. The sediments were subjected to enormous pressure with the result that they were crystallized, converting the beds of limestone into marble and the sand into quartz. This process is known as metamorphism.

At some period in early geologic time a great cataclysmic event occurred. The earth's crust, in what is now eastern Canada and northeasten United States, was subjected to immense pressure from within. The exact time and nature of this event is not known. However, there exists unmistakable geologic evidence that such an event actually did occur. It covered many thousands, possibly millions, of years. It may have been the result of a collision of drifting continental land masses, causing pressure to be exerted against the Grenville rocks resulting in some of the rocks buckling downward to great depth and others thrust upward to a distance of many thousands of feet. As a result of this event, whatever it might have been, a mighty mountain range was formed. This range, one of the oldest on the face of the earth, is known as the Laurentian Range. It has its origin in Labrador and covers most of eastern Canada. A spur crosses the St. Lawrence River at Thousand Islands and enters New York State. Here the mountain mass divides into five more or less parallel ranges reaching from Lake Champlain on the east to the Black River on the west, and the Mohawk Valley on the south. This structural feature of being arranged in long, nearly parallel ridges or ranges, is probably due to numerous faults or fractures within the earth's crust. These five mountain ridges form the rugged Adirondack Mountain chain and the great Adirondack Wilderness. The wilderness comprises about one fourth of the total area of New York State and is about the size of the state of Vermont. Within it, in addition to the five mountain ranges, are found more than 1,500 lakes and ponds of numerous shapes and sizes, many rivers and streams, gorges of various types and a primeval forest.

The ranges of the Adirondack Mountain chain run approximately parallel to each other from northeast to southwest. They are, on an average, eight miles apart. The history of the Saratoga Spa is concerned only with the two easternmost of these ranges, the only ones to traverse the Saratoga quadrangle. The most easterly of these is the Palmerton Range which has its origin in Sugarloaf Mountain on the shore of Lake Champlain. It runs south-southwest along Lake George, crosses the Hudson River, which has cut a channel through it near Glens Falls, and continues south in Saratoga County to Saratoga Springs where it can plainly be seen in that part of the town where the mineral springs are located. The name Palmerton is that of a band of Indians who settled in the area now known as Wilton which had earlier been called Palmerton. The other range, the next one to the west, is the Kayaderosseras Range. It also rises near Lake Champlain in the area of Crown Point and runs south into the western part of Saratoga County. This range derives its name from the old Indian hunting ground which it traverses.

After the Precambrian (Grenville) rocks were laid down there followed a period of millions of years during which the region was above sea level. It is known that in ancient times the Adirondack Mountains were much higher than they are today, probably as high or higher than the Himalayas of today. Over the years erosion has removed thousands of feet of surface material.

During the early part of the next geologic era, namely the Cambian period

PERIOD	FORMATION	SECTION	DESCRIPTION OF FORMATION
Quaternary	Glacial		clay, sand, gravel larger stones
Ordovician	Canajoharie		shale and limestone
	Glens Falls		shales and limestone
	Amsterdam		limestone
Cambrian	Little Falls		limestone and dolomite
	Hoyt		limestone, dolomite Cryptozoan fossils
	Theresa		dolomite sandstone
	Potsdam		sandstone
Precambrian	Grenville		metamorphic crystalline rocks

Columnar section of the geologic formations of the Saratoga area.

of the Paleozoic Era, the sea again impinged on the area, coming in from the east and spreading westward. At no time did it cover the dome of the Adirondacks, only the edges. Marine sediments were deposited in the water, layer upon layer over millions of years. The depth of the water varied from time to time, though it was never very deep. The fossils found in the deposits are those of shallow-water animal life.

The earliest geologic deposit to be laid down in this Cambrian sea was the Potsdam sandstone. This rests directly on the Grenville precambrian crystalline rocks, the basement layer of the area. It consists mainly of an accumulation of coarse sand and gravel.

Above the Potsdam formation are found transition beds of sediments gradually phasing from sandstone to dolomite limestone for a thickness of from ten to two hundred feet. This formation is known as the Theresa Passage by some geologists, including Ruedemann. By others (Clarke 1910) it is designated as the Galway formation, named for the town of Galway where it is well represented.

Overlying the Theresa formation is a hard, light gray, compact series of layers which were laid down in the upper (late) Cambrian sea. According to Colony (1930) they are composed chiefly of very massive beds of dolomite, rough in texture, gray in color and made up of closely interlocking crystals of dolomite. This formation is known as Little Falls dolomite (limestone) and is the last Cambrian rock to be laid down.

The lower more calcareous, fossiliferous layer of the Little Falls dolomite which lies directly over the Theresa Passage is considered by some geologists to be a separate phase of the formation. Ulrich and Cushing, in 1910, termed this phase the Hoyt limestone, named for the Hoyt quarry four miles west of Saratoga Springs where it is plainly seen. In this layer are found beds of well preserved specimens of cryptozoön fossils. It was originally believed that these forms belonged to the animal kingdom, hence the name cryptozoön (hidden animal). Later they were assigned to the vegetable kingdom when it was determined that they were a form of algae, the earliest, lowest form in the vegetable kingdom. An unusually fine display of these upper (late) Cambrian fossils may be seen in an exposed Cryptozoön reef a few miles west of Saratoga Springs in Lester Park where a tablet with the following information has been erected.

> "The fossils on the surface of this rock are the remains of marine plants or algae which grew on the bottom of the ancient Cambrian sea. They are among the oldest plants of the earth. They grew in cabbage shaped heads and deposited lime in their tissue. This ledge has been planed down by the action of the great glacier which cut the plants across showing their concentric interior structure. The scientific name of the plant is *Cryptozoön Proliferum Hall*."

One half mile south of Lester Park are the Petrified Gardens where extensive cryptozoön beds may be seen. These beds are the off-shore sea bottom of the Paleozoic (Cambrian) sea which covered the area many million years ago.

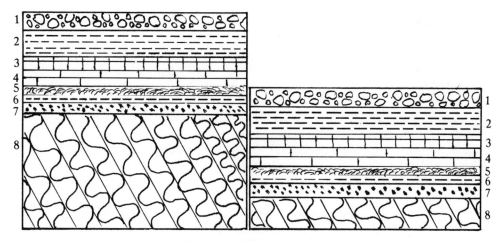

Diagram of Saratoga Fault

Formations: 1. Glacial drift; 2. Canajoharie; 3. Amsterdam; 4. Little Falls; 5. Hoyt;
6. Theresa; 7. Potsdam; 8. Precambrian.

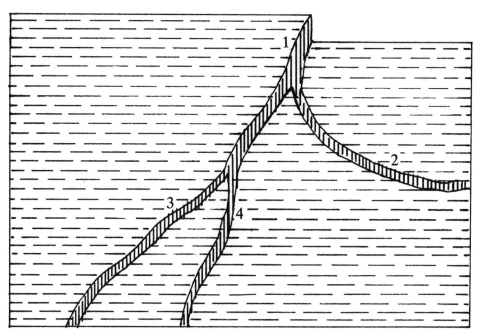

Diagram of the McGregor Fault and its branches
1. McGregor Fault; 2. Gurn Spring Fault; 3. Woodlawn Fault; 4. Saratoga Fault.

The conditions existing at that time were obviously favorable for the growth of these prehistoric life forms which flourished in this shallow sea water. Over a period of time, the lime secreted by these plants built up reefs which preserve these forms so beautifully to the present day.

A striking feature of this limestone formation shown clearly at the Petrified Gardens is the series of solution channels which occur throughout the area. These channels have been enlarged by the solution of limestone along the joint planes or cracks. This is of interest in relation to the mineral waters of the area since the mineral waters are known to circulate in these channels in the Little Falls limestone.

After the Cambrian period, northern New York was again raised above sea level, and there followed a long period of erosion before the area, except for the Adirondack "island," was again submerged under the Ordovician sea. During this period more of North America was covered by the sea than at any other time except during the Precambrian period. The deposits laid down in the Saratoga area in the early part of this period were mainly limstone and are designated the Amsterdam limestone. During the latter part of the period, the sediments deposited as the sea floor sank were mostly muds and sands. These formed shale and sandstone making up the formation known as the Canajoharie shale.

Transition beds of mixed shale and limestone between the Amsterdam and Canajoharie layers are known as the Glens Falls formation.

No deposits more recent than the Ordovician period are found in the Saratoga quadrangle. It is, therefore, assumed that the area was not submerged beneath sea level again except for a brief period during the Quaternary period, and that, after being upraised after the Ordovician period, it has continued as dry land ever since.

The rocks of the Saratoga region are cut by a series of faults. These faults are the result of breaks in the rock or fractures in which the rock on one side of the fracture has slipped above or below the rock on the other side so that the strata are not continuous, the level of the strata being higher on one side of the fracture than on the other.

Just when these great faults were formed is not certain. It is likely that they are the result of more than one disturbance. It is believed that some minor faulting occurred during the Precambrian time. It is likely that considerable faulting occurred during the Paleozoic era after the depostion of Ordovician sediments when the Adirondack "island" was elevated and the margins sagged below the level of the sea.

Two large main faults cross the Saratoga quadrangle. The westernmost of these, the Hoffman's Ferry fault, crosses the extreme northwestern corner of the quadrangle. There are related subsidiary faults running roughly parallel and to the east of it. The second major fault is the McGregor fault, so named because its great 1,400 foot scarp may be seen along the east side of Mt. McGregor, having Precambrian rocks on the upthrow side and Canajoharie shale on the downthrow side. This fault extends north, as a very visible feature

Upthrow side of Saratoga Fault which forms the background for High Rock Park

A portion of the Great Reef of Cryptozoon Proliferum at the Petrified Gardens near Saratoga Springs

of the landscape, to Lake George where it forms a prominent scarp along the west side of the lake, passing westward away from the lake a little farther north. South of Mt. McGregor near King's Station, about four miles north of Saratoga, a branch fault sets off from the main fault toward the northeast. This is the Gurn Spring fault. About a mile north of Saratoga Springs the main McGregor fault divides into subsidiary faults. One of these, the Woodlawn fault, runs off in a southwest direction. Another branch, the Saratoga fault, continues into Saratoga Springs where it is intimately related to the springs of the area. It may plainly be seen to the west of the High Rock Spring where its upthrow side, composed of Little Falls dolomite, forms a backdrop for the area of High Rock Park.

At the present time we are in the last great period included in the geologic time scale, the Quaternary period of the Cenozoic era. At the beginning of this period a major climatic event occurred due to the fact that the immense ice sheets of the Pleistocene age spread over the northern part of North America and Europe. Nearly four million square miles of North America were covered with ice of depths sufficient to cover the highest mountains. There were three great centers on the North American continent from which the ice flowed. The easternmost of these, the Laurentian ice sheet, spread from northern Canada down over New York State covering the entire state with the exception of the southern shore of Long Island.

Over the estimated one half to one and a half million years of the glacial era, ice sheets advanced and retreated several times, resulting in inter-glacial periods when the climate became warmer and vegetation flourished.

There occurred during the ice epoch a scouring and planing of the terrain by the ice and the debris frozen in it. Great amounts of material, ranging from small rocks to large boulders, were carried by the ice in its movements. This accumulation was spread over the land as the ice receded. The debris deposited varied from region to region and made up the surface soils and sub-soils overlying the bedrock in the area. It consisted of sands and clays and also of coarse fragments of gravel and larger stones and boulders derived from mountainous areas. The thickness of this till varies from one place to another. In some areas it is scarcely visible while is others it reaches a depth of two hundred feet.

The effect of glaciation may plainly be seen in Lester Park and the Petrified Gardens where the surface rocks of the area have been planed down to the level of the cryptozoon reefs, producing a spectacular exposure of these remarkable beds.

As the final ice sheet retreated northward it left in its wake bodies of water occupying the valleys. Some of these were of considerable size. One of the larger ones was known as Lake Albany. It reached as far south as Kingston and as far north as Whitehall, totally covering the Saratoga area. Deposits laid down in this lake by streams which flowed into it consisted of fine clays and sand. They now form the topsoil of the region.

When Lake Albany subsided to the 320-foot level, the Saratoga plain emerged as land surface. This marked the end of the glacial period.

The streams of the area, Kayaderosseras Creek and Coesa (Geyser) Creek, had their origin in the glacial period. Both emptied into Lake Albany until it subsided. They then eroded their way through the glacial debris and rock of the region to form their present channels.

The mineral waters of the Saratoga region are found in a natural reservoir in the sandstone or dolomite layers of the earth's crust, namely the Amsterdam limestone, the Little Falls dolomite and the Hoyt limestone. They occupy channels and cavities formed by the solution of the limestone in these rocks. The channels are connected on different levels by passageways making it possible for the waters to circulate freely throughout the whole area. As they circulate they find egress to the earth's surface at a fault that connects with the surface. The cause of the rise of the water in natural flow is due to the carbon dioxide gas with which the water stored in the channels is saturated. When an opening is found in the rock at or near the surface, the gas released from the water forces the water to rise and flow out on the surface. It is interesting to note that wherever the mineral waters are found, Canajoharie shale forms the surface layer of rocks. Because it is impervious to water, the shale prevents the mineral water from reaching the surface except along fault lines where the surface is broken. In the same way, surface water is prevented from reaching and mixing with the mineral waters.

It can be seen that for many years since the earth was formed, nature has produced geologic formations that have made possible the existence of the mineral waters of Saratoga.

4

Composition of the Mineral Waters

"She wieldeth her wand and a potent sway,
Distilling, with magical alchemy
These healing waters, all may quaff.
To her is given the guardian care
Of the living fountains pure and fair;
Ever—forever—to blend and measure
The portions that form the crystal treasure."
—"The Song of the Fountain"

The question may reasonably be asked, "What is a mineral water?" It is a fact that all waters, with the exception of carefully distilled waters, contain certain salts. So the question arises as to what extent the water must contain dissolved minerals in order that it may be called a mineral water. This amount has been set at fifty grains per gallon. It will be seen from accompanying analyses that the Saratoga mineral waters fit comfortably into this category.

The composition of the Saratoga mineral waters has remained fairly constant over the years. From the simple crude analyses of the early years to the sophisticated, accurate determinations of modern-day chemists, the analyses have shown the presence of the same constituents in approximately the same amounts and proportions. That all of the waters from all of the springs have the same source is apparent since they all contain the same constituents and vary from one another only in their concentration and relative amounts of these constituents. The waters containing the highest content of minerals are those coming from the deepest wells which are the wells in the Ballston area. These wells are the farthest south of the active mineral springs. It has been found that the depth necessary to drill through the strata to strike mineral water increases from north to south. The wells in the Ballston area are deeper than those in Saratoga and the waters have a higher content of minerals. The wells at the Geysers are deeper than those in the city of Saratoga Springs and they are stronger in minerals and carbon dioxide gas. Individual components may be erratic in their distribution and may not follow this pattern absolutely. It will be noted, for example, that the Old Red Spring is higher in iron (ferrous bicarbonate) than is the Hathorn #1 Spring which is farther south. It is this relatively high iron content which is one of the reasons that has caused the Old Red Spring to be known as the "Beauty Spring" since the iron it contains can be readily assimilated by the human body in the treatment of anemia.

In most of the springs, sodium chloride (table salt) is the most abundant dissolved substance. A notable exception is the Old Red Spring in which the content of the calcium salt (calcium bicarbonate) exceeds that of the sodium salt. This may explain why this water has proven so effective in the treatment of skin disease. Years ago calcium was frequently a component in prescriptions for skin lesions.

Calcium bicarbonate, magnesium bicarbonate, sodium chloride and potassium chloride form the bulk of the dissolved substances in the waters. It is thought that the alkaline earth compounds, calcium and magnesium carbonates as well as iron carbonate found in the waters, are derived from the limestone rocks in the area. The presence of carbon dioxide gas in the water makes it better able to dissolve these substances from the rocks through which they pass.

Lithium in the form of lithium chloride was first discovered in the Hyde Franklin Well in Ballston Spa. The discovery led to a campaign advertising the fact and proclaiming lithium to be very important medically. Needless to say, this led to increased patronage of the well. Lithium is used today for certain diseases of the nervous system.

Dr. John Steele was the first to detect iodine in the mineral waters. When this element was discovered in the President Spring in High Rock Park the name of the spring was changed to the Iodine Spring. We know today that iodine is a very important element in our bodies. It is especially involved in the metabolism of the thyroid gland.

In addition to the minerals mentioned above, the waters contain compounds of barium, ammonium, bromine and, in common with all natural waters of whatever origin, they contain variable small amounts of silica and alumina, probably derived from the rocks in which they are stored under the ground.

A striking feature of the Saratoga mineral waters is the fact that they contain only a negligible amount or no sulfate. In no way can they be labeled "sulphur waters."

Carbon dioxide gas is an outstanding feature of the Saratoga waters. It is this component that gives the waters their palatable taste. Part of this gas is combined with certain elements forming bicarbonates. This combined portion is not apparent on observation. Some of the gas is combined with the water itself, making the water slightly acid and, therefore, better able to dissolve certain substances contained in the rocks through which it passes. As the water approaches the surface from the depths of the earth it is under less and less pressure as it rises. This allows the gas to escape from the water in the form of bubbles. This escape continues after the water reaches the surface until, finally, the amount of gas remaining in the water is equivalent to the volume of the water, that is, the water holds in solution only one volume of the gas after it has stood for some time at atmospheric temperature and pressure. As the gas is given off, the water becomes less acid. This results in the settling out of such substances as calcium, magnesium, and iron carbonates previously dissolved from the rocks through which the carbon dioxide saturated water passed while underground. These substances settle out as sediment in a glass if the water is being used as a beverage or, if the water is allowed to flow on the ground, the carbonates form a lime-like substance known as travertine or tufa seen around the fountains.

The amount of carbon dioxide gas in the water varies from well to well, the average being three or four volumes of gas to one volume of water. Some wells have decidedly more. The Lincoln Spring water is one of the most highly charged waters. It is the water from this group of springs that is used for the mineral baths given at the spa bath houses.

A significant part of the beneficial effect the waters have on the human body may well be due to the so-called "trace" elements they contain. These are elements which are contained in such minute quantities that they are scarcely detectable and can often be demonstrated only by very refined spectrochemical techniques. Until about fifty years ago these elements were considered to be of little, if any, importance to the body. However, their function in the human body is now being recognized as increasingly important as more research is done. With the advent of the spectroscope, new techniques have been available and a remarkable picture of these elements in the mineral waters has been revealed. It has been found that these trace elements are important, even vital, in the functioning of all living organisms including humans. Baudisch tells us that one part of manganese in forty million parts of water can determine the life history of certain fungi, and that one part of iodine in twenty-five million parts of water is vital for the health of London.

Among the many trace elements that have been found in the Saratoga mineral water are boron, bromine, chromium, cobalt, copper, gallium, iron, lithium, manganese, molybdenum, nickel, lead, radium, strontium, tin, thallium, zinc and zirconium.

Strock studied the composition and origin of these waters from a geochemical standpoint by quantitative spectrochemical analyses of groups of elements, especially trace elements, isolated chemically from the waters as well as from the rocks of the area. He was the first to find zirconium in these or any other mineral waters. He also detected the presence of tin, manganese, cobalt and nickel.

Interesting research on trace elements was carried on at the Saratoga Research Institute by George Heggan and Carl Edwards in the 1950's. The work was done in conjunction with the Albany Medical College under a grant of the U.S. Public Health Service. The study was directed primarily at the

Immersion in Lincoln Spring showing accumulation of carbon dioxide bubbles on the skin

trace element content of human and animal species for the purpose of detecting and measuring significant differences, if any, between normal and cancerous tissue. By means of the spectroscopic method they determined trace elements in animal and human tissues and made some very important observations on the presence and relative amounts of trace elements in both normal and cancerous tissue.

That the Saratoga mineral waters are radioactive has been known for many years. Radium was extracted for the first time in 1898 by Madam Curie, from ore mined in the Johahimstall Mine in Bohemia. Two years later, Herr Dorn, a German, discovered the existence of radon, a radioactive gas generated from radium.

Thereafter, a number of scholars discovered that radon was contained in the waters of various spas. Bad-Gestein, a spa in Austria, despite having a chemical composition not much different from that of pure water, was known to have remarkable curative powers. Its action was a mystery among researchers until it was shown that the water contained radon. Dr. Sandler, a young scientist, carried on active medical research on this water and showed that it had a favorable effect on patients suffering from arthritis, gout and many other diseases which had been considered incurable.

The Japanese have measured radon concentration in their spas and have set up an Institute for Radioactive Spring Research at Ikayama University to carry on full-scale research. It was found that inhabitants who lived for many years near Misasa Spa, a powerful radioactive spa in Japan, show a lower rate of sterility and lower mortality from cancer as compared with inhabitants of other districts.

Radon has also been proven to be effective in other conditions such as rheumatism, circulatory disorders and hypertension. Institute scientists note that the positive effects obtained at their spas are not solely due to radon, but are also the result of the waters' dissolved materials and its mechanical and thermal effects on the body.

In his research on radioactivity, Dr. McClellan found that the radon in the Saratoga mineral waters is absorbed through the skin. He determined that the mild degree of radioactivity present in these waters is "insufficient to produce any damage, temporary or permanent, to any living organism."

A report on the waters by the Bureau of Mines, Washington, D.C. states that the radioactivity is due in an unusual degree to dissolved radium salts, therefore, they contain a permanent agent which will produce emanations indefinitely.

In 1913, Dr. Paul Haertl made the following observations: "All deep natural mineral springs derive much of their virtues, aside from their mineral and other contents, from radioactivity. This is a term that is used a great deal for advertising purposes, but there are instruments for exactly measuring the radioactivity. The estimate made by the Bureau of Mines in Washington does not present the full radioactivity of the springs at Saratoga because samples were obtained under conditions unfavorable for exact determination. I am convinced that many of the emanations of the waters now forcibly expelled from the borings are lost through the agitation of the water."

The value of the presence of radioactivity in the mineral waters has been a moot question for some time. The final word on the matter has not as yet been written. However, there is much evidence to show that the radioactivity has a favorable physiologic effect on the human body. Unfortunately, the springs at Saratoga have been penalized by over-zealous laws on radioactivity requiring that signs be displayed warning that the waters might be injurious to health because of the radium content. How ridiculous and unfair can laws be? If the mineral waters have deleterious physiologic effects, they have yet to be demonstrated!

It is not beyond the realm of reason that at least part of the favorable results obtained by the use of mineral waters, previously not explainable on the basis of then current scientific knowledge, may be due to the radioactivity of the waters. Could this not be the reason that the artificial mineral waters, which seemingly are the exact chemical counterpart of those found at springs, do not have the same beneficial effect?

The iron content of the mineral waters was of special interest to Dr. Oskar Baudisch. He came to the Saratoga Spa in 1935 as Director of Research. His research on the Saratoga mineral waters dated back to 1923 when he was associated with Yale University and later with the Rockefeller Institute for Medical Research. As an authority on magneto-chemistry, he worked on the iron molecule. In the course of his research he investigated the iron contained in Saratoga mineral water. He demonstrated that the iron contained in the water, in spite of the relatively small amount in solution, exceeded much larger amounts in therapeutic value as a remedy for anemia. This effect he showed to be due to the fact that the peculiar internal structure of the specific iron molecule contained in the water was similar to that of the iron molecule contained in the hemoglobin of blood. For this reason the iron in the water can be readily assimilated in the body and is, therefore, more readily available to the body than are other forms of iron.

That the composition of the Saratoga mineral waters is complex is indeed an understatement. As time goes on and more scientific discoveries are made, we are finding out that these waters are truly complex. At the present time our empirical knowledge of their value far exceeds scientific explanation.

Mineral springs have been enjoyed by mankind because they have improved and restored health through the ages. Perhaps some day our scientific knowledge of these waters will equal our empirical knowledge, providing the answer to the question of why these waters produce the beneficial results they do.

A chart showing the analyses of the waters of Saratoga Spa can be found in the Appendix on page 284.

5

Origin of the Mineral Waters

"He sendeth the springs into the valleys,
which run among the hills."

—Psalm 104:10

For many years, geologists have speculated on the problem of the origin of the Saratoga mineral waters. Though several logical theories have been proposed, the question remains unanswered. To date, no one theory has satisfactorily answered all of the questions involved.

Dr. Steele, a resident of Saratoga Springs who had studied the Saratoga mineral waters intensively, wrote in 1838 in his book on the waters, "Much interest has been excited about the source of these singular and interesting waters, but no researcher has as yet satisfactorily answered the mystery." He concluded, after some speculation, "Its production is therefore unaccountable."

According to geologists, waters coming from beneath the surface of the earth are classed in three groups: *meteoric* - waters which are derived from rainfall, *magmatic* - waters contained in igneous rocks which were formed by crystallization of the molten mass evicted from deep within the earth, and *connate* - waters derived from sedimentary rocks formed by the laying down of sediments in ancient seas.

Controversy has arisen as to which of these three sources fits the case of the Saratoga mineral waters. The final answer will probably be a combination of all three.

Dr. T. Sherry Hunt, Chemist of the Geological Survey of Canada, in an article entitled "Chemistry of Natural Waters," published in the *American*

Journal of Science and Arts in 1865, believed that these waters, as well as other mineral waters he studied in the eastern United States and Canada, are derived from Paleozoic strata laid down in ancient seas. That is, he believed them to be connate.

Dr. Charles F. Chandler, in a paper published in the *American Chemist* magazine in 1871, expressed the view that the mineral springs at Saratoga probably have their origin in the Potsdam sandstone layer of rock underlying the area. He believed that the surface waters of the Laurentian hills flowing down into the earth penetrate this porous sandstone and become saturated with minerals derived partly from the rocks and partly from the sandstone layer above. He did not explain the presence of the carbon dioxide gas, saying only that "down in the rocky reservoir the water is charged with gases under great pressure."

Another early publication on the source of the Saratoga mineral waters is that by Charles F. Fish published in 1881 in the *Popular Science Monthly*. In this article he discussed two different theories held by scientists at the time.

Advocates of the first theory note that there is a great watershed lying to the west of Saratoga Springs in which are found many ponds, lakes and streams. To the west, hills and mountains rise to several hundred feet above sea level. All of the streams which drain this region flow to the east. The various strata of the west side of the McGregor fault also dip in this direction. Thus it is believed that the subterranean drainage is in the same direction. The advocates of this theory believe that the waters of this area permeate the soil and the underlying strata of rocks resulting in the disintegration of the rocks and the solution of their various constituents in the water. In the process, new compounds are formed with the evolution of carbon dioxide gas which dissolves in the water increasing its solvent power, enabling it to dissolve more material from the rocks. The water flows downward and eastward until it reaches the Saratoga fault where it is able to escape through the crevices in the rocks and rise to the surface. Thus by the simple law of gravitation and hydrostatic pressure the waters reach the surface of the ground as springs. The head pressure to accomplish this is furnished by the water stored in lakes and ponds on the higher altitude. The advocates of this theory contend that the minerals in the mineral water are those that were contained in the ancient seas in which the deposits forming the rocks were laid down. Thus they believe the waters to be connate.

The advocates of the second theory, the deep-seated origin theory, agree with adherents of the first theory that the source of at least some of the water comes to the fault from the elevated land to the west. They disagree, however, on the source of the minerals which they contend are not the result of percolation through the rock, but rather have a deep-seated source. They believe that, until the water reaches the fault, it is unimpregnated with minerals and gas. They propose that the fault extends downward into the very fiery depths of the earth and that, since the substances contained in the waters closely resemble those substances which appear when volcanoes erupt, the source is similar: the depths of the earth. So, the source of the minerals and gas in the mineral waters is believed to be the molten interior of the earth, obtained by the process of sublimation and subsequent absorption. They contend that the waters are magmatic in origin and further substantiate this theory that impregnation occurs at the fault by the fact that wells driven in the ground west of the fault yield fresh water.

Dr. James Kemp, in a paper entitled "The Mineral Springs of Saratoga," published in 1912, discussed at length the various theories on the source of the mineral springs. He rejected the idea that the springs derived their mineral content from ancient sea water contained in the local strata, citing the absence of abundant brine springs in the area. In considering the source of the carbon dioxide gas in the water he expressed the opinion that the most likely source would be expiring volcanic or igneous action, noting that the copious emission of the gas is one of the characteristic features of inactive volcanoes. He considered the volcanic plug at Northumberland, about ten miles northeast of Saratoga Springs, to be significant in this connection. The plug is a volcanic mass first recognized as such in 1901. It is the only purely volcanic rock to be found anywhere in New York or New England west of the Connecticut valley. Dr. Kemp was convinced that the plug was truly volcanic. He admitted that no one could attribute the carbonic acid gas in the mineral water to the Northumberland plug itself, but argued, "The plug does serve to show the former existence of volcanic action and, unless it has been thrust westward into its present position by some great reversed fault from an original situation farther east, as outlined by Professor Cushing, it may be considered significant to this extent." His final conclusion on the origin of the mineral waters was as follows, "The explanation which appeals most strongly to the writer is that the carbonic acid gas, the chlorides, bromides, iodides, flourides and sodium carbonate are deep-seated. The sodium carbonate might in part or in whole be derived from the feldspar in the old crystalline rocks. The carbonated waters take calcium and magnesium carbonates from the limestone encountered in their upward journey more especially from the Little Falls dolomite. They mingle with artesian waters from the west, and may furnish a good portion of the motive power toward the close of the ascent. The greatest vents lie in or near the fault which passes through Saratoga Springs, but not all are demonstrably on it. The Gurn Spring is near a branch. The course of the fault is less clear at the Geysers, at Ballston and at Round Lake."

Cushing and Ruedemann, in a paper entitled "Geology of Saratoga Springs and Vicinity," published in 1914, disagreed with Kemp on the significance of the volcanic knob at Northumberland as related to the source of carbon dioxide gas in the Saratoga mineral waters. They did not completely reject his theory but considered it unlikely. They argued that the volcanic knob at Northumberland is no evidence whatsoever of underground igneous action in the general region or of the existence of present day magmatic water underground. They cited two difficulties in the way of unqualified acceptance of this theory of the origin of the Saratoga waters: there is no evidence of igneous action of any recency in the vicinity, or anywhere else in the eastern United States and, the Saratoga waters are not thermal waters.

Cushing and Ruedemann believe that the Saratoga mineral waters are confined underground to the area of the district which has a shale cover, that is, the district lying to the south and east of the Saratoga fault. Here, in cracks and crevices in the dolomite layer of rocks, they circulate until the Saratoga fault is reached where they have access to the surface as springs. The head necessary to supply pressure for their ascent to the surface is obtained from the mountains to the east of Saratoga Springs. They believe that the waters are mixed waters, having their source partially in a deep-seated metamorphism of the crystalline rocks deep in the earth, and partially from a connate source.

The Saratoga Springs Commission created by the Legislature of 1929 "to make a comprehensive study and survey of the mineral springs at Saratoga" engaged Professor R.J. Colony of Columbia University to make a geological study of the springs. In his very complete report he commented on the origin of the Saratoga mineral waters, treating the waters and the dissolved substances separately as follows:

> (a) Origin of the waters: It is believed that most, if not all, of the water is of meteoric origin, and that the source is the Adirondack mountain mass. This is a region of heavy precipitation, in which are many lakes, ponds, swamps and streams. It is broken by great faults, the glacial cover is favorable, and in the Saratoga section the highland mass is divided into two parts by a buried river valley filled with glacial debris, stretching from Corinth southward, that most surely influences the distribution of ground water. The mountain mass is, moreover, in fault contact with the rocks of the Saratoga basin, so that there is every opportunity for the water to find its way into the limestones of the Saratoga area.
>
> (b) Origin of the dissolved substances: With the exception of lime, magnesia, iron, silica and alumina, that are judged to be obtained from the reservoir rocks by the solvent action of heavily carbonated waters, the components are believed to be derived from a subjacent igneous mass at depth, that may be later in geological age than the crystalline rocks of the Adirondacks and the crystalline floor on which the sediments were deposited; but still very old in geologic time, and nowhere appearing at the present surface. Emanations given off from such deep-seated masses are the very last end products of expiring vulcanism.
>
> The peculiar composition of the mineral waters precludes a marine origin for the dissolved components, and also derivation from connate salts in the rocks; these are of marine source in the first place and partake of the character of marine salts. The lack of sulfates in the mineral waters together with the large amount of chlorides, and the presence of bromides and iodides, and the very large quantity of carbon dioxide with which the water is supersaturated is a very peculiar assemblage of components that can be explained in no other way than by derivation from a deep-seated

source. The water is largely meteoric, but the dissolved substances
probably originate at depth.

Dr. Lester Strock, research chemist of the Baruch Research Institute of the
Saratoga Spa, deduced a new theory of the origin of the mineral waters. The
new theory was intended, in addition to accounting for the abundant common
constituents in the water, to be a working hypothesis to suggest possible
origins for trace elements and their characteristic ratios in the water.

An attempt was made to trace the origin of the more abundant constituents
in Saratoga water to known geological formations of the region. The geochemical study entailed the use of spectrochemical analysis of the water with
particular emphasis on the lesser abundant and rare constituents, the so-
called trace elements. The study included consideration of the following
points: the composition of actual geological formations and deposits of the
vicinity; their possible contributions to the mineral in the Saratoga water; the
possibility of subterranean waters in the formations concerned, reaching
specifically the Saratoga region by means of known structural geological
features of the whole region involved; the fact that the properties and dissolv-
ing power of underground waters undergo changes as they penetrate the different formations.

In his detailed study of the composition of the waters and of the rocks of the
area, Strock concluded that a source beyond the immediate vicinity of the
springs was essential for any explanation of the various constituents contained
in the waters. He felt, for example, that it is highly improbable that the large
quantity of sodium chloride (common salt) in the waters is obtained from the
rocks of the area. He determined that sources much richer in sodium and
chlorides must be involved. He reasoned that a probable source for these con-
stitutents, and probably others, might be the natural brines originating from
salt deposits derived from evaporation of ancient sea waters as found in the
Central New York salt beds in the Salina division of the Silurian formation of
the state. Since the Salina formation reaches to within forty miles of the
Saratoga region, it is reasonable to assume that at least some of the salts in the
mineral waters have their origin in this brine. Favorable geological structures
exist which readily permit the movement of subterranean water from the
Salina formation, or other strata known to contain brine waters, to the Saratoga region.

Underground waters have leached these salt beds, then penetrated lower to
older geological formations by way of fault lines, cross joints and bedding
planes. These "early" Saratoga waters pass through the limestone downward
and eastward into the Schenectady basin and the Little Falls dolomite of the
Saratoga area. They find their way into the numerous parallel faults running
north from the Mohawk River toward the Saratoga region. They are forced
northward through channels and fissures in the dolomite by the head of water
supplied from the west.

In their course from the Salina beds to the Little Falls dolomite, the waters leach certain elements from the rocks through which they pass. One of these elements, iodine, is leached from a "fossil iodine-rich soil" bordering the Salina sea, and from numbers of iodine-rich fossil seaweeds. Iodine is fifty-three times more abundant in Saratoga mineral water than in sea water.

Strock believed that those remaining elements not derived from distant sources, such as salt beds and dolomite, were contributed by the sedimentary rocks of the region. There are abundant limestone beds along the course the water follows to Saratoga. These and the dolomite in which the waters circulate in the Saratoga area supply an adequate source of calcium for the waters. The potassium could be supplied in part from the Camillus lime mud rock overlying the Salina rock salt, which could also supply the bromine.

Strock's conception of the genesis of the Saratoga mineral water is explained in the accompanying table reprinted in the *Publication of Saratoga Spa*, No. 14, 1944, from the *American Journal of Science*, vol. 239, December 1941.

GENESIS OF SARATOGA MINERAL WATER
(L. W. Strock—1940)
FACIES I. (High Saline)

(a) $\underline{\underline{K}}$ and $\underline{\underline{Br}}$: Camillus overlying Salina Salt Beds.

(b) $\underline{Na}$ and $\underline{Cl}$: Salina Rock Salt Beds.

(c) $\underline{I}$, Na, K, $\underline{Ca}$: Formations between b and d, particularly: Medina Sandstone, Utica and Schenectady Shales, Trenton formation (mostly limestones), also Limestone adjacent to (d) and Potsdam sandstone.

CO_2 — Added here at latest, if (a) to (d) is continuous series.

(d) $\underline{Ca}$ and $\underline{\underline{Mg}}$: Little Falls Dolomite.

FACIES II. (Low or No Saline)
(Essentially surface waters containing only traces of Cl and CO_2)

(e)   Local overlying Shales — Canajoharie (and Chazy Basin?)

(f)   Little Falls Dolomite

(g)   Grenville Gneiss and Igneous Complex

Note: Doubly underlined means nearly sole source.
    Singly underlined means 50% or more of total.

Oskar Baudisch supported the belief that the Saratoga mineral waters are of marine origin by his work on isotopes, mainly of potassium, and by his work on rare elements using the refined method of spectroanalysis, namely ultraviolet light spectroscopy.

He felt that the assumption that the waters are solely of magmatic or volcanic origin is no longer tenable. He explained his position as follows:

> Recently new light has been thrown on the question of the leaching out of underground material which hundreds of millions of years ago was deposited out of shallow warm sea water and which now, at least partly, furnishes the parent material for the salts in solution in Saratoga mineral water. It becomes apparent, indeed, that the Saratoga mineral water is stored sun energy and that most all of its constituents represent the remains of organic life processes of the plankton or drifting small micro and macro organisms which once inhabited the shallow water of the Cambrian sea half a million years ago.
>
> In the late Cambrian era a notable succession of barrier reefs, composed entirely of species of lime secreting algae, Cryptozoön, bordered the Adirondacks. There are several facts showing that the Cryptozoön limestone, which is to be seen in a most spectacular exposure in the "Petrified Gardens" near Saratoga Springs, is of organic origin. The lime has been secreted during the life process of small algae.
>
> The question now arises how can we prove that the Cryptozoön reefs or remains of the plankton life of hundreds of millions of years ago and the Saratoga waters have any relationship with each other. The ordinary chemical analysis of the water cannot give us the answer to this question. It is, however, conceivable that quantitative spectrum analysis of the trace elements of both the Cryptozoön reefs and the Saratoga waters might also give us a clue to the relationship between the two.

Baudisch felt that he found the answer to the question of the source of the waters by the use of the so-called "tagged atoms" of elements or "tracer" isotopes. In his experiments, potassium, unique among the elements considered necessary for sustaining life since it alone is radioactive, was used.

Working with an isotope of potassium (K^{41}) Baudisch showed the close relationship of this particular form of potassium to that found in sea water and in the cryptozoön formation of Lester Park and the Petrified Gardens in the vicinity of Saratoga. He noted that the chemical composition of Saratoga mineral water is closely related to sea water. He felt that the elements found in the mineral water were derived from the remains of living organisms whose basic constituents would be the same as those found in the human body. Since the cells of all living things contain the same elements in the same form, the elements of the Saratoga mineral water are of value to the human body and are, therefore readily assimilated by the body to be used as building blocks in reconstructing cells.

There are certain basic facts concerning the origin of the Saratoga mineral waters which, in general, are accepted by all investigators. These are:

• The mineral water springs bear an intimate relationship to the faults of the area.

• The mineral waters are found in the limestone and dolomite layers of the rocks of the area.

• The surface of the downthrow side of the fault is composed of an impervious layer of Ordovician shales which prevents the accession of the waters to the surface except along fractured fault lines.

• The Saratoga mineral waters all have a common origin. As shown by analysis, waters from all of the springs contain the same constituents, differing only in the degree of concentration of these constituents; the springs from the deepest strata in general, being the most concentrated.

The final word has not as yet been written on the origin of these waters. Therefore, the origin of the Saratoga mineral waters still remains a matter of speculation.

6

The Mineral Springs of Saratoga

"He opened the rock and the waters gushed out;
They ran in the dry places like a river."
—Psalm 105:41

The naturally carbonated mineral waters of Saratoga are a precious natural resource and are the area's greatest asset. It can realistically be said that the waters are the veritable "raison d'etre" of Saratoga Springs. These waters flow from the earth heavily charged with carbon dioxide gas and with many vital minerals in solution. The various springs have diverse characteristics and range from powerful saline cathartic waters to those so lightly mineralized as to render them palatable for use as a beverage. As they reach the surface of the earth their temperature is approximately 50°F the year round.

The number of free-flowing springs found on the surface of the ground is relatively small. Most of these have been found in the vicinity of the city of Saratoga Springs. Many other springs have been obtained by drilling through the ground surface layers of gravel, sand and underlying shale to the bedrock beneath. The mineral waters lie chiefly in the Little Falls dolomite layer of the subsurface rocks of the area. They may also be found in the overlying layer of limestone rock, circulating freely in solution channels until encountering a break in the rock. Upon reaching a break or fault, the waters are able to make their way to the surface of the ground to appear as bubbling springs or to be lost by mixing with surface water. It is very likely that many springs have been lost in this way with the result that they have never been discovered. A covering of slate over the limestone layer of rock serves as a roof which prevents the escape of the mineral waters except at the site of the springs and the spots where well holes have been drilled down to the bedrock dolomite layer. The slate covering also prevents the surface water from reaching the mineral waters and mixing with them.

Most of the mineral springs have been obtained by drilling. The site for drilling is usually chosen where bubbles are detected issuing from the ground at which point a well hole is drilled until mineral water is struck. This occurs at various depths depending on the location. In some areas mineral water is obtained at a depth of a hundred feet; in other areas it is necessary to penetrate to a depth of a thousand feet or more. In general, the depth increases from north to south, the wells of Ballston Spa being deeper than those in Saratoga Springs. On drilling, when the orifice of the spring is found, a tube is inserted through the drill hole and cemented to the rock around the orifice. This prevents contamination with surface water. The mineral water is conducted to the surface through the tube thus inserted.

There is a striking relationship between the faults traversing the area and its springs, all of which arise in close proximity to the faults. Most of the springs of the Saratoga Springs area emerge along the eastern side of the Saratoga branch of the McGregor fault. The upthrow side of the Saratoga fault may be seen behind the High Rock Spring on the west side of High Rock Park where it rises to a height of thirty to forty feet. The main McGregor fault is plainly visible to the west from Route 9 just north of Saratoga Springs.

The Saratoga fault has been traced in Saratoga Springs from the High Rock area south along a line through Congress Park to Congress Street and Broadway where it makes a western turn, after which it turns south again. Its exact course from here on is lost in drift and rubble so that it is less clear at the Geysers, Ballston Spa and areas south of there. This fault line along which springs occur may also be traced north of Saratoga Springs through Gurn Spring to Argyle in Washington County and even beyond. It is assumed that if the same fault is not there, then another one is probably present where mineral springs have appeared on the surface.

Mineral springs in this region have been found over a very large area, a distance of approximately sixty-five miles, reaching from Albany on the south to Whitehall on the north. From Albany, the line may be traced in a northwesterly direction to Round Lake and the village of Ballston Spa and from there to Saratoga Springs. The line then takes a course slightly east of north to Gurn Spring and then runs slightly north of east to Argyle in Washington County. From here it runs to Whitehall, a total distance of sixty-five miles.

The southernmost mineral spring discovered along this range was near the Hudson River in Albany. In 1826 Messrs. McCullock and Boyd were boring in North Broadway for water for a brewery. At a depth of 465 feet they struck carbonated mineral water and carefully tubed the well. Subsequently, these men drilled a second well not far from the first. At a depth of thirty feet a mineral water vein was struck. As drilling was continued, they found, at different depths, sulfuretted hydrogen, carbonated hydrogen and finally carbon dioxide gas. The mineral water was found in a layer of rock known as Hudson

River slate. This well was found to be connected with the first one drilled since, when large quantities of water were drawn from one, the level of the other receded. On chemical analysis, the water proved to be similar to the mineral waters of Ballston Spa and Saratoga Springs.

The owners, when they discovered that they possessed mineral springs, made the area into a "mineral garden" with fountains and carefully land-scaped grounds. However, the mineral water was not commercially successful so was abandoned after a time in favor of the original idea of beer.

Between Albany and Round Lake, a distance of about twenty miles, no mineral springs have been found. In 1875 a drill hole was put down in Round Lake and at 1,300 feet, a flow of mineral water similar in composition to Saratoga mineral water was struck. The well was tubed and, for a while, the Methodist Camp Ground Community enjoyed their own private mineral water spring. Some time later, in an attempt to revive the spring when its output diminished markedly, the hole was torpedoed. After the explosion the flow was lost completely.

In the early years several mineral springs were discovered in Ballston Spa. The most well-known is the Old Iron Spring, still widely used. Among the others were the United States Spring, the Fulton Chalybeate Spring, the Franklin Sulphur Spring and the several Sans Souci Springs.

More springs are found following a course roughly along Route 50 toward Saratoga Springs and the State Reservation. In the State Reservation, the Saratoga Spa, in the area known as The Geysers, are many spouting springs. The first of these, the Geyser Spouting Spring, was drilled in 1870 and many more have been drilled since. A little to the northeast, toward Broadway in Saratoga Springs, is found a group of springs known as the Lincoln Group. The mineral water from these springs, being very highly carbonated, is used in all of the bath houses of the Saratoga Spa.

Going farther north in the city of Saratoga Springs are more springs, some of which are running and some of which have been capped. Those now running are the Columbian and Congress Springs in Congress Park, the Hathorn #1 Spring on the corner of Spring Street and Maple Avenue opposite Congress Park, and, farther north on High Rock Avenue in High Rock Park, the High Rock Spring and others of that group. Most northerly of all is the Old Red Spring.

A group of springs which formerly played a very active part in Saratoga life, located about a mile northeast of Saratoga Springs, was called the Ten Springs. These springs, which are no longer running, were located in parks known as Excelsior and Eureka Parks. Among these springs were the Excelsior, White Sulphur, Lithia, Eureka, Minnehaha, Brook, Taylor's Alexander, Taylor's Washington and Taylor's Jackson or Union Springs.

About a mile north of Saratoga Springs, Gurn Spring emerges from rock. The vent is some feet below the capping of gravel and is no longer visible.

Ten miles northeast of Gurn Spring lies the Vita Spring whose water is similar to that of the Gurn Spring.

In South Argyle, about fifteen miles northeast of Saratoga Springs, near the Moses Kill, is found Reid's Spring. This in "an acidulous carbonated water something like the Saratoga waters." It is recorded that the people of the vicinity used it for raising their dough preparatory to baking their bread, no yeast being necessary.

In the village of Whitehall, thirty-nine miles northeast of Saratoga Springs, is found a mineral spring called the Adirondack Spring. It is very lightly carbonated and contains only about one-tenth the mineral content of the Saratoga waters.

A little east of Saratoga Springs in the township of Saratoga is a group of four mineral springs called Quaker Springs, all located within about two hundred yards of each other.

The area of New York State known geologically as the Saratoga Quadrangle has been blessed with a precious and valuable resource, the naturally carbonated mineral waters. These springs were highly prized by the Mohawk Indians, and even worshiped by them. They placed great confidence in their healing powers. The early white settlers also came to value the springs which even proved to be commercially lucrative. In the heyday of the springs, the nineteenth and early twentieth centuries, there were as many as a hundred or more springs actively running at a time. At present, this number has been reduced to only a few.

Over the years, Saratoga has known many mineral springs. Some have come and gone and others, like Tennyson's Brook, seem to go on forever. Basically they are all similar in that they all contain the same minerals, and all are charged with carbon dioxide gas. They vary widely, however, in the concentration and proportion of the minerals contained, and in the degree of carbonation. Each spring is distinctive as will be seen by the analyses and each, because of its specific composition, has a unique therapeutic application.

A list describing the springs of the Saratoga area with their location follows. It will be noted that many of the springs have had more than one name.

"A" SPRING (SARATOGA "A" SPRING)

The site of this spring, which was discovered in 1785, was on the east side of a steep bluff near the railroad embankment just north of the Old Red Spring on Spring (High Rock) Avenue on the road leading to the Ten Springs. The spring no longer exists as a running spring since its site is buried in rubble alongside the new highway arterial.

It is believed that the "A" designation of this spring stood for alum which gave its water an astringent sweet-sour taste.

In 1865 George Weston purchased the property, tubed the spring, built a bottling plant and bottled the water, which he claimed was the most effective mineral water in the world.

In 1867 the bottling house burned. The spring was at that time retubed to a depth of thirty-two feet through solid rock. A new company was formed with Mr. J.F. Henry as president. Mr. Henry was well known as the leading druggist in America and the largest dealer of proprietary medicines in the world.

ABEL'S SPRING

This spring was located at the White Sulphur Springs Hotel on the southeast shore of Saratoga Lake.

Both Gene Tunney and Jack Dempsey drank it when they trained at Luther's White Sulphur Spring Hotel for championship fights.

ADAM'S SPRING (ORENDA SPRING, CONGRESS #2 SPRING)

See Orenda Spring.

AETNA SPOUTING SPRING (VICHY SPOUTING SPRING)

Name given to a spouting well, discovered in 1872 on the margin of the little lake near Geyser Spring and just across the water from the Triton well. The spring was not open to the public.

AINSWORTH SPRINGS #1, #2, & AINSWORTH'S FAVORITE SPRINGS

These springs were drilled in the late nineteenth century by Seymour Ainsworth, a contractor, on the site of the trolley station on the southwest corner of Broadway and Congress Street.

ALEXANDER'S SPRING (TAYLOR'S ALEXANDER SPRING)

One of the springs found in Taylor's Ten Spring woods.

ALNOBA SPRING (CLARK #2 SPRING)

See Clark #2 Spring.

APPOLOS SPRING

This spring was named in a list of springs in the 1887 edition of *Saratoga Chips* by N. Sheppard. To date research had revealed no further information on it.

ARONDACK SPRING (KISSINGEN SPRING, HYPERION SPRING)

This spring was originally drilled in 1872, under the name Hyperion Spring, to a depth of 192 feet on the east side of Geyser Lake a short distance from the Triton Spring. The original officers of the spring company were Edward S. Sargent, Henry O. Read, William C. Jones, Charles P. Sumner and E. S. Churchill.

On January 8, 1887 the Saratoga Kissingen Company was formed from the original company with a capital of $100,000. In 1902, when the French government started suit against the Saratoga Vichy Company because the American firm had used the name "Vichy" without permission, the Saratoga Kissingen Company, fearing a similar suit by the Bavarian government on the use of the name "Kissingen," quickly renamed their spring "Arondack." Bottling of the water was continued until about 1915.

ARONDACK EAST & ARONDACK SOUTH SPRINGS

These springs are listed on a map of springs and wells in Saratoga Springs by William P. Hill dated August 4, 1909.

ARTESIAN SELTZER SPRING

This spring is listed in a list of springs in the 1887 edition of *Saratoga Chips* by N. Sheppard.

AWASA SPRING (PANDORA SPRING)

Awasa is an Iroquois word meaning "where the bear drinks." This spring, which was formerly called the Pandora Spring, was located in Dandaraga (the Vale of Springs). In this very beautiful setting the water bubbled into a large glass bowl over the spring. The Vale of Springs no longer exists. The area is now included in the Saratoga Performing Arts Center.

BAKER SPRING

Located in Geyser Park, Baker Spring is listed in William P. Hill's 1909 *Map of Springs and Wells in Saratoga Springs*. It was also listed by Kemp in 1912.

BARREL SPRING (SELTZER SPRING)

See Seltzer Spring.

BENEDICT'S SPRING

From *Allens' Analysis*, 1844: "This fountain is located some three miles west of Saratoga Village. It is a light water comparatively if we speak of the ingredients common to it and the other mineral springs of our village. But it contains, in addition to the carbonic acid and carbonates, sulphuretted hydrogen, which constituent, together with its associates, entitles it to more attention than it has ever received."

BIG RED SPRING

A new mineral spring drilled in 1976 on the grounds of the Saratoga Thoroughbred Race Track on Union Avenue, it is located west of the paddock walking area. It is 300 feet deep and has three jet fountains. In 1977 an attractive white pavilion from the Excelsior Spring was placed over it.

It was named after the famous race horse Man-O-War, whose nickname was Big Red.

BRIDGE SPRING

This spring is one of the many geysers drilled in Geyser Park.

BROOK SPRING

This spring was located within a few yards of the Excelsior Spring in Excelsior Park.

BROWN'S NEW BETHESDA SPRING

Located at 21 Phila Street. Described in a directory printed in a local newspaper as "cathartic, alterative and tonic."

CARLSBAD SPRING (MORCK SPRING, REDMOND SPRING)

This spring was drilled in Geyser Park west of the Vichy Spring in 1885. The flow was abundant. The water is similar to Hathorn #2. It is highly charged with carbon dioxide gas.

CHAMPION #1 SPOUTING SPRING (GYANTWAKA)

This is one of the many springs drilled in the Geyser Spring area east of the Delaware and Hudson railroad tracks in Geyser Park by the famous well driller, Mr. Jesse Button. It was drilled in 1871, a year after the Geyser Spring had been drilled. At a depth of 300 feet, Mr. Button reached the great mineral reservoir that underlies the area, making this spring the fountainhead of the mineral spring system of Saratoga. The water spouted with great force to a height of 25 to 30 feet. It was tubed with a pipe that extended above the ground and was fitted with a nozzle having a smaller opening than the pipe. To relieve the pressure that accumulated in the system with this smaller orifice, the nozzle was removed daily allowing the water to spout to a height of 80 feet or more. In order to get maximum tourist attraction value from this procedure, it was done at five o'clock every afternoon, the time the Delaware and Hudson train went by. During the winter months the water formed a column of ice up to 30 feet in height and several inches in diameter.

The water was bottled by the Champion Spouting Spring Company.

This was one of the 18 of 163 mineral springs left running when the Saratoga Springs were taken over by the State of New York. It was retubed and resealed in 1916.

CHAMPION #2 SPOUTER SPRING (FORMELL'S CREEK SPRING)

Drilled in Geyser Park near Champion Spouter Spring #1. It was retubed and resealed in 1916.

CHAMPION #3 SPOUTER SPRING

Drilled in Geyser Park near the Delaware and Hudson railroad tracks, not far from Champion Spouter Spring #1. It was retubed and resealed in 1916.

Photo by Howard S. Maguire

Big Red Spring

Columbian Spring

Collection of the Saratoga Spa

Champion #1 Spouting Spring 1871   *Collection of George Bolster*

Collection of George Bolster

Champion #2 Spouting Spring

Coesa Spring, circa 1912

Congress Spring

From engraving by P.R.B. Pearson, 1873

*Empire Spring and Bottling House. The site was
later occupied by the Van Raalte mill. The spring
still runs in the basement of the building*

From engraving by P.R.B. Pearson, 1873

Excelsior Spring, located in Excelsior Park

Geyser Spring showing hole in ceiling cut to accommodate spouter

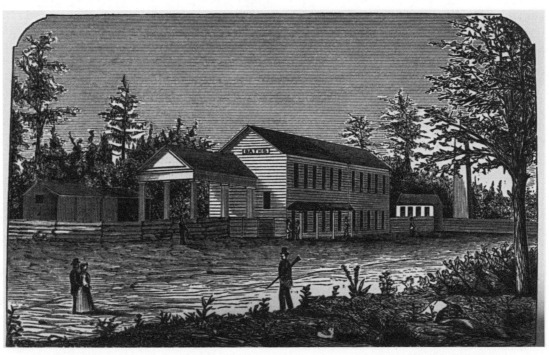

Hamilton Spring and Bath House as it appeared in 1840

CHIEF SPRING

This well was a spouter located at the intersection of South Broadway and the road running to Eddy's Corners and Saratoga Lake. It was drilled in September 1899 and found to be a rich source of carbon dioxide gas. It was owned by the Chief Natural Mineral Water Company. Jerry Stiles was manager of the company.

CLARENDON SPRING (WASHINGTON SPRING)

See Washington Spring.

CLARK #1 SPRING (ZALAMA SPRING)

Zalama means "sweetheart" in Iroquois.

Situated in Geyser Park in a picturesque ravine near Geyser Creek. It was retubed and resealed in 1916.

CLARK #2 SPRING (ALNOBA SPRING)

Alnoba means "warrior" in Iroquois. This spring is situated in Geyser Park in a picturesque ravine near Geyser Creek.

CLARK #3 SPRING (SPRUDEL SPRING)

Situated in Geyser Park in a picturesque ravine near Geyser Creek.

COESA SPRING

This spring, one of the geysers in Geyser Park, is located on Route 50 in a small pavilion with a Tennessee marble fountain in which the mineral water bubbles up into a glass bowl. It is a saline alkaline water. The balance between saline and alkaline give Coesa a laxative as well as an effective antacid quality. It should not be taken with food, but before meals. It has been recommended by physicians because of its value in the treatment of liver and gall bladder diseases.

Coesa was one of the 18 of 163 springs left running when the Saratoga Springs Reservation was formed and the springs taken over by the State of New York.

COESA #2 SPRING

Located in Geyser Park.

COLUMBIAN SPRING

This spring was discovered in 1803 by Gideon Putnam as he was clearing land around the Congress Spring. It is located one hundred feet southwest of the Congress Spring in Congress Park just south of the Broadway entrance. In 1806 it was tubed by Gideon Putnam. In 1823 it was purchased, along with the Congress Spring and surrounding land, by John Clarke, who constructed a

Grecian pavilion over it in 1840. In 1865, after the Congress and Empire Spring Companies merged, the water was bottled.

The water is rich in iron and has a high content of carbon dioxide gas. At one time it was called the "headache" spring, because some people experienced a headache after drinking a quantity of it.

In 1981 the City of Saratoga Springs found the spring which had dried up and disappeared in 1884. They tubed it and again built a Grecian pavilion over it similar to the one John Clarke had constructed. This project was financed by the Saratoga Historical Society.

CONDE DENTONIAN SPRING

This spring is listed by Kemp (1916). No further information is given.

CONGRESS SPRING

In 1792, fifteen years after the Battle of Saratoga, Nicholas Gilman, an adjutant general in the Continental Army who had served in that battle, decided to revisit the scene where he had served. Together with his brother, John Taylor Gilman, a member of the Continental Congress who was later to become governor of New Hampshire, he went to Saratoga and spent the night at the tavern of Benjamin Risley, father of Mrs. Gideon Putnam. The following morning he and his brother and others went hunting along an Indian trail to the site of the present Congress Park. One of the brothers noticed a trickle of water coming from a small hole in the rocky embankment near a stream which ran through the area. On tasting the water, they found that it was carbonated mineral water similar to that of the High Rock Spring near Mr. Risley's tavern. There was much excitement over the discovery. It was agreed by the guests at the tavern that the new spring should be called the Congress Spring in honor of the member of the hunting party who was a member of Congress.

The spring was located on land that belonged to the Livingston family, who had acquired it from Isaac Lowe, an heir of Rip Van Dam, one of the patentees of the land under the Kayaderosseras Patent.

In 1802 the spring was tubed by Gideon Putnam who in 1804 excavated the spring fifteen feet west of the original outlet. This he did by rerouting the stream, which ran by the spring, to expose an area from which bubbles were coming. He then excavated an eight foot deep hole at the location and put in a ten inch square wooden tube which he fixed firmly to the rock below.

In 1822, John Clarke of New York City purchased the Congress Spring with land surrounding it. In 1823, he and a colleague, Thomas Lynch, began to bottle the water and sell it all over the United States and Europe. He improved the grounds surrounding the spring, and made the water available at the spring free to all. He placed an awning over the spring which was later replaced by a beautiful Doric structure. Dipper boys were engaged to serve the water to the patrons. The following sign was posted at the spring: "Reports have been circulated relative to the mode of furnishing water at the spring. The proprietor thinks it due to himself and the public to say that all pitchers, jugs and kegs for family use will be filled gratuitously by the boys in attendance, and that any remuneration given to the boys will be exclusively for their benefit. John Clarke."

Following the death of John Clarke in 1846, Clarke's daughter and stepson, William B. White, took over the business and managed it until White's death in 1864. At that time, Chauncey Kilmer, president of the Empire Spring Company, purchased the business and merged the two companies. In 1879 B. B. Hotchkiss purchased the business and in 1904 the Congress Spring was sold at auction for $75,000.

Mineral water rights to the Congress Spring, as well as to other springs in Saratoga Springs, were acquired by the State of New York when acquisition for the formation of the Saratoga Springs Reservation was begun.

In 1913, engineers of the Reservation drilled and revived the old spring. On several tests it was found to be polluted. It was, therefore, discontinued. In 1939 tons of stone were poured into the pit which contained the spring. In 1963 steps were taken by the city to reactivate the spring and restore the site to its nineteenth century appearance. The fountain was set on a new pump base. However, state and county laboratory tests confirmed that the water was still polluted, so the spring was abandonned.

In 1976 water from the Congress IX Spring, which was found not to be polluted, was piped from that spring to the fountain of the original Congress Spring. The Congress IX lies a little north of the original Congress Spring in Congress Park. A replica of the original Greek pavilion with Doric columns was placed over the spring by the Saratoga Historical Society.

Professor Chandler, respected chemist of the School of Mines of Columbia University, had this to say about Congress water: "The peculiar excellence of the far famed Congress Spring is due to the fact that it contains very much less iron than any other spring, and that it contains, in the most desirable proportions, those substances which produce its agreeable flavor, and satisfactory medicinal effect; neither holding them in excess, nor lacking in anything that is desirable in this class of waters."

Perhaps more than any other spring, the Congress Spring is responsible for the nationwide and worldwide reputation of Saratoga Springs.

CONGRESS IX SPRING

This spring lies to the north of the original Old Congress Spring. It is water from this well that is currently piped in to the Congress fountain under the pavilion in Congress Park.

CONGRESS #2 SPRING (ORENDA SPRING, ADAMS SPRING)

See Orenda Spring.

CRYSTAL SPRING

This spring was excavated and tubed in 1870 by Charles P. Brown, a prominent jeweler and optician of Saratoga Springs. The site of excavation was on the west side of Broadway south of Congress Street on the grounds of the Park Place Hotel which was owned by Mr. Brown. The water which did not rise to the surface, but had to be pumped, was crystal clear. However, it had a very strong odor of sulphuretted hydrogen which detracted from its attractiveness as a beverage. The owner tried to compensate for this by giving the spring an attractive name, "Crystal Spring." The water was bottled and sold under this name.

The Park Place Hotel was destroyed by fire in 1871, and was rebuilt as the Grand Central Hotel.

DEUEL SPRING

This spring is listed in *Saratoga Illustrated* by R. F. Dearborn (1873).

DIAMOND SPRING

A spring in Saratoga State Park belonging to the Vichy Company was located a few feet north of the Vichy Spring.

DITCH WELL #2

This spring was located in Geyser State Park near Geyser Creek on land previously owned by the General Carbonic Gas Company.

DR. STEELE'S SPRING (PAVILION SPRING, ROYANCH SPRING)

See Pavilion Spring.

ELIXIR SPRING (RED SPRING #2, NEW RED SPRING)

See New Red Spring.

ELLIS SPRING

This spring was located in Geyser Park on land previously owned by Robert Ellis in a deep valley on the side of one of the principal branches of the Kayaderosseras. About two miles south of the village immediately under the embankment of the railroad, the Ellis is between the Glacier and Geyser Springs. Unlike many other springs at Saratoga, it issues in a horizontal position from the side of a hill. It is a very fine chalybeate and is not bottled.

ELLSWORTH #1 SPRING & ELLSWORTH #2 SPRING

Located in the State Park along the right of way for a possible trolley line connection between Lincoln tract and Ferndell Bottling Works. Both produced water similar in character to most of the mineral water springs in the Lincoln tract. It was purchased by the state in 1916.

ELMWOOD SPRING (MONROE SPRING)

See Monroe Spring.

EMPEROR SPRING

Retubed and resealed in 1916 with the water brought back to a condition of purity that had not been known for many years, it is located in High Rock Park just south of the High Rock Spring. The Emperor is one of the most important springs on the Reservation since the demand for its water is greater than for that of any other spring on the Reservation excepting perhaps Hathorn #1.

EMPIRE SPRING (WALTON SPRING, NEW CONGRESS SPRING)

This spring is located in the northern part of the village on Spring (High Rock) Avenue at the head of Circular Street, near the base of a high limestone bluff a few rods above the Star Spring and about three fourths of a mile from the Congress Spring. It was found about 1793 when Jacob Walton purchased Lot #12 in the 16th allotment of the Kayaderosseras Patent. For over fifty years it was known as the Walton Spring. It was not until 1846 that the spring was tubed by Messrs. Weston and Co., the early proprietors. They made extensive improvements in the grounds surrounding the spring, landscaping and planting trees. In 1861, the spring was purchased by D. A. Knowlton and in 1864, the spring and bottling works were sold for $65,000 to Chauncey Kilmer, who also purchased the Congress Spring Company. In 1865, the Congress and Empire Spring Company was formed. It was dissolved in 1884 and the two springs became separate entities. In 1904, the Empire Spring Company was sold at public auction for $76,500 to Joseph Clark, owner of a textile company. The property was converted into a textile mill. The spring still flows in the basement of the Van Raalte mill.

EUREKA SPRING

This spring was discovered in 1866. It was located in the midst of beautiful Eureka Park, situated northeast of the village about a mile from the High Rock Spring. In 1866, it was purchased and developed by Anthony Dyett, who built a bottling plant and bottled the water in unique round-bottomed bottles.

EXCELSIOR SPRING

This spring is located in a beautiful valley a short distance northeast of the village of Saratoga Springs, near the center of a park known as Excelsior Park, in the Valley of the Ten Springs. The principal entrance of this park is on Lake Avenue one half mile east of Circular Street.

The spring is one of the original ten springs in the Valley of the Ten Springs, land owned by the Taylor brothers, purchased by them in 1794. The springs were discovered in 1814.

In 1858 H. H. Lawrence purchased some 25 acres in the Valley which included the Excelsior Spring. He retubed it, bottled the water and sold it worldwide. Lawrence landscaped the surrounding grounds, creating beautiful Excelsior Park.

An advertisement in *The Saratoga Journal* of June 8, 1882 ran as follows:

> By far the pleasantest way to reach this spring is by the shady winding walk, or the romantic bridle path through Excelsior Park, or you can drive by way of Lake Avenue to and through the park; but if you haven't a carriage at your disposal, nor a horse which you can ride, and don't care for beautiful scenery, and the healthful exercise of a mile walk, buy a ticket for and take your seat on one of the pleasant cars of the Saratoga Lake Railway and get out at Excelsior Station which is in the center of the Valley of the Ten Springs and within the border of Excelsior Park. Mr. Henry Lawrence, the proprietor, will receive you courteously.

FAVORITE SPRING (AINSWORTH'S FAVORITE)

Developed in 1880, this spring was located opposite Congress Spring on the site of the trolley station (later the Broadway Drink Hall) on the corner of Broadway and Congress Street. It was owned by Seymour Ainsworth who erected a two story building on the site. The spring expired after a short time.

FERNDELL SPRING (STATE SEAL, SARATOGA SOFT SWEET SPRING)

In response to requests for a non-carbonated, non-mineral spring water, a systematic survey was made of the many sweet water springs in Geyser Park. Samples were taken from fifteen different springs of still water and analyzed in the Reservation laboratory by "Doc" Ant. The results were exceedingly favorable. Upon evaporation, all of the water showed less total solids than the principally marketed pure still waters. The spring showing the smallest total of solids was found in a ravine near the Willow Gate of Geyser Park and was chosen for development. The water was originally marketed under the name Saratoga Soft Sweet Spring Water. This name, however, was found to be too cumbersome to use commercially, so was changed to State Seal Water. It is quite free from minerals, as the upper stratum of sand is entirely sealed off from the more soluble rock below by an impervious table of clay; the water bubbles forth from the sands which are silaceous and insoluble in water.

This water is recommended by physicians where a mineral-free water is indicated. It is also ideal for general use where a non-chlorinated water is desired.

FLAT ROCK SPRING (IMPERIAL SPRING)

This spring was discovered shortly after the High Rock Spring became known to the early settlers in 1767. Its water very closely resembles that of the High Rock Spring. It is located behind the City Hall on Lake Avenue in the city parking lot. Originally, it was located on the edge of a marsh at the foot of a steep bank which terminated the west side of the valley. It was tubed by Henry Walton, who also built a Chinese pagoda over it. For many years it was one of the only known springs in Saratoga with a dipper boy in attendance to serve the many summer visitors who patronized the spring. A bath house was kept at this spring by Gardner Bullard.

When the Pavilion Spring, a short distance away, was tubed in 1839 the Flat Rock Spring disappeared. In 1880 it was noted "The Flat Rock Spring still exists, but it is covered by the tanneries." In 1978 the spring was revived. It was tubed in its location in the city parking lot behind the City Hall and piped to the Broadway sidewalk in front of the City Hall. The original Chinese pagoda was reinstalled and the spring became one of the main attractions on Broadway.

FLAT SPRING #1

Located in Geyser Park on land previously owned by The General Carbonic Company.

FLAT SPRING #2 (KARISTA SPRING, IRON SPRING)

See Karista Spring.

FLAT SPRING #3

Located in Geyser Park on land previously owned by The General Carbonic Company.

FORMELLE'S CREEK SPRING (CHAMPION SPOUTER #2 SPRING)

See Champion Spouter #2 Spring.

FORMALSEK SPRING

Shown on a map of Springs and Wells in Saratoga Springs by William R. Hill, June 24, 1909. No further information provided.

FOUNELLE CREEK SPRING

Listed in a list of springs, 1912. No further information provided.

FRESH WATER SPRING

Flowing from the hillside in the northeast corner of the Casino grounds, the spring is popular with city residents.

GEYSER SPOUTING SPRING

A new era in the history of the mineral springs of Saratoga was ushered in in February 1870 when this spring, the first spouting geyser, was drilled within the walls of a nut and bolt factory by Jesse Button, a well-known, experienced well driller. On Ballston Avenue, about a mile south of the village, the factory was situated in a pleasant ravine bordering on Coesa Lake at the base of a beautiful cascade of fresh water falling over the 22-foot falls. Mineral water was reached at a depth of fifty-two feet below the 80-foot overburden of shale marking the western bank of the Vale of Springs. When the vein was struck, the water spouted to a height of twenty feet, hitting the ceiling of the room. Later the factory owners cut a hole through the roof of the building to accommodate the spouter. The factory was transformed into a very attractive pavilion, and the spring became a tourist attraction. The building was open at all times for free inspection and the public was invited to visit the spring, examine the wonderful natural phenomenon and taste its agreeable water. Bus service from the village to the spring was provided for the convenience of visitors. As many as 150,000 registered in the visitor's book in one year. The spring was purchased by the State of New York in 1911 and retubed in 1912. The water has been bottled from the beginning and is one of the three mineral waters bottled by the state.

The water is cathartic and very agreeable as a beverage. It is strongly charged with minerals and carbon dioxide gas. At the present, it is available to the public at a twin fountain just to the west of the bottling plant on the Reservation. The other water available at the fountain is State Seal Water.

GLACIER SPRING

A few months after the successful drilling of the Spouting Geyser Spring in February 1870, Gibbs and Son, flour dealers, engaged Mr. Jesse Button, the same well driller, to drill a well for them near their mill. Close to the R and S railroad tracks and directly opposite the original spouting geyser, mineral water was struck at a depth of 220 feet. However, since the well was not a spontaneous spouter, the project was considered a failure and work was abandoned. A year later, in 1871, a second drilling was attempted. This time, at a depth of 300 feet, a beautiful spouter was struck, which spouted water to a height greater than that attained by the Geyser Spring. The well was tubed and named The Glacier Spouting Spring. It was called "the most remarkable fountain in the world." It discharged through a one and one half inch nozzle from four to eight gallons per minute of perfact water and gas suds to a height of 80 feet.

GOVERNOR SPRING

This spring is located in High Rock Park just east of the High Rock Spring on what was originally Star Spring property. It was bored in 1908 through 35 feet of clay and 135 feet of rock. Since its boring coincided with the date in June 1908 when Governor Hughes signed the Reservation Bill into law, the spring was appropriately named the Governor Spring.

At present, the spring is tapped into a fountain in High Rock Park on a slab also containing the Peerless Spring and the Seltzer Spring. Each of these mineral springs, though lying in close proximity to each other, has a distinctly

— Holman

different taste. The Governor is a chalybeate water strongly impregnated with carbon dioxide gas.

GUNPOWDER SPRING (IODINE SPRING, PRESIDENT SPRING, STAR SPRING)

See Star Spring.

GYANTWAKA SPRING (CHAMPION SPOUTING #1 SPRING)

See Champion Spouting #1 Spring.

HAMILTON SPRING

Located directly behind Congress Hall (now the site of Saratoga Springs Library) a little northeast of Congress Spring at the corner of Spring and Putnam Streets, this spring was discovered and tubed by Gideon Putnam in 1809. He named it after General Hamilton. At the time of the spring's discovery, Putnam Street ran through Congress Park to East Congress Street. A bath house covered by a lovely Doric pavilion was moved from the Congress Spring to the Hamilton. Here the first "Kur" treatment began, as guests from Putnam's Tavern, erected in 1800, came to be cured.

HATHORN #1 SPRING   *Spg & Putnam*

This spring was discovered in 1868 by Samuel Freeburn, a stone mason engaged at the time in constructing the foundation for the new ballroom of Congress Hall, which lay across Spring Street from the main Congress Hall.

The new spring was named Hathorn in honor of the owner of the property. In May 1869 it was drilled to a depth of 1,006 feet, the deepest in Saratoga. There is some question, however, about the depth, since some of it may have been the result of replication due to faulting. Unfortunately, the core of the boring was lost so this question could not be resolved.

The spring became one of the most famous and one of the most profitable of the Saratoga mineral springs. Its water was consumed more than any other water in Saratoga. By 1911 its natural flow ceased and the water had to be pumped.

In 1912 it was tubed by the state and it began flowing again with a moderate mineralization and a fair amount of gas. Its low mineralization was considered a good thing in as much as its indiscriminate use might have worked harm were it more highly mineralized.

The Hathorn water was bottled and sold throughout the United States and Canada.

HATHORN #2 SPRING

This spring is the most southerly of the Geyser Park group. It was discovered in 1890. Located on Route 50, very accessible to the public, it is highly patronized. During the summer season it has been necessary to station a state trooper at the spring to maintain an orderly use of the water by the large number of people who come to drink the water before breakfast. Its use has always been an important part of the ritual of taking the "Kur" at Saratoga.

One of the three mineral waters bottled and sold under the auspices of the State of New York, its water has been claimed by some physicians to be the most valuable water yet discovered at Saratoga. It is famous for its cathartic properties.

HATHORN #3 SPRING

Located not far from Hathorn #2 spring on Route 50, this spring was discovered in 1905. In 1916 retubing and resealing markedly increased the available flow. The water flows from a Tennessee marble fountain with drinking cups provided by a girl in charge. Noted for its cathartic properties, it is claimed by some to be the strongest water of the saline group of the Saratoga mineral waters.

HARPER SPRING

Located in State Park, this spring was included in a list of springs in 1912 by King and also listed by Dunn in 1974. Research has revealed no further information.

HAYES SPRING (HURLBURT #1 SPRING)

Located in Geyser Park on the west bank of Geyser Creek opposite the famous Island Spouter.

According to tradition, inhalation of the gas emitted from this water will relieve sinus congestion and will be effective in the treatment of the common cold. There is an opening in the concrete structure over the spring where the gas may be inhaled.

Over the years this water has been used in the treatment of gall bladder and liver diseases.

HIGH ROCK SPRING

This was the first of the mineral springs of Saratoga to become known to the early settlers. It was located at the base of an escarpment to the west of the brook which ran through marshy ground. Attention was first drawn to the site by the great numbers of game and wild animals that frequented it as a salt lick.

The spring is covered by a unique conical structure, resembling a miniature volcano, composed of tufa or travertine, which is a deposit of carbonates laid down from water as it flowed over the top of the mound, as it was known to do in earlier days. The carbonates came out of solution from the water as the carbon dioxide gas, which made the water acid, was released. As long as the water is underground and under pressure, the carbon dioxide gas stays in the water, but when it reaches the surface of the earth where pressure is reduced, it is given off from the water in the form of bubbles. Over the years carbonates have formed at the mouth of the spring, forming the mound and embedding the sticks and other material in it. The cone is 37 inches in height and 25.6 inches in circumference at the base. On the summit there is a circular aperature 10 inches in diameter.

When the Kayaderosseras Patent was partitioned by ballot on February 22, 1771, lot #12 of the 16th allotment, on which the High Rock Spring is situated, came into the possession of the Rip Van Dam estate. Since Van Dam, the original petitioner, had died in 1745, the executors of the estate sold the spring to Isaac Lowe, Jacob Walton and Anthony Van Dam.

In 1783, after a visit to the High Rock Spring as a guest of General Schuyler, George Washington tried to purchase the spring, but was unable to do so, because Mr. Lowe would not release his interest.

In 1826 the spring was purchased by Mrs. Eliza White, a widow, who in 1828 married John Clarke, owner of the Congress Spring. They, and later their children, under the name of Clarke and White, bottled and sold the High Rock water.

The spring was sold to Seymour Ainsworth and W.H. McCaffrey in 1865. In an attempt to eliminate any lateral outlets to the spring, and thereby secure water in greater abundance and of better quality, they decided to do a thorough job of retubing it. Accordingly, they employed a number of men to undermine the mound and, with a powerful hoisting derrick, lift it off and set it aside to explore the spring. Dr. Charles F. Chandler of Columbia University School of Mines, in a lecture on the mineral waters reported in *The American Chemist* in 1871, gives the following description of the exploration of the spring:

> Just below the mound were found four logs, two of which rested on the other two at right angles, forming a curb. Under the logs were bundles of twigs resting upon the dark brown or black soil of a previous swamp. Evidently some ancient seekers after health had found the spring in the swamp, and to make it more convenient to secure the water, had piled brush around it, and laid down the logs as a curb. But, you inquire, how came the rock which weighed several tons above the logs? The rock was formed by the water. It is composed of tufa, carbonate of lime, and was formed in the same manner as stalagmites and stalagtites are formed. As the water flowed over the logs, the evaporation of a portion of the carbonic acid caused the separation of an equivalent quantity of insoluable carbonate of lime which, layer by layer, built up the mound. I hold in my hand a large fragment of the rock; it contains leaves, twigs, hazelnuts and small shells, which, falling from time to time upon it, were crusted and finally imprisoned in the stony mass.
>
> Below the rocks the workmen followed the spring through four feet of tufa and muck. Then they came to a layer of solid tufa two feet thick, then one foot of muck in which they found another log.

Below this were three feet of tufa; and there, seventeen feet below
the apex of the mound, they found the embers and charcoal of an
ancient fire. By whom and when could this fire have been built? The
Indian tradition went back only to the time when the water overflowed the rock. How many centuries may have elapsed since even
the logs were placed in position? A grave philosopher of the famous
watering place, remembering that botanists determine the age of
trees by counting the rings on the section of the stem, and noting the
layers in the tufa rock, polished a portion of the surface and counted
eighty-one layers to the inch. He forthwith made the following
calculation:

High Rock, 4 feet, 80 lines to the inch	- 3840 years
Rock and tufa, 7 feet, low estimate at	- 400 years
Tufa, 2 feet, 22 lines to the inch	- 600 years
Muck, 1 foot	- 130 years
Tufa, 3 feet	- 900 years
Time since the fire was built	5870 years

As I have seen half an inch of tufa formed in two years on a brick
which received only twenty grains of carbonate of lime in a gallon, I
am inclined to think our antiquarian's estimates are not entirely
reliable.

On completion of the retubing operation, the owners of the spring constructed a colonnade over it at the cost of $6,000. It was of Gothic architecture
surmounted by a mosque-like dome crowned by an immense gold eagle.

In 1872 Ainsworth and McCaffrey went bankrupt, and the spring was sold
at auction for $16,000. The Saratoga High Rock Spring Company, formed
with William G. Fargo as president, continued operation of the spring water
business until 1904 when it was sold to W. E. Barnes and W. S. Henry for
$25,000.

A few years later the property was purchased by the Village of Saratoga
Springs. Together with Congress Park, the site was to be constructed and
maintained by the village as a park under an agreement made with the
Saratoga Springs Reservation Commission in which the village owned the property and the state owned the spring rights. On the three and one half acre
site, the smallest of the Saratoga Springs Reservation parks, High Rock Park
was constructed. Next, the state constructed a pavilion over the tufa core from
which the bubbling High Rock water could be dipped and served to visitors.
The original land around the spring was swampy and wet, but filling operations raised it until it was high and dry, giving no indication of the ancient
swamp once surrounding the site. The cone of tufa, however, which had been
replaced in its origianl position, was comparatively depressed below the level
of the filled in land. Accordingly, one looked down into it from the sides of the
pavilion.

In 1969, a granite marker in High Rock Park, engraved with an Indian
prayer, was dedicated. Mrs. Brenton Taylor was chairman of the nineteen-

member committee planning the project. The occasion was sponsored by the Chamber of Commerce, with speakers including State Supreme Court Justice Michael Sweeney and Mayor James Benton.

At present, High Rock Park is included in the Urban Cultural Park plan of Saratoga Springs. The waters of three mineral springs, in addition to the High Rock, are available at fountains to the south of the High Rock Spring. These are waters from the Governor, Seltzer and Peerless Springs. A marker has been erected at the site giving the history of the High Rock Spring.

HOUSE SPRING
Located in the State Park, this spring is listed by Kemp (1912) and by Dunn (1976). No further information is available.

HURLBURT #1 SPRING (HAYES SPRING)
See Hayes Spring.

HYPERION SPRING (ARONDACK SPRING, KISSINGEN SPRING)
See Arondack Spring.

IMPERIAL SPRING (FLAT ROCK SPRING)
See Flat Rock Spring.

IODINE SPRING (GUNPOWDER SPRING, PRESIDENT SPRING, STAR SPRING)
See Star Spring.

IRON SPRING (KARISTA SPRING, FLAT WELL #2)
See Karista Spring.

ISLAND SPOUTER
Located in Geyser Park on a small island in Geyser Creek opposite Hayes Spring.

JACKSON SPRING (UNION SPRING)
See Union Spring.

JUDE'S WELL (ROSEMARY SPRING)
See Rosemary Spring.

KARISTA SPRING (FLAT SPRING #2, IRON SPRING)
Karista means "iron" in Iroquois language.

This spring is located on the west side of Geyser Creek in one of the most scenic parts of Geyser Park.

One of the 18 of 163 springs left running when springs were taken over by the state. Retubing and resealing in 1916 markedly increased its available flow. In 1925 an attractive pavilion and a new fountain were erected over the spring.

This water is one of the strongest ferruginous waters in the world. It may be obtained only at the spring and is not bottled.

When in the 1930's it was decided to give mud pack treatments at the Spa, it was necessary to find a certain type of humus mud. Such mud could only be found on land which had once been in a certain type of valley where leaves were blown for thousands of years, with drainage that would permit the leaves to decompose without putrifying. Geologists surveyed many areas in search of the ideal mud. They finally found it around the Karista Spring where the mud was very strongly impreganted with iron from the water.

KISSINGEN SPRING (ARONDACK SPRING, HYPERION SPRING)

See Arondack Spring.

LAFAYETTE SPRING

Located on west side of Geyser Creek, a short distance south of the Champion Spring.

LAFAYETTE SPRING #2

Locate in Geyser Park near Lafayette Spring.

LELAND SPRING

Drilled by and named for owner, Charles E. Leland, owner of the Clarenden Hotel. Located near Washington Spring on South Broadway where St. Peter's Academy now stands.

LEVENGSTON SPRING (PUTNAM SPRING, PUTNAM CONGRESS SPRING)

See Putnam Spring.

LINCOLN GROUP OF SPRINGS

These are springs which were drilled from 1896 to 1910 on South Broadway on land owned by the Lincoln Spring Company and the Natural Carbonic Gas Company. They were drilled from 350 to 425 feet deep through dolomite. All extraordinarily highly carbonated, these springs were valuable for yielding carbon dioxide gas for bottling. In 1911 they were taken over by the State of New York and the pumping of the water for gas was stopped. There were somewhere between eighty and a hundred wells on the property of the two gas companies. They were designated by numbers and letters and were not named as other springs were. Most of them have been capped. However, some are now used to supply the mineral water used in all of the bath houses at the Spa, their high carbon dioxide content making them especially ideal for this purpose. Five ample wells furnish 24,000 gallons per day for the Lincoln Bath House alone during the summer season. There, during the morning hours, one hundred baths, each using sixty gallons of the mineral waters, are given per hour.

Some of the Lincoln water is used in fountains for drinking purposes. From 1920 to 1960 there was a fountain opposite the main entrance of the casino. Lincoln water was piped to it from the Spa Reservation. This line also supplied a fountain at the northeast corner of Putnam and Spring Streets (now public parking lot) and provided a supplemental supply to the Putnam or Saratoga baths on Phila Street. Over the years the line became corroded and was finally abandoned.

LITHIA SPRING

One of the springs in the Ten Spring Woods, it was named for its high lithia content. A porthole over this spring would burn with a blue flame when ignited.

MAGNESIA SPRING (UNITED STATES SPRING)

See United States Spring.

MAGNETIC SPRING (SLOCUM SPRING)

Located on Spring (High Rock) Avenue opposite High Rock Park. It was discovered in 1873 by William P. Slocum. The water was used principally for bathing purposes. It was claimed that the Magnetic Bath House was the only one in Saratoga Springs that had porcelain-lined tubs, a steam boiler and electric bells. This spring ceased to flow and was filled up in 1914.

The following advertisement was used to publicize the baths:

> Magnetic water baths are a remedy for rheumatism, neuralgia, nervous prostration and diseases peculiar to women. They have a powerful effect also in relieving weariness and exhaustion. They produce healthy sleep; they are at once a tonic and a stimulant, and are very cleansing and softening to the skin. The water has worked wonderful cures in cases of dyspepsia, liver difficulties, kidney troubles and weakness of the lungs.

MENNONEBE SPRING

Located in Geyser Park, this spring had an intimate relation to the Geyser Spring. It showed an increase while the Geyser decreased in flow. On account of its great similarity to the Geyser Spring and, because it constituted an unwise drain on the valuable well, the Mennonebe Spring was filled with concrete and closed in 1919.

Hathorn Spring #3 showing crowds gathered to drink this strong cathartic water before breakfast

High Rock Spring in 1840 with Saratoga Fault in background

From engraving by P. R. B. Pearson, 1873

Section of High Rock showing layers accumulated over the remains of a fire built at the spring hundreds of years ago

From engraving by P. R. B. Pearson, 1873

Iodine Spring in 1842. Later named Star Spring

Island Spouter in winter

Karista Spring

Pavilion Spring

From engraving by P. R. B. Pearson, 1873

Patterson Spring

Collection of the Saratoga Spa

Bath House of Putnam Spring. This building was later occupied by the Saratoga Bath House

Star Spring and Bottling House as it appeared in 1870

MINNEHAHA SPRING

One of the springs in the Ten Springs Woods, not far from the Excelsior Spring.

MONROE SPRING

Located on the east side of Maple Avenue, a little north of the Flat Rock Spring, it lay in the rear of Elmwood Hall, also known as Ford's Institute, at 48 Maple Avenue. The building was razed in 1974.

MORCK SPRING (CARLSBAD SPRING, REDMOND SPRING)

See Carlsbad Spring.

MORIARTA SPRING

One of the Lincoln Spring group on South Broadway on land of Lincoln Spring Company which had previously belonged to Moriarta.

NEW CONGRESS SPRING (EMPIRE SPRING, WALTON SPRING)

See Empire Spring.

NEW RED SPRING (RED SPRING #2, ELIXIR SPRING)

See Red Spring #2.

NEW YORK DAM SPRING

This spring in Congress Park was capped and sealed in 1916.

NOLAN SPRING

A private spring in the rear yard of the Putnam mansion on Whitney Place just southeast of Congress Park and presently the site of the Presbyterian-Congregational Church.

Two bores were made; one was dry, the other yielded mineral water.

OLD HURLBURT SPRING

Located in Geyser Park. Listed in Dunn (1974) and W. Kemp (1912). No further information available.

OLYMPIA SPRING

Located in Geyser Park. No further information available.

ORENDA SPRING (ADAM'S SPRING, CONGRESS #2 SPRING)

Located in Geyser Park, the water from this spring cascades over a 30 foot embankment into Geyser Creek below. This action results in a vertical structure 30 feet high and 2 to 5 feet thick made up of tufa or travertine, composed mainly of carbonates deposited from the water flowing over it. It is, in a sense, a miniature Yellowstone of the east, except that it is about 93% carbonates from cold water, rather than silicates from hot water. According to Strock, research chemist at the Simon Baruch Research Institute, the travertine is built up at the rate of 2 tons per 1,000,000 gallons of water.

Travertine has an interesting physical structure, and has a few singular features:

• It is radioactive. Minute amounts of radon and other radioactive materials dissolved in the water become highly concentrated in the tufa.

• It affords an open air, above ground, exhibition of cave-type travertine formation. However, it forms more rapidly and is, therefore, coarser than the underground variety.

• The rapid formation of the tufa gives rise to a sort of "instant fossilization." Twigs and leaves and other objects are quickly coated with the carbonates and become fossils.

The water has one of the highest potassium iodide contents among the Saratoga waters. Scientists of the Simon Baruch Research Institute believe that this iodide passes off in fumes and that it is possible here to inhale the iodine required for the human body. This belief has added a new technique distinctive to the Saratoga Spa.

The formation of travertine from the Orenda Spring may plainly be seen looking south from the bridge over Geyser Creek which is on the path between the ticket office on Route 50 and the main building of the Saratoga Performing Arts Center.

PANDORA SPRING (AWASA SPRING)

See Awasa Spring.

PARADISE SPRING

Located in Geyser Park. Listed by Dunn (1974). No further information is available on this spring.

PATH SPRING

Located in Geyser Park. Listed by Dunn (1974). No further information is available on this spring.

PATTERSON SPRING

This spring was discovered in 1886 on the property of Alexander H. Patterson on the south side of Phila Street, one block east of Broadway and it soon became one of the most popular springs in Saratoga. Quite radioactive, the water was considered one of the strongest diuretics, superior as a cathartic and alterative, and a delicious beverage. The water was bottled and indications for its use included "kidney and liver complaints, rheumatism, diabetes, heartburn, dyspepsia, sour stomach, sick headache, malaria and weaknesses of women." The fine drink hall with its forty foot ceiling built to dispense the water served between 1,500 and 2,500 persons daily.

PAVILION SPRING (DR. STEELE'S SPRING, ROYANCH SPRING)

This fine fountain was first discovered by Dr. John H. Steele in 1816. It was located southeast of the Flat Rock Spring on the Willow Walk in the rear of the Columbian Hotel between Lake Avenue and Caroline Street. Because it lay in the midst of a deep morass buried under 40 feet of alluvial deposit somewhat remote from its source in the rock, tubing it was extremely difficult, and all attemtps failed until 1839 when Daniel McClaren finally succeeded at great expense of money and effort. After this spring and the United States Spring were successfully tubed, the surrounding swamp was drained, filled and landscaped. An attractive colonnade, one of the most elegant in the village, was placed over the two springs.

Possibly because of the enormous expense involved in making this fountain accessible, Mr. McClaren decided to place a tax on the water, charging fifty cents for an individual and one dollar for a family for the privilege of drinking it. This stirred up great protest in the community. Meetings were held and the owner of the spring was denounced. The tax was known as "The Saratoga Stamp Act." Needless to say, the tax was withdrawn and people were allowed free use of the water.

The water was much used both at home and abroad. It was a great favorite of the people of German extraction who sometimes mixed it with wine. The free acid of the spring was most abundant, and passed in great quantities from the mouth of the fountain. Its water was not so heavy as that of the Congress Spring, but the liberal quantities of free gas present imparted a very smart, pungent taste, and induced many to think it the strongest water of the valley. This taste, so characteristic of all Saratoga mineral waters, was enhanced by drinking from a metallic cup, instead of the glass tumblers generally used. The reason is obvious to those who have studied the principles of galvanism.

This water was bottled and shipped all over the eastern United States.

PEERLESS SPRING

This spring is located on the east side of High Rock Avenue about ten feet from the Magnetic Spring. The lessee of the Magnetic Spring bath house formerly provided free service of the water to the public during the summer months while the bath house was in operation.

At present, the water from this spring is piped in to High Rock Park and flows from a fountain on a concrete slab on which are also located fountains supplying water from the Governor and Seltzer Springs.

The water is very palatable, fine alkaline, saline water of moderate strength.

POLARIS SPRING (RAVINE SPRING)

A spouter still running in Geyser Park just to the east of Geyser Creek, south of the Island Spouter. Its water shows very high radioactivity.

PRESIDENT SPRING (IODINE SPRING, GUNPOWDER SPRING, STAR SPRING)

See Star Spring.

PUMP WELL #4 (TALLULAH SPRING)

Tallulah means "leaping water" in Iroquois.

Located in Lincoln Park on land previously owned by the General Carbonic Company, this water was considered an excellent digestive and valuable table water. It had a high bicarbonate of soda, a low sodium chloride and an unusually small iron content. Its radioactivity was higher than any other spring on the reservation. This well was retubed and resealed in 1916.

PUMP WELL #5

This well was located in Lincoln Park on land belonging to the General Carbonic Company which had previously belonged to the Shonts estate. It was retubed and resealed in 1916.

PUTNAM SPRING (LEVENGSTON SPRING, PUTNAM CONGRESS SPRING)

This spring was discovered in 1835 by Mr. Lewis Putnam, then the oldest living resident of Saratoga Springs. It lies on Phila Street opposite the Patterson Spring. At the time of its discovery, it was regarded as the richest chalybeate water in the Saratoga group. It was a very popular water, used by both local citizens and visitors. Many were particularly attached to this water, using it instead of the Congress for cathartic purposes, with good results. It was used also for mineral baths given in the Levengston Bath House under which the waters of the spring emerged. This fine bathing establishment, previously owned by Mr. Putnam, was acquired by the State of New York in 1911.

PUTNAM CONGRESS SPRING (PUTNAM SPRING, LEVENGSTON SPRING)

See Putnam Spring.

QUA SPRING

Located on High Rock Avenue opposite the High Rock Spring, its water was bottled. The spring was owned by the Arthur Qua family.

QUEVIC SPRING

This spring was located in Excelsior Park not far from Excelsior Spring. It was drilled just before the turn of the century. Because Mr. Lawrence, the owner, greatly admired Queen Victoria, he named the spring after her. Queen

Victoria was shortened to Quevic, and the water bottled under that name.

In 1948 the spring and bottling plant were sold to Carl Touhey. The plant burned to the ground in 1966. In 1967 the property and spring were sold to the Saratoga Vichy Spring Company, who had contracted to bottle the waters for the company after the fire. In 1973 the Saratoga Vichy Spring Company was sold to William White, Jr., who continued bottling the water.

RAVINE SPOUTER SPRING (POLARIS SPOUTER SPRING)

See Polaris Spouter Spring.

RED SPRING (OLD RED SPRING, BEAUTY SPRING)

This valuable spring was the second one of the mineral springs of Saratoga to become known to the early settlers. It was discovered very shortly after the High Rock, about 1770, probably by Samuel Norton, a very early settler at the High Rock. Located about 55 yards north of the High Rock Spring, its name derives from the fact that a deposit of iron forms in the water on standing. On leaving the spring the water is clear, sparkling and pleasant to taste. The total mineral content is somewhat lower than that of the other springs, while it is relatively much higher in iron.

The first bath house to be constructed in Saratoga was built near this spring in 1784. Bryan's bath house was used by visitors with all kinds of eruptive skin diseases. The spring was often called the bathing spring or the beauty water spring.

In 1870, the Red Spring Water Company was formed by John A. Carpenter, Lewis E. Whitney and Eli Samtel. Extensive excavation was done in order to tube the spring. A second vein of mineral water was found, which was also tubed. The new spring was called New Red Spring or Red Spring #2. In 1871 a bottling plant was built, water shipped within the United States.

From the beginning, this spring has been famous for its phenomenal curative properties when used in cases of skin disease or for inflammation of the eyes. The testimonials on its value are legion, and there is scarcely a true Saratogian who cannot relate at least one incident of a cure by the "Beauty" water. One such testimonial, taken from *The Saratogian* of July 20, 1955, may illustrate the case in point:

SARATOGA WOMAN FINDS SHINGLES CURE
IN RED SPRING SPA WATER

Mayor Mallery and Mrs. Lottie F. Katz of this city have joined in executing sworn affidavits which they hope will be instrumental in convincing an ailing public of the beneficial effects of the Saratoga mineral water.

Mrs. Katz, who with her husband, conducts a news and novelty store opposite Convention Hall, deposes that since January 2, 1953, or a period of more than two years, she has suffered from shingles. Her face and head were covered with a rash "not pleasant at times," and the cause of great pain and suffering.

"Injections by two physicians did not help," she adds, and, "when I consulted one physician about bathing the parts in Red Spring water, I was informed that the treatment was too severe."

"However, my husband and I felt that the pain and suffering could be no worse, so I started applying packs soaked in Red Spring water, and to my great pleasure my skin has cleared and the pain and suffering has disappeared." The result was accomplished in about three weeks, she said.

This statement in the form of a letter to the mayor, and notarized, explained the reason for writing as: "You wanted a testimonial on the value of the mineral waters of Saratoga Springs."

"I feel," she adds, "that there are many thousands of people who would be benefited if they were to try the waters of our city and I deeply regret that the doctors do not see fit to recommend these waters."

"I sincerely hope that my experience will serve as an example for thousands of people who must be suffering as I was."

The major part of the testimonial is to substantiate Mrs. Katz's statement. Mayor Mallery is an acquaintance and saw her regularly during the period she was afflicted with the disfiguring and painful ailment.

Of particular interest in connection with the affliction is a timely article featured recently in a nationally circulated weekly magazine which referred to shingles as "incurable" insofar as there is no effective remedy known to medicine.

RED SPRING #2 (NEW RED SPRING, ELIXIR SPRING)
See New Red Spring.

REDMOND SPRING (CARLSBAD SPRING, MORCK SPRING)
See Carlsbad Spring.

ROSEMARY SPRING (JUDE'S WELL)
Located on the grounds of the Grand Union Motel on South Broadway. In 1964 it was drilled to a depth of approximately 452 feet, and was the first new well drilled in Saratoga Springs in more than half a century. The gazebo over the spring is from the Rosoff house grounds on Union Avenue, next to the Racing Museum on the east. The white marble slabs used at the spring are from the original sidewalk in front of the old Grand Union Hotel.

An antique flower urn covers the well. It has two cups attached to it for drinking purposes.

ROYAL SPRING
This spring was located on the southwest corner of Lake Avenue and Henry Street. It was bored in 1887 to a depth of 693 feet and is remembered for the fact that its water was put up in brown crocks.

ROYANCH SPRING (PAVILION SPRING, DR. STEELE'S SPRING)
See Pavilion Spring.

SARATOGA "A" SPRING ("A" SPRING)
See "A" Spring.

SARATOGA SOFT SWEET SPRING (FERNDELL SPRING, STATE SEAL)
See Ferndell Spring.

SELTZER SPRING (BARREL SPRING)
This spring is located in High Rock Park about 150 feet south of the High Rock Spring. It was discovered in 1792. In 1793, along with the other springs in the High Rock area, it came into the possession of Jacob Walton. He developed a path to the spring and embedded a barrel in the marshy ground around it thus providing a dam to contain the water which was used for bathing. This led to its being called "the Barrel Spring."

In 1860 the spring was purchased by Dr. J. P. Haskins, who properly tubed it and placed a glass tube 3 feet long and 15 inches in diameter over it, making an attractive display of bubbling water which was enjoyed by many visitors. The water was sold in bottles and in tanks of 10 or 20 gallon capacity.

This spring is the only seltzer spring in the United States. It is a rival of the famous Seltzer Spring in Nassau, Germany, which it very closely resembles. It is unsurpassed for mixing with red or white wines.

At the present, the water flows on a slab at the south end of High Rock Park.

SHONTS #1, #2, and #3 SPRINGS
Located in the State Park, these springs are listed in Kemp (1912) and in Dunn (1974).

SLOCUM SPRING (MAGNETIC SPRING)
See Magnetic Spring.

SMALL ROCK SPRING
From reliable accounts given by three visitors to the High Rock Spring in the late 1700's and early 1800's, there apparently was a second similar spring located near the High Rock Spring which has since disappeared. This was known as the Small Rock Spring.

SPRUDEL SPRING (CLARK #3 SPRING)
See Clark #3 Spring.

STAR SPRING (IODINE SPRING, GUNPOWDER SPRING, PRESIDENT SPRING, WALTON SPRING)

Located in High Rock Park north of the High Rock Spring, it was first called the Gunpowder Spring because of the odor of gunpowder at the spring.

In 1784, a four foot high protective curb was placed around the outlet of the spring and it was renamed President Spring.

In 1834 it was tubed, found to contain iodine and renamed Iodine Spring.

The Star Spring Company was formed in 1865, the spring was again renamed the Star Spring and the "finest bottling house in Saratoga" was erected. The water was supplied in bottles as well as in large 15 gallon tin-lined barrels. This spring was sometimes referred to as the Walton Spring after it came into the possession of Jacob Walton in 1793.

STATE SEAL WATER

See Ferndell Spring.

STRONG SPRING

This spring was drilled in the courtyard of Dr. Strong's Sanatorium on the east side of Circular Street between Phila and Spring Streets, the site of the former Father's Hall of Skidmore. The sanatorium was founded in 1835 under the name Remedial Institute.

The spring had to be capped as the result of a lawsuit brought by Henry H. Hathorn, who won a claim based on the allegation that Dr. Strong's spring adversely affected the flow of the Hathorn #1 Spring.

SWAMP ANGEL SPRING

Located in State Park, it was listed by Dunn (1976).

TALLULAH SPRING

See Pump Well #4.

TAYLOR'S JACKSON SPRING (UNION SPRING)

See Union Spring.

TAYLOR'S WASHINGTON SPRING

Located in Ten Spring Woods.

TEN SPRINGS

A group of springs discovered in 1814 on property owned by John and Ziba Taylor, located northeast of High Rock Park and north of Lake Avenue.

TOWNSEND RAILROAD SPRING

Included in the book *Empire Spring* by E. Emmons, M.D. (1849)

TRITON SPOUTING SPRING

A pipe well 192 feet deep on the east side of Geyser Lake, it was drilled in 1872, the fifth spring to be drilled in Geyser Park area. It was protected by a little frame building which also served as a bottling house.

UNION SPRING (JACKSON SPRING)

This spring is one of the original springs of the Ten Springs group in the Ten Spring Woods. It was discovered by John Taylor on his property, located near the center of what is now Excelsior Park, about 165 feet west of the Excelsior Spring. Originally it was known as the Jackson Spring.

Along with the property including Excelsior Spring, the spring was purchased by Henry H. Lawrence in 1859. It was retubed in 1865 and sold in bottles as well as in special patented 30 gallon barrels lined with pure block tin.

Professor C.F. Chandler of the Columbia Universtiy School of Mines, analyzed the water, giving the following report: "This water is of excellent strength. It is especially noticeable that the ratio of magnesia to lime is universally large, which is a decided advantage. The water is also remarkably free from iron which is a great recommendation."

UNITED STATES SPRING (MAGNESIA SPRING)

This spring is located only ten feet from the Pavilion Spring behind the Columbian Hotel on Pavilion Place between Lake Avenue and Caroline Streets. It was originally in a very swampy area of forty feet of alluvial deposit. Its original owner, William H. Walton, sold the property to Daniel McClaren in 1839. The new owner invested a large sum of money to improve the property and tube both the Pavilion, and later, this spring. He erected a handsome structure over the two springs, making an interesting tourist attraction.

Though located very close to the Pavilion Spring, its water was distinctly different. It was used extensively to mix with wines, and was bottled and widely distributed.

VICHY SPRING (SARATOGA VICHY SPRING)

This well was drilled in 1872 in Geyser Park not far from Geyser Lake. A fine vein of mineral water was struck at 180 feet. In composition, it strikingly resembled the water of the famous Vichy Spring in France, having a higher bicarbonate of soda and lower salt content than any other spring of the Saratoga group. The water was bottled by the Saratoga Vichy Spring Company.

In 1902 suit was brought by the French Government against the Saratoga Vichy Spring Company because of the use of the name "Vichy." It ended in the Supreme Court, and a favorable judgment was awarded the Saratoga Vichy Spring Company. Strongly in their favor was the fact that they had used the name "Vichy" for over 25 years before the suit was brought.

The water may be used as a mixer because it is low in iron and the mineral content is controlled. It does not precipitate iron, which would cause a dark cloudiness, when mixed with alcohol, as is the case in the other mineral waters.

VICTORIA SPRING

This well was drilled 204 feet deep at the Geysers in 1892. It was reputed to be a clear, sparkling, delicious mineral water. It was bottled and sold until 1911, when the water ceased to flow and could only be obtained by pumping. It was capped and sealed in 1916.

WALTON SPRING (EMPIRE SPRING, NEW CONGRESS SPRING)

See Empire Spring. The Star Spring was sometimes referred to as The Walton Spring after it came into the possession of Jacob Walton in 1793.

WAGMAN SPRING

This spring was owned by the proprietor of Elmwood Hall. Situated just south of High Rock Park, it was not a flowing spring. Water was obtained by means of a hand pump.

WASHINGTON SPRING

This spring was the first tubed by Gideon Putnam in 1806. It was located in the court of the Clarendon Hotel on South Broadway where St. Peter's Academy now stands. In 1828 a commodious bath house was erected near the spring. There were billiard tables and bowling alleys in the bath house, and nearby was a pond stocked with speckled trout for fishing. The grounds in the vicinity were very picturesque, and were lighted every evening by gas.

The spring was purchased in 1856 by John H. White, stepson of Clarke, who began bottling its water in 1859. It was a chalybeate (iron) water, having tonic and diuretic properties.

WHITE SULPHUR SPRING - EUREKA PARK

This is the only sulphur spring in Saratoga Springs. Located in Eureka Park at the north end of Spring Valley, it was tubed in 1868 and was said to be unsurpassed by any sulphur spring in the state. Sulphuretted or hepatic waters acquire their peculiar properties from beds of pyrites or by passing through strata of bituminous shale and foetic-oolitic beds. These are regarded as organic sulphuretted waters, while the others are mineral. The water of this spring was remarkably clear and discharged 20,000 gallons a day.

A fifty room bath house was constructed next to the spring. It had excellent, accommodations with facilities affording warm and cold sulphur baths.

WHITE SULPHUR SPRING - SARATOGA LAKE

This once famous spring is located on the east side of Saratoga Lake about a mile south of Snake Hill. It lies in a beautiful ravine through which runs a small stream which is fed by fresh water springs. The course of the spring to the brook is marked by a deposit of sulphur. The water is strongly charged with sulphuretted hydrogen.

Steamboat service on Saratoga Lake, two trips per day, was enjoyed by patrons of the spring, its bath house and the White Sulphur Springs Hotel. The hotel was located on Saratoga Lake near the spring.

WINDMILL SPRING

Located in the State Park, further information is not available.

ZALAMA SPRING (CLARK #1 SPRING)

See Clark #1 Spring.

7

The Mineral Springs of Ballston Spa

*"Mineral springs are a national asset, and
any nation which fails to make use of these
gifts of nature causes loss and damage to
the economic strength of its people."*
—Oskar Baudish

Ballston Spa is a charming village about seven miles southwest of Saratoga Springs. It is situated in a valley through which runs a small stream which is a branch of Kayaderosseras Creek.

Mineral springs were first discovered in this area around 1769 during a survey and partition of the land of the Kayaderosseras Patent. To defray the expense of surveying, a plot of land which lay about two and a half miles south of a recently discovered mineral spring was set aside to be sold.

It was this plot of land that the Reverend Eliphet Ball and his parishoners purchased with the idea of founding a new parish in the area. The Reverend Ball, a cousin of George Washington's mother, was a Congregational minister in the Town of Bedford, Westchester County. He and his loyal parishoners, with all their earthly possessions, moved to the new site to begin a new life. By mutual consent the place was called Ball's Town, later contracted to Ballston.

At the time there was some opposition to the name. A strong contingent wanted to call the place McDonaldville, after the McDonald brothers who had settled just south of there in 1763. The McDonalds developed a prosperous farm near the lake, later called Ballston Lake. However, Reverend Ball's followers won out and the settlement became known as Ballston. As springs were developed, Spa was added to the name. Ballston Spa developed as a springs resort area several years before Saratoga Springs became known.

In 1772 a gentleman by the name of Benjamin Douglas purchased a plot of land of about 100 acres just west of the first spring to be discovered, the Old Iron Spring. Mr. Douglas came from Lebanon Springs, a community thirty miles east of Albany, where mineral springs had been discovered and developed, so making the town a flourishing resort. Sir William Johnson's papers reveal the fact that he visited these springs several times.

Douglas sought to get a head start in developing Ballston Spa as a prosperous resort area around its mineral springs as had been done at Lebanon Springs. He immediately built a log house on his land for the accommodation of visitors who came to partake of the mineral waters. He was so successful that, by 1790, he found it necessary to increase his facilities by enlarging the building.

At about the same time that Benjamin Douglas arrived in Ballston Spa, Peter Ferris also arrived. He purchased and settled a plot of land next to the land owned by Mr. Douglas. He too provided for the accommodation of visitors.

In 1792, Mr. Nicholas Low of New York City erected a large house next to the spring and opened it as a boarding house. By 1803 he saw the need for a deluxe hotel to accommodate people seeking a luxurious environment during their visit to the springs. Accordingly, he built such a place, a three story wooden building, 100 feet long with wings 50 feet long. He called it Sans Souci, "without cares," named after the palace built by Frederick the Great in 1745 at Potsdam, Germany.

The enterprising citizens of Ballston Spa provided attractive, comfortable accommodations for visitors to the springs from the time the springs were first discovered in 1769. With such inviting accommodations, Ballston Spa was a flourishing resort when Saratoga was still a wilderness. Ballston Spa was at least twenty years ahead of Saratoga Springs in development as a resort town. It was incorporated as a village in 1807. It was not until after Gideon Putnam planned and developed the village of Saratoga Springs that it took hold as a resort area where the benefits of its springs could be enjoyed by visitors.

A list of the springs of Ballston Spa which are situated in a deep valley through which passes a branch of the Kayaderosseras Creek follows:

ARTESIAN LITHIA SPRING

This spring was discovered in 1866 by workmen drilling for oil. It was located on Saratoga Avenue on the site now occupied by a knitting mill.

When the drill reached a depth of 650 feet there was an explosion which shot the drill 20 feet into the air. This was followed by a spouting of water 50 feet high.

On analysis by Professor C.F. Chandler of Columbia University School of Mines, the water proved to be a strong mineral water with a high lithium

Ballston Spa, circa 1860

Artesian Lithia Spring, discovered in 1866 while drilling for oil

content. A spring house and bottling plant were built at the spring, and the surrounding grounds were landscaped.

The water was bottled and sold under the name Artesia Lithia Spring Water. Great emphasis was placed on the lithium content of the water, and fantastic claims were made as to its medicinal value.

BISCHOFF SPRING

This spring is located on Milton Avenue on the north shore of a branch of Kayaderosseras Creek on the property of the Bischoff Chocolate Factory. It was drilled in 1930. At present, it is not flowing.

CHAPMAN SPRING (GLEN SPRING)

See Glen Spring.

COLUMBIAN SPRING

This spring was drilled in 1767 on Malta Avenue on the property of Samuel Hides. It was located about 200 feet from the famous Franklin Spring. Its depth was 715 feet.

FRANKLIN SPRING

See Hides Franklin Spring.

FULTON CHALYBEATE SPRING

Information on this spring, rich in iron, is not available.

GLEN SPRING (CHAPMAN SPRING)

This spring was drilled in 1861. It was located just below the woolen mill dam. Its flow lasted only three years.

HIDES FRANKLIN SPRING (COMSTOCK)

Samuel Hides was a blacksmith in Ballston Spa and a prominent citizen. He had a great interest in spiritualism and frequently claimed to have made contact with departed spirits through a medium. In 1867 he believed that he made contact with the spirit of Benjamin Franklin and was advised by the spirit that on his property there existed a spring with superior medicinal value, and that he should develop it for "the healing of the nation."

He owned 30 acres of land on Malta Avenue on which several wells had already been drilled. After his seance with Franklin's spirit, he engaged drillers in 1867 to drill what was to be the well for "healing the nation." At a depth of 715 feet water was struck and a geyser spouted over 50 feet in the air. When analyzed, the water showed extremely high mineral content.

After a time Mr. Hides' name was added to the name of the spring and it became known as the Hides Franklin Spring and the water was bottled as Hides Franklin Mineral Water.

In later years the spring was housed in a round bottling building made of cobblestones. The building was razed in 1951 and houses were built on the property.

LAFAYETTE SPRING (WASHINGTON SPRING)

See Washington Spring.

LOW'S SPRING

The second spring discovered in Ballston Spa, located in Gordon's Creek, its water was used in the first baths.

LOW'S WELL

The third spring discovered in Ballston Spa, it was the most popular of the day and was a member of a group of springs collectively called "Sans Souci."

OLD IRON SPRING

This spring was the first discovered in Ballston Spa, and the last one to remain running. It was discovered by Beriah Palmer in 1769 while making a survey of the 14th allotment of the Kayaderosseras Patent. It is located near the stream that runs through the valley. In the early days it flowed out of a barrel which was sunk around it. Its appeal to cattle and wild animals made the area very unsanitary. To protect it, the citizens of the village erected a marble curb around it, with flagging surrounded by a handsome iron railing.

In 1874 the spring was retubed. The same vein was struck 50 feet north of the original site.

PARK SPRING

This spring is one of the Sans Souci group of springs and is located behind the Medbury Hotel. It has nearly the same compositon as the United States and Low's Springs, except that it contains a much larger proportion of iron oxide than any of the waters in the vicinity.

SANS SOUCI SPRINGS

The Sans Souci Springs was a group of mineral springs all owned by Nicholas Low, the owner and proprietor of the Sans Souci Hotel. The first of these springs to be discovered was Low's Spring near Gordon's Creek (also known as Jack's Spring). Until its discovery, only one other spring had been discovered in Ballston Spa.

Low built a bath house by this spring where mineral baths were very popular with the hotel guests. This did much to enhance the attractiveness of the Sans Souci Hotel and Ballston Spa as a watering place.

Other springs in the Sans Souci group were Sulphur Spring, Park Spring, which was located behind the Medbury Hotel and the New Spring.

In 1870 George Smith, then owner of the Sans Souci Hotel, selected a spot just outside of the hotel's main hall on a center line with the central corridor, and had a well drilled. At a depth of 690 feet a vein of very fine mineral water was struck. The well was tubed and a small pavilion was built over it. The water was bottled and for a time sold well under the name Sans Souci Spouting Spring Water. However, the bottling was stopped in 1870 and the well was capped.

Years later, Joseph Peshette retubed the spring to a depth of almost a thousand feet and Sans Souci Water was again bottled and sold until the time of Mr. Peshette's death in 1967. Later it was purchased and again bottled until 1970. The spring still remains, though inactive, in a small building in the center of the block.

SULPHUR SPRING

One of the Sans Souci group of Springs.

WASHINGTON SPRING (LAFAYETTE SPRING)

This well was first drilled in 1817 and lasted only two years. In 1824, it was drilled again 100 feet south of the Iron Railing Spring. In 1828 it was rechristened The Lafayette Spring. It became extinct in 1874 when the Old Iron Spring was retubed 50 feet north of its original site.

WASHINGTON LITHIA SPRING

Drilled in 1868 to a depth of 612 feet, this spring was located at the base of the railroad embankment just below the fairgrounds.

Its water was analyzed in 1876 by Dr. C.F. Chandler of Columbia University School of Mines and found to be rich in lithium. It was bottled by the Washington Lithium Spring Company until 1896 when the company was dissolved.

The spring is currently owned by the Village of Ballston Spa. There is still a small flow of water in the abandoned casing. If retubed and reactivated, the spring could be beneficial to the people of Ballston Spa.

WEST SPRING

This spring was drilled in 1897 by George West near his bag mill on the south side of the branch of the Kayaderosseras Creek which runs through the village.

The spring has been abandoned and the site is now a parking lot.

UNITED STATES SPRING

This spring was located at the northeast corner of Bath and Washington Streets. Owned by James Jack, the water was used, along with water from Sans Souci Springs, in the bath house on the north side of Washington Street east of Bath.

8

The Kayaderosseras Patent

"The health of nations is more important than the wealth of nations."
—Will Durant

The area of Saratoga County in which the Saratoga Spa lies was once part of the County of Albany. It was not until 1791 that Saratoga was set off as a separate county. The lands in the Saratoga area were originally inhabited by Mohawk Indians. This expanse of virgin forest, lying in the foothills of the Adirondacks, the natural habitat of many species of wild animals, was revered by the Mohawk tribe of the Iroquois nation as their favorite hunting ground. They believed that the mineral springs found in the area were a gift of the great god Manitou, to be used by them to restore the health of their ailing members and, to preserve the well-being of those who used them wisely. Because they considered these waters sacred, they kept their presence a closely guarded secret.

The early history of this whole area is one of controversy and bloodshed. The controversy came when the white settlers tried to purchase the land from the Indians and settle it. In many cases the Indians felt that the land was being fraudulently wrested from them and they resisted with violence. Settlers were killed and homes and villages burned by the Indians when they felt that there was no other recourse after warning the settlers that they had no right to occupy the territory.

Some of the lands in the county were honestly and legitimately secured by the colonists, however, and were released without resistance on the part of the Indians. In consideration of a purchase price in money or goods, the colonists were given a deed to the land by the Indians. This was confirmed by the colonial government with a land grant. Following this a warrant was issued for the preparation of a patent issued by the Crown to certain of its subjects for that special tract or parcel of land.

Several such patents were issued in the early years of the colonial period. One of the earliest of these, the Van Schaick Patent, was granted May 31, 1687 to Anthony Van Schaick. It included the present town of Waterford on the Hudson and a considerable tract of land adjacent to it in the Town of Half Moon.

Another early grant was made by the Appel Patent for land on the north side of the Mohawk River which extended three miles back into the woods towards Ballston Lake. In his petition to the Crown in 1708, William Appel stated that twenty years before a field of corn on the north bank of the Mohawk in the County of Albany had been planted by him and his partner, Harmanus Hagadorn. At the time it was ready for harvest the Mohawks, who were on the warpath against Canada, had encamped on it and destroyed it. The loss was estimated at $400.00. In consideration of this the Indians had given them a deed to the land which was signed by four sachems of the tribe. The petition further stated that Mr. Appel had been wounded in 1690 when the hostile tribes from Canada burned Schenectady.

Some time later the Saratoga Patent was issued to Colonel Peter Schuyler, Robert Livingston and several others for a tract of land bordering on the Van Schaick land and extending north along both sides of the Hudson and reaching back for a distance of six miles on either side. The land was called by the Indians, "Se-rach-ta-gue," which meant "Hillside country of the Great River." The sale had been negotiated as early as 1684. The negotiation was not completed, however, until 1702 when conveyance of the deed was made "for and in consideration of divers goods to Philip Schuyler and Robert Livingston, yeomen of the City of Albany." It was conveyed by two "Maquas Indians, owners and proprietors of the land." They described themselves as "Joseph, the Indian by them called Ta-jon-min-ha-ge and Hendrick, by them called De-han-och-rak-has." Hendrick later fought under Sir William Johnson at Lake George and was slain near Bloody Pond. Later, when the proprietors of the Kayaderosseras Patent acquired their title, they obtained a release from Schuyler and Livingston for their interest in that part of the Saratoga Patent that was included in the Kayaderosseras Patent.

Over the years other patents were issued for land in what is now Saratoga County. Some of the largest of these were the Northampton Patent, the Clifton Park Patent, the Niskayuna Patent, the Dartmouth Patent, the Livingston Patents, the Patent to John Glen and forty-four others and the Wilson and Abeel Patents.

Probably the most important and certainly the most well-known patent issued in what is now Saratoga County was the Kayaderosseras Patent granted by Queen Anne on November 2, 1708 in the seventh year of her reign.

The area involved was very large, some 800,000 acres or more. The tract included not only almost all of the present Saratoga County, that is all the land which had not previously been assigned by former patents, but also some adjacent areas in Warren, Montgomery and Fulton counties.

The earliest known record of this grant is dated April 22, 1703 when Governor Lord Cornbury granted to Samuel Shelton Broughton, attorney general and member of the New York City council, a license to purchase for himself and "others" a certain tract of unappropriated land known as Kayaderosseras. This was granted with the provision that the purchase be confirmed by letters patent within one year of the date of the petition.

For reasons that are not entirely clear, the purchase was not completed until October 4, 1704. On that date Broughton agreed to purchase the lands from the Mohawk sachems Joseph, Hendrick and Cornelius, who apparently represented three Mohawk clans. The price to be paid was stated as sixty pounds. The deed as actually signed bears marks of Joseph, Hendrick, Amos and Gideon. The mark of Cornelius does not appear. Just why Amos and Gideon should have signed is not known. Actually only two of the original three were represented instead of the three whose members made the deal. This fact was later used by the Indians as an argument against the legality of the treaty.

Over the next four years repeated attempts were made, first by Broughton and later, after his death by his heirs, on the basis of this deed, to establish legal title to the land by having a patent issued by the Crown. However, the necessary papers were never issued. It has been said that the reason for this was the fact that "neither Broughton nor anyone else for him had ever paid money directly or indirectly" to the governor. In addition, Mary Broughton, widow of Samuel, had returned to England and had taken the Indian deed with her so that it could not be produced.

Finally on September 23, 1708 a new petition for the tract was presented to the governor by Nanning Hermanse on behalf of himself and the "others" included in Broughton's petition of 1703. In the petition he stated that, although the senior Broughton, by a license from Governor Cornbury, did make a purchase of the tract, Broughton had not obtained a patent for it. He asked that the land be granted to the thirteen petitioners in thirteen undivided shares.

On November 2, 1708 the Kayaderosseras Patent was issued to Nanning Hermanse and his twelve associates. He was successful in establishing legal title to the land where his predecessor Broughton had failed. The famous patent was issued by Lord Cornbury, Governor, acting for Queen Anne. It formally granted to the petitioners the huge Kayaderosseras tract in thirteen undivided shares on condition that they or their heirs "shall within the Time and Space of Seven Years now following from and after the date hereof, Settle, Clear and make Improvements of . . . some Part or Parcel thereof."

In spite of the fact that great effort had been expended in securing title to the land, very little, if anything, was done by the patentees about the provision that it should be settled within seven years. Petition after petition was filed asking for more time for settlements to be made. They found it extremely difficult to take possession of the land because the Indians did not recognize the title, declaring that the white man was fraudulently trying to take their land from them. A permit for a survey was obtained from the governor in 1732. There is, however, no available record that such a survey was ever made.

Meanwhile the Mohawk Indians, from whom the land was alleged to have been purchased, became very concerned over the threatened loss of their precious hunting grounds. At intervals, they complained to Sir William Johnson about the whites who claimed the tract.

Finally, through the influence of Johnson, a conference was held at Albany in June 1754. The basic aim of this conference was the preservation of Anglo-Indian friendship. Lieutenant Governor DeLancey of New York was requested to explore the complaints of the Indians and to satisfy their demands, if possible. During the conference he held a special meeting with the Mohawks to discuss a deed to the Kayaderosseras tract. What apparently was the original Broughton deed of 1704 was read to the Indians. In examining both the deed given by the Indians and the patent issued by Queen Anne it was found that the land described in the deed was far less than that granted in the patent. Canandagara, spokesman for the Mohawks, explained to the members present that the Indians did not trust the "writings," a term used to designate the deeds which had been secured by the white man from the Indians. Canandagara claimed that the deeds had been obtained fraudulently and that his people feared that they would be dispossessed as a result. He noted that there was an old man present who had no recollection of the land ever being purchased. He stated further that his people would never have sold such a valuable property for the paltry sum of sixty pounds.

Faced with this dilemma, DeLancey was at a complete loss as to how to settle the matter and make payment satisfactory to the Indians. He informed them, however, that he would lay the matter before the King, who, he believed, would see that they were justly treated.

Shortly after the conference in a letter to the Board of Trade, he urged their cooperation in resolving the matter. He pointed out that "the land had been first granted to thirteen persons or tenants in common, but by purchase and devises the claimants had increased to such a number that it would be impracticable to divide and settle it." He suggested that "it would be of great service and security to our northern frontier if the grant were cancelled."

Because the controversy had heated up to such a threatening point, the Crown found it necessary to have one qualified person to manage Indian affairs. Accordingly, on February 17, 1756, Sir William Johnson was commissioned by George II as "Sole Agent and Superintendent of the Affairs of the Six Nations and their Confederacy in the Northern parts of North America." This enabled Johnson to actively protect the interests of the natives. He found himself in the impossible position of having to please both the Indians and the patentees of the great tracts.

The Lords of Trade, realizing that the problem of the extravagant land claims was one of the principal causes of the serious unrest in the colony, requested Sir Charles Hardy, then Governor of New York, to recommend to the New York Legislature that they consider the advisability of passing a law to "vacate and annul" the exorbitant and fraudulent Kayaderosseras Patent. They were not anxious to see the matter brought to the courts because they realized it would be a "long and involved process." Accordingly, on July 6, 1756, Goldsbrow Banyer, New York merchant and councilman, placed before the council a message from Governor Hardy stating that the Lord Commissioners for Trade and Plantations had requested "the interposition of the legislature in passing a law for vacating and annuling these exhorbitant and fraudulent patents." In spite of the fact that it had been requested by the Lords of Trade and was heartily supported by the Governor and Lieutenant Governor, no action was taken by the Legislature.

On March 20, 1760 the Indians again appealed to Johnson. They complained that nothing had been done to satisfy their claims though they had been promised earlier that the Kayaderosseras affair would be settled to their satisfaction. They said "We are afraid it will be forgot, and then we must be a ruined people." Johnson promised to lay their complaints before the King.

Another attempt was made by the Lords of Trade in 1764 to have the Kayaderosseras Patent cancelled. They appealed to the Legislature through Lieutenant Governor Cadwallader Colden. Again the effort failed when the Legislature declined to cooperate. The Board of Trade then asked Colden to send them an authentic copy of the patent and deed to place before Parliament. The Board reasoned that, since there was no proof of actual settlement of the tract, Parliament might vacate the patent.

In a letter sent November 6, 1764 to the Board with the copy of the deed and patent, Colden discussed the matter of property rights as viewed by the Indians. He pointed out that they considered all lands to be held in common and that only by occupancy can land be distinguished as private property. He contended that for this reason no individual Indian can give title to the lands. He further noted that the Indian deed to Kayaderosseras had been negotiated by three sachems and that only two of the three had signed it. Amos and Gideon, the co-signers, were unidentified Indians and were not parties to the deed. He also noted that the Indians had no conception of English miles and that the land area included in the patent was much greater by far than that described in the original Indian deed. He sent a copy of this letter to Sir William Johnson and asked him to assist the Indians by supplying evidence that would support the Indian claim that the patentees had made few, if any, attempts to settle the land.

Johnson cooperated fully in this matter. He put forth great effort to have the patent vacated and thus secure justice for the Mohawks. He said everybody knows "the whole thing to have been a notorious fraud." His efforts, however, met with little or no success.

When the Indians saw that nothing was being accomplished in their behalf they became desperate. Johnson, in a letter to Lieutenant Governor Colden dated February 27, 1765, expressed anxiety and showed that he was convinced that the matter had become serious and might escalate to the point of involving the whole colony. He pointed out that the affair had gone beyond the bounds of the Mohawk tribe and the six Iroquois nations and had reached the Ohio Delawares. They all believed that the Mohawks deserved better treatment than they had been given. Johnson feared that the Indians might take matters into their own hands with catastrophic results to the colonists. He felt that the colony could be "in more trouble fifty times than the patent was worth."

Finally, a committee of Kayaderosseras patentees made a move to bring about a settlement by offering a quit claim deed to part of the tract. They requested Johnson to lay the proposal before the Indians for their consideration. Unfortunately, it cannot be determined from Johnson's letters and memoirs just what happened to this proposal.

In 1766 Sir Henry Moore, Governor of New York, made a sincere attempt to settle the dispute. He spent four days in the Mohawk country conferring with their chiefs. They informed him that they were looking for the justice from England that had been denied to them in America. They declared that they would allow no settlement on their land that was taken under fraudulent claims. They believed that the government should cancel the Kayaderosseras grant.

In a letter to the Secretary of State, the Earl of Shelburne, Moore reported on his visit and stated that the Mohawks wanted the government to cancel the Kayaderosseras grant. He listed their reasons for the request as follows:

> 1st.   They deny that it was ever their intention to convey so large a tract of land as the patent describes which according to some accounts contains 600,000 acres and according to others 900,000 acres.
>
> 2nd.   They acknowledge that some of their brethren did intend to sell a small tract which is included in this patent, but that it bears no manner of proportion to that mentioned in the deed.
>
> 3rd.   That the deed of sale was executed only by two of their tribes without the concurrence of the third, which makes it void, as no lands can be disposed of in a fair and equitable sale, without the consent of all the three tribes denominated by them, the Turtle, the Wolf, and the Bear.
>
> 4th.   That they never received any consideration of the sale nor do the patentees pretend that they ever did.
>
> 5th.   That they have been informed that some goods were sent to Schenectady, which were to be given to them instead of money, but the person with whom they were intrusted gave it out that the house in which they were lodged was burn't, and the goods destroyed so that they never had the least gratification for the land either in goods or money.

Governor Moore then met with patentees of the tract and suggested that they surrender the patent to the Crown. Understandably, the suggestion met with no success. He found that they had made so many divisions and subdivisions of the original tracts that the number of proprietors had reached one hundred and thirty with the result that "every family of any consideration in the Province is concerned in it, as well as the principal lawyers of the country. Whether application is made to the assembly or to the courts of justice there is not the least probability of success as the very persons interested in the event will in either case be the judge in his own cause." They had hopes that, since the court had done nothing about settling this grant, it would have to be settled in America, in which case a result favorable to them would be assured.

Finally in May 1768 the claimants, desperate to have the affair settled, gave Governor Moore complete authority to settle the matter in such manner as he deemed appropriate. Accordingly, after a few details, such as a proper survey, were settled, he called together the three principal Mohawk chiefs and, with two agents of the patentees and in the presence of Sir William Johnson, negotiations were carried on. An agreement was reached that was acceptable to both the patentees and the Mohawks. According to the terms of the agreement "the patentees released to the Indians a large tract of land in the western portion of the grant. They also relinquished all claims to those lands that had legally been granted to others. The Indians, on their part, released all claim to the remainder of the patent, provided the patentees paid them five thousand dollars."

This land grant controversy, like many others in the colonies, was resolved only after much effort had been expended over a long period of time. It is an illuminating example of colonial land fraud practices.

The Kayaderosseras Patent was partitioned among the patentees by ballot on Friday, February 22, 1771. Lot #12 of the 16th allotment came into possession of Rip Van Dam by this balloting. Having died in 1746, his property went to his heirs, who were the first white men ever to exercise jurisdiction over the High Rock Spring which lay in this allotment.

The original Kayaderosseras Patent is preserved under special glass. It is in the County Building on Woodlawn Avenue in Saratoga Springs, in the office of the County Historian, a copy of which is included in the appendix at the end of this book.

9

The Early Settlers

"Drink of this crystal fountain
And praise the loving Lord
Who from the rock mountain
This living stream outpoured
For emblem of the holy fount
That flows from God's eternal mount."
—William Blake

Saratoga lies on historical ground. Through its hills and along its trails the mighty Mohawk tribes of the great Iroquois Confederacy of Nations made their way to attack their enemies, the Algonquins of Quebec. Many a bloody struggle took place on this ground when the Mohawks, who were greatly feared by all their enemies because of their extreme cruelty in war, fought to defend their favorite hunting ground which they called Kayaderosseras.

From the writings of the early French explorers recorded in the Jesuit Relations we learn that in 1642 Mohawks returning from a raid on Quebec brought with them, among other captives, Pere Isaac Jogues, a Jesuit priest who had come to New France in 1636 to work with the Indians. Pere Joques was captured, along with several of his converts, during the raid. It is recorded that the group stopped by a spring of mineral water on their way back to Iroquois territory, where they were refreshed by the bubbling waters. This is the first recorded instance of a visitor to what probably was one of the mineral springs of Saratoga.

During the many years in which the French and their allies, the Algonquins, fought the British and their allies, the Iroquois, it is more than likely that other non-Indians visited the springs at Saratoga, lying, as they do, in the path between Quebec and the Mohawk Valley.

In 1687 Governor Dongon of New York offered land to any who would settle the area. This was an attempt to increase the population and to balance the increased military strength in French Canada, a result of the French adding several hundred Indian warriors to their forces.

Governor Dongon's offer was not accepted. The hazards of living in the area, which was an exposed frontier at the time, were too great. Settlers were in constant danger of attack and massacre. The Schuyler family had built a stockade on the south side of Fish Creek at the junction of the Hudson River. This was attacked by the Indians in November 1747 and, along with twenty houses, was burned to the ground. Thirty families were killed and scalped, and about sixty others were taken prisoner. This was only one of many such attacks. The area remained in constant danger of such attacks until the Province of Canada was finally subjugated by the British in 1759 when General Amherst marched up the Hudson and the shore of Lake Champlain to capture Montreal and take complete control of the province.

Just when the famous High Rock Spring first came to the attention of the early settlers is not certain. The charming story of Sir William Johnson being carried in 1767 to the spring by the Mohawk braves for treatment of a wound he had received in the Battle of Lake George in 1755 cannot be corroborated. It is documented by careful research of the Sir William Johnson papers that in 1767 and again in 1768 Sir William visited "the springs on the New England border" as he went or returned from the shore near Long Island. These "springs" would have referred to Lebanon Springs which lie in this location and were discovered in 1766. In 1771 Johnson did visit "a spring lately discovered to the north-ward of Schenectady," a spring referred to as "the spring at Kayaderosseras," which must have been the High Rock Spring. This visit of Sir William Johnson is accurately documented.

It is possible that the first early settlers to come upon the High Rock Spring may have been surveyors, surveying the land of the Kayaderosseras Patent which had finally been settled through the intervention and dedicated effort of Sir William Johnson in 1768. In a letter to Dr. Joshua Fisher of Boston written by Dr. Samuel Tenney, a regimental surgeon in the Continental Army, stationed near the Saratoga battlefield during the Revolutionary War, Dr. Tenney told of visiting "some mineral springs in the vicinity of this place." He went on to say, "They were unknown (except to the Mohawks in whose country they are found) 'till about thirteen years ago; at which time they were discovered by some surveyors. The land for several miles around them is a wilderness." The letter, which was published in *The Memoirs of the American Academy of Arts and Sciences*, is dated September 1, 1783. This would pinpoint the discovery of the springs as 1770. It is known that the Old Iron Spring in Ballston Spa was discovered in 1770 by surveyors surveying the land of the Kayaderosseras Patent in that area, and the same is likely true of the springs of Saratoga. It is interesting that the springs are not mentioned in the Kayaderosseras Patent of 1708, but "the Crown reserved to itself all gold and silver mines."

After 1770 several attempts at settlement of the High Rock Spring area were made. The first person known to have come with serious intention of settling was Dirck Scowton, a young pioneer who had previously settled on the bank of the Hudson River near Waterford. In 1773 he made his way over a trail which led from the Hudson River to the east side of Saratoga Lake, thence across the lake to the mouth of the Kayaderosseras Creek and up the creek to an old Indian trail which led to the High Rock Spring. He made a clearing on top of the hill at the rear of the spring, on which he built a cabin and planted a crop. Here he remained, trading with the Indians, until the summer of 1773 when he had a serious misunderstanding with the Indians and was driven away by them.

A year later, during the summer of 1774, John Arnold, an ambitious young man from Rhode Island, came with his family to the High Rock Spring and appropriated Scowton's cabin, which he converted into a rude tavern to accommodate visitors to the spring. He left the spring during the winter months and returned to his former home on the bank of the Hudson. After two summers he abandoned the project and left permanently.

John H. Steele, M.D., in his *Analysis of the Mineral Waters of Saratoga and Ballston*, published in 1817, includes an account of the appearance of the springs at the time that Arnold and his family arrived there. It was related by Mr. Thomas Arnold, a son of John Arnold, who in 1774, at the age of nine years, came with his family to the High Rock Spring. At the time he related the story to Dr. Steele, Arnold was a highly respected farmer who was living in the Town of Stillwater about eight miles from Saratoga. His account is as follows:

> The valley along the brook was covered by large trees of hemlock, elm and maple; and the bank on the west side of the valley with a thick growth of overgrown white pine, while the opposite side was a perfect thicket of yellow and pitch pine.
>
> The High Rock and Flat Rock were the only springs at that time known. The hole or opening at the top of the High Rock was at times nearly filled with water, but this only happened in wet weather. The water usually stood some inches below the top of the hole where its surface was in a constant state of agitation. This agitation when the hole was nearly full of water, would, at times, cause it to surge over and run down its sides, but this very seldom happened. There was nothing like a constant discharge from the top of the rock at any time. The water, however, was at all times so high as to be easily dipped with the hand. There were the remains of a small hut or cabin near the rock, probably the one built by Sir William Johnson.
>
> The Flat Rock covered a quantity of ground of several rods in extent; it was considerably elevated above the marsh or swamp which surrounded it; the surface was flat and hard, and was perforated in numerous places, where the water stood in little pools, through the bottom of which it was constantly bubbling up. The marsh and grounds about the rock were much broken and trodden up by the footsteps of wild animals which flocked here in great numbers to drink the water, of which, there is every reason to believe, they were

voraciously fond. Deer and moose would, at times, when in pursuit of this beverage, apparently lose their wildness and suffer themselves to be closely approached, and they were frequently shot by the Indians, and other hunters, while regaling themselves at this fountain.

The woods abounded with wild game. Bears, deer, wolves and moose were seen almost every day; and the small stream which ran through the valley was the abode of beaver and great quantities of salmon trout.

There were sixteen cabins occupied by different families of Indians, all in sight of Arnold's house. These Indians were principally employed in hunting and fishing, and although frequently intoxicated, they were generally inoffensive and friendly.

In the fall of 1776, Samuel Norton, a Welshman who had previously settled in New Bedford, arrived on the scene and took possession of the house abandoned by Arnold. Before coming he had obtained in writing a permit from Isaac Lowe to "occupy and improve a farm near the salt spring at Saratoga." Lowe had obtained title to the land by purchase from the heirs of Rip Van Dam to whom it had been assigned on partition of the Kayaderosseras Patent. Norton made further improvements in the house, but stopped suddenly in 1777 when he heard of the approach of the British army toward Saratoga. Concerned about the safety of his family he left Saratoga never to return. He joined the British army and died before the end of the war. Isaac Lowe's property was confiscated when he left the country during the Revolution.

General Philip Schuyler, a resident of Schuylerville, visited the High Rock Spring several times during the 1770's. It was, however, not until the Revolution was over, and he was free from active military duty, that he had time to indulge his wish to make use of the spring. In 1783 he cut a path through the wilderness from his home in Schuylerville to the High Rock Spring. There he first pitched a tent and later built a cabin. This he occupied every summer until his death. While at the cabin he hosted several illustrious visitors. One of these was General Washington, who, while stationed at Newburgh in 1783, awaiting the final signing of the peace treaty, decided to tour the battlefields of the upper Hudson area. He journeyed to Albany where he was joined by Governor Clinton and Alexander Hamilton. The group went on horseback to General Schulyer's home in Schuylerville. With General Schuyler they toured the areas where the battles of Saratoga had taken place. From there they visited Fort Edward, Lake George and Crown Point, returning by way of Saratoga.

General Washington's diary discloses the fact that he spent a night in the log cabin as the guest of General Schuyler, and that he drank the waters of the High Rock Spring. He was so impressed with the mineral water that he tried to purchase the spring. This fact is substantiated in a letter he wrote to Governor Clinton on November 28, 1788 as follows: "I am sorry we have been disappointed in the mineral spring at Saratoga and the purchase of that part of the

Oriskany tract on which Fort Schuyler stands, but very glad you have succeeded upon such very advantageous terms in the purchase of 6000 acres adjoining, for you have certainly obtained it immensely cheap." He was unsuccessful in his attempt to acquire the High Rock Spring because Henry Livingston had already secured perfect title to the land by purchase from the Commissioners of Forfeiture who had confiscated the property when Lowe abandoned it during the Revolution.

General Washington's enthusiasm for the High Rock Spring was transmitted to his friends both by word of mouth and by correspondence. One person who was duly impressed by this enthusiasm was Colonel Otho H. Williams, a distinguished officer who had fought in the Revolution. He made the journey from his home in Baltimore to Saratoga to seek treatment for the rheumatism from which he had suffered for some time. Following his visit he gave the first recorded written account of the living conditions at Saratoga in a letter to General Washington dated July 12, 1784 as follows:

> Dear Sir: After I had the pleasure of seeing you in Philadelphia, I made an excursion to New York and from there up the North River as far as Saratoga. One motive for extending my tour so far on that course was to visit springs in the vicinity of Saratoga which I recollect you once recommended to me as a remedy for the rheumatism. They are now frequented by the uncivilized people of the back country; but very few others resort to them, as there is but one small lodging house within several miles of the place. Corporal Armstrong and myself spent one week there which was equal to a little campaign for the accommodations were very wretched and provisions exceedingly scarce. The country about the springs being uncultivated, we were forced to send to the border of the Hudson for what was necessary for subsistence.

He went on to describe some experiments he had performed on the waters. The accommodation he referred to was probably the Norton house.

A son of Samuel Norton came to the springs in 1783. He laid claim to the property which his father had abandoned during the Revolutionary War, and made significant improvements on it. He remained there until 1787 when the property was sold to Gideon Morgan. Morgan sold it to Alexander Bryan that same year.

Alexander Bryan was born in Connecticut of Acadian parents. After living for a time in Dutchess County, New York and marrying there, he moved to Half-Moon, a small settlement on the Mohawk River in southern Saratoga County. Here he kept a tavern which, being on an important crossroads, was frequented by people of different loyalties. He must have been an extraordinarily shrewd man, for he became the trusted confidant of both the British and the Americans during the Revolution. He was employed as a spy by both General Gates and General Burgoyne. Both sides had complete confidence in him and trusted him with their most secret information. The truth was, however, that his loyalty lay with the Americans. It was he, who under orders from

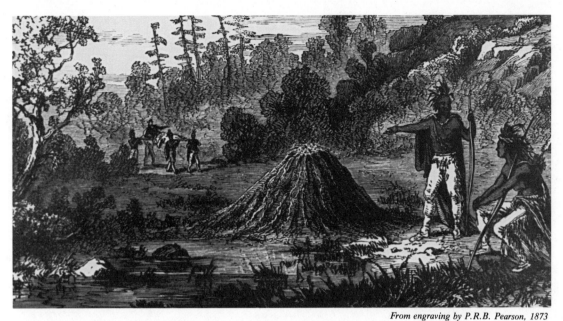

From engraving by P.R.B. Pearson, 1873

Sir William Johnson being carried on a litter to High Rock Spring

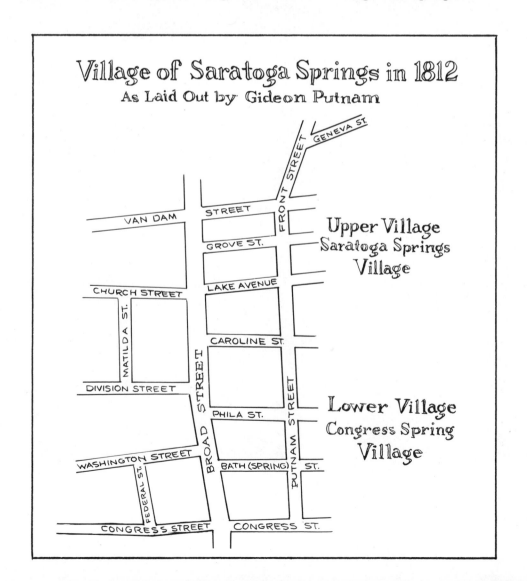

Village of Saratoga Springs in 1812
As Laid Out by Gideon Putnam

GENEVA ST.

FRONT STREET

Upper Village
Saratoga Springs
Village

VAN DAM STREET

GROVE ST.

LAKE AVENUE

CHURCH STREET

MATILDA ST.

CAROLINE ST.

DIVISION STREET

BROAD STREET

PUTNAM STREET

Lower Village
Congress Spring
Village

PHILA ST.

WASHINGTON STREET

FEDERAL ST.

BATH (SPRING) ST.

CONGRESS STREET

CONGRESS ST.

View of Congress Park in 1816. Congress Hall, built in 1812, may be seen in the background

Saratoga in 1820

General Gates, gained admission to the British camp at Fort Edward and to General Burgoyne. The British were en route to Albany to join forces with General Howe. Bryan was able to bring back to General Gates at Bemis Heights the valuable information that the Burgoyne forces had crossed the Hudson and were advancing toward Stillwater.

The Morgan property which Bryan had purchased was located on the corner of Rock and Front Streets on the cliff above the High Rock Spring. On this site he built a blacksmith shop and an additional log building where he opened a tavern. He was the first permanent settler at the springs after the war. After thirty years of tavern keeping, he retired and left Saratoga. He died at the age of ninety-two.

A marker erected by the State of New York marks the site of the Bryan cabin. It reads:

ERECTED 1832

On the site of the log cabin inn of Alexander Bryan,
Revolutionary scout, the building standing presently on
the site was built by Johnson Bryan, Alexander's son, in 1832.

The year 1789 saw the arrival in Saratoga of a man who was destined to become so important in the annals of the springs that he would later be known as the founder of Saratoga. This man was Gideon Putnam, who arrived in Saratoga with his family accompanied by his brother-in-law, Dr. Clement Blakesley and his family.

Gideon Putnam, a descendent of the famous Israel Putnam, was born in the town of Sutton, Massachusetts in 1764. He married Doanda Risley of Hartford, Connecticut, settling in Middlebury on the site now occupied by Middlebury College, and later in Rutland, Vermont. In 1789, he came to the Five Nations or Bemis Flats near Saratoga Lake where he built a cabin and planned to make a home. His brother-in-law, Dr. Clement Blakesley, with his wife, the sister of Mrs. Putnam, also settled there. This place proved to be very inhospitable to the settlers. Even the elements seemed to contrive against them. A violent rainstorm blew up one night. It flooded the surrounding country and covered the cabin floor, threatening to submerge them and all their belongings. In the darkness they were caught in a life-threatening situation. But luck was with them. Fortunately a neighbor, Zophar Scidmore, who lived on higher ground, knew that some new families had recently moved in on the flats, and he realized that their lives were at risk. He thereupon took his sailboat and hastened to their rescue. Making several trips he brought the Putnam and Blakesley families to his home and sheltered them under his hospitable roof.

This calamity was too much for Gideon Putnam to bear. He and Dr. Blakesley and their families abandoned Bemis Flats as soon as the storm was over. With their families and possessions, they made their way to the springs at Saratoga.

On arriving in Saratoga, Putnam looked about and, on viewing the lush growth of forest trees and the rich soil, he said to his wife, "This is a healthy place, the mineral springs are valuable, the timber is good and in great abundance, and I can build me a great house."

He leased three hundred acres of land a short distance west of the High Rock Spring from Derick Lefferts, one of the original purchasers of the Kayaderosseras Patent. On this land he built a house, put in crops and established himself as a permanent settler.

Dr. Blakesley built a log cabin on the cliff behind the High Rock Spring where he and his familiy lived for only three years before leaving permanently.

In 1791 Benjamin Risley, father of Mrs. Gideon Putnam, arrived in Saratoga and acquired a boarding house on the corner of what later became Front and Rock Streets, directly opposite and only a short distance from the tavern occupied by Alexander Bryan. Thus he became a rival of Bryan, his neighbor on the opposite corner. Encouraged by his success when the venture became profitable, he purchased more land on the north side of Rock Street, between Catherine and Front streets from Katrina Van Dam and others. Here he constructed two other houses which he opened as a tavern and a boarding house. It was at Mr. Risley's boarding house that the Gilman brothers were staying when they discovered the Congress Spring in 1792.

Gideon Putnam, meanwhile, cut lumber on the land he had leased and, during the winter months when he was not busy with his garden, made staves and shingles. In the spring, he carried them to the Hudson River, floating them to New York City on a raft. There he found a ready market for his product and by 1791 he had accumulated enough money to purchase the land, build a sawmill and hire a neighbor to assist him in producing more lumber and shingles. Soon he had sufficient funds to acquire additional land. In 1802 he purchased from Henry Walton an acre of land in the lower village opposite the Congress Spring at the site where the Grand Union Hotel later stood for many years. After clearing the land, he built the first seventy-foot section of Union Hall, which consisted of a large living room, two parlors and a large kitchen on the first floor, and lodging rooms on the two floors above. The building was later enlarged to contain four hundred lodging rooms. He called the place "Putnam's Tavern." The natives called it "Putnam's Folly." To them the idea of building such a large tavern in the midst of an uninhabited wilderness was the height of folly. The tavern sign, with a picture of Putnam and a wolf, is still preserved in the museum in the Casino in Congress Park in Saratoga Springs. This image of a wild place inhabited by wild animals was realistic since the location of the tavern was in swampy ground in a forest which was indeed inhabited by many species of wild animals. One day a passerby, within earshot of Gideon Putnam, remarked when he saw the building, "That man has forgotten the admonition of John Rogers, 'Build not your housetop too high.'"

In 1805, Gideon Putnam purchased still more land from Henry Walton. This tract extended from the east side of Congress Street to the lands of Jacobus Barhyte, the present Yaddo, which lies east of the race track. The village of his dreams was laid out on the west side of this land. His plan for the village showed him to be a man of great vision, as well as a person with fine public spirit. In addition, he was fortuantely blessed with keen business ability.

He planned the streets of the village to be broad so the springs could be in the middle where they would be public property and accessible to all. Congress, Hamilton and the Columbian Springs were all included in the original plan in this way. Broad Street, the present Broadway, was laid out in front of Union Hall 120 feet in width. Along either side of the street, elm trees were planted. Congress Street was laid out perpendicular to it, sixty-six feet in width. Other streets leading into Broad Street were planned: Caroline Street to be named after his granddaughter, Phila Street to be named after his daughter, Washington Street to be named after his son and so on.

West of Broad Street, on land he had purchased when he built Union Hall, he reserved an area for a burial ground. Also reserved was a plot for a house of worship to be deeded to the first congregation of whatever denomination would agree to erect an appropriate structure. This plot was later deeded to the Baptist church by Putnam's heirs.

When Putnam told his wife that he contemplated laying out a large public park around Congress Spring, she asked him to make a garden of the rocky ledge that runs behind the spring. She quoted to him:

> "If you'd have a mind at peace
> A heart that cannot burden
> Go find a gate that opens wide
> upon a little garden."

To which he replied, "Now you have found a God's garden and around it we shall develop a great park."

In 1804 Gideon Putnam retrieved the Congress Spring which had practically stopped running. Noticing bubbles coming from the village brook near the spring, he changed the course of the brook so as to expose the site where the bubbles came from the ground. At that spot he excavated an eight foot hole and put in a ten inch square wooden tube to the point of origin of the spring.

In 1806 Gideon Putnam tubed the Washington Spring and a short time later he tubed the Columbian and Hamilton Springs. He built a bath house just north of the Congress Spring for the use of patrons of Union Hall as well as local residents. This he later moved to the Hamilton Spring.

Construction of Congress Hall was begun in 1812 on the site of the present Saratoga Springs library building. One day, as Gideon and some of his workmen were inspecting the building, the scaffolding on which they were standing gave way and the whole group was catapulted to the ground below. One man was killed and all the others injured. Putnam suffered several fractured ribs as well as other injuries. He never fully recovered from the results of the fall. In December of that year he developed pneumonia and died.

Congress Hall was finally completed in 1815 and was sold to Mr. Van Schoonhoven.

With the death of Gideon Putnam, Saratoga lost its greatest benefactor. He died before his dream village had been completed. As a result, it was not built exactly as he had planned it. The streets were made narrower and the springs, instead of being located in the middle of the streets, reverted to private ownership. One wonders how different Saratoga Springs might have been if Gideon Putnam had lived longer.

Ironically, Gideon Putnam was the first one to be laid to rest in the cemetery he had set aside in his village plan for that purpose. A monument to him and his wife, Doanda, is the most imposing one in the little burial ground which still exists on Beekman Street.

10

Saratoga in the Victorian Era

"After going to Long Branch and frolicking
in the waters,
I relish going to Saratoga and letting the
waters frolick in me."

—Josh Billings

The village of Saratoga Springs was greatly enriched by having had Gideon Putnam as one of its citizens for the twenty-three years he made his home there. His contributions enhanced the life of the whole community and he left a substantial framework on which to build an outstanding village. He laid out the streets with vision and foresight, tubed several of the springs and built a mineral water bath house, thus promoting Saratoga Springs as a health resort. He built a large hotel and started construction on another.

At the time of Gideon Putnam's death, Saratoga Springs consisted of two villages; the southern portion was then called "Congress Spring Village" and was distinct from "Saratoga Springs Village" or the "Upper Village."

The village of Saratoga Springs was incorporated by an act of the Legislature in 1827. At that time the inhabitants numbered about 2000. There were approximately 300 dwellings clustered more or less at the two extremes of the village; in the north end around the High Rock Spring and in the south end around the Congress Spring. There were but four streets in the corporate bounds of the village running north and south. They were Broad Street which ended on the north at Rock Street; Putnam-Front Street, running from Congress Street to Lake Avenue as Putnam Street and extending to the northern part of the village as Front Street; Matilda Street running from Division Street to Church Street; and Federal Street connecting Congress and Washington Streets. The streets running east and west were Congress Street, which at that time extended both east and west from Broad Street; Washington Street, Division Street and Church Street extending west from Broad Street, and Bath Street (later Spring Street), Phila Street, Caroline Street, Lake Avenue, Grove Street and Geneva Street, running east from Broad. Bath Street, Phila, Caroline and Lake all ended at Putnam Street, everything being swamp between Putnam Street and the sand bank where Circular Street is now. Van Dam Street crossed Broad Street, running both east and west, Geneva Street extended from Front Street to the Ten Springs.

The streets were clean and attractive with their fine kept lawns, gardens and trees. The well-built houses projected a feeling of neatness and comfort. The whole village exuded an atmosphere of salubrity, and showed that the citizens took great pride in their village.

In the business section of the village were a number of stores and shops as well as a printing office and other places of business. A reading room located just beyond the United States Hotel housed a circulating library and a supply of newspapers from all parts of the country. A record book was kept here into which the arrivals and departures of visitors were copied once a day from the books of the principal houses. If anyone was expecting a friend and wished to know if he had arrived, he had only to refer to this list and look for his name. There were five meeting houses or places of worship scattered throughout the village.

Since there were no manufacturing or mercantile pursuits in the village, it obviously owed the prosperity which it enjoyed to its phenomenal characteristics as a watering place. The reputation of the mineral springs had spread and people came from great distances to enjoy the health-giving properties of the waters. With this increasing popularity more and more springs were discovered and tubed. By 1830 the following springs were actively flowing: The High Rock, the Congress, the Columbian, the Washington, the Hamilton, the President, the Monroe, the Flat Rock, the Red and the Ten Springs.

The need for more accommodations for visitors was met by the construction of larger and more magnificent hotels, and by the citizens of the village opening their homes to seasonal guests.

The Columbian Hotel, begun in 1808, was completed and opened for guests in 1809. It was built on Broad Street south of Lake Avenue by Jotham Holmes, an innkeeper, who had kept a house near the High Rock Spring.

Just north of the Columbian Hotel on the east side of Broad Street, the Pavilion Hotel, built by Nathan Lewis, was opened May 26, 1819. This fine hotel stood on the corner of Broad Street and Lake Avenue on the site of the present City Hall. It had a two-story front with a large wing on Lake Avenue, containing the office, bar, kitchen and so forth. A one-story piazza ran the length of the front of the building. It was surrounded by handsome grounds which reached to Grove Street, beautifully landscaped with gardens, trees and walks.

In 1823 John Ford built the original part of the United States Hotel on the west side of Broad Street north of Union Hall. It was a fine three-story brick building with a colonnade rising to the second story in front. Its two-story piazza ran the length of the front of the building raised high above the level of the street.

In its early days Saratoga Springs had its share of illustrious visitors. In 1825 Marquis de Lafayette was feted at a dinner given by Saratogians on the occasion of his first visit to this country after the Revolution. In the same year Joseph Bonaparte, brother of Napoleon and exiled former King of Spain living in this country, was a guest at the United States Hotel along with his sister, Caroline Murat and his two daughters. It all, Bonaparte spent five seasons in Saratoga Springs. During this time he visited the establishment of Jacobus Barhyte, on the site of the present Yaddo Estate. Impressed with the natural beauty of the place, and desirous of making a home in Saratoga Springs, he offered Barhyte $20,000 for the place. Barhyte was overwhelmed by the large offer. After he recovered from his astonishment, he refused the offer saying, "If it's worth that much to you, it's worth that much to me." Bonaparte also tried to purchase the High Rock Spring in 1824, but again was unsuccessful. He had hoped to establish a fine estate in Saratoga Springs, but being frustrated in his attempt to purchase the property, he later bought a beautiful estate in Bordentown, New Jersey.

An idea of the impression this early Saratoga Springs made on its visitors may be gained from the letters of Almira Hathaway Reid, age 29, of Fairhaven, Massachusetts, wife of a New Bedford whaling captain. She had journeyed for eight days by sloop, steamer and stage to reach Saratoga Springs where she hoped to improve her health. A letter dated August 12, 1826 reads as follows:

> About half past seven we arrived safe at Saratoga Springs where we have taken lodgings at a private boarding house, where there are a number of invalids; about thirty dined today. Every house, almost, in town is a boarding house and all are full to overflowing; a number of elegant houses are built on purpose to accommodate travelers; they cannot give a stranger a night's lodging, and I am told numbers have to return as they came or go to Balls-town.
>
> I drank two tumblers of water this morning from the Congress Spring. I dislike the taste very much, but it is not as bad a dreg as I have taken. At 11 o'clock I took a tumbler from the Flat Rock Spring, found that equally unpleasant, but feel very good courage to try the efficacy of spring water as a number here have benefited in similar complaints.

On August 17th she wrote as follows:

> Today has been excessively warm and the continual passing of the stages and carriages raised one constant cloud of dust which renders it unpleasant; but I must think Saratoga a pretty place. The main street is tolerably level and very broad. A number of elegant boarding houses such as the United States, Columbian Hotel, Montgomery Hall, Union Hall, Pavilion and Congress Halls, beside many

private genteel houses.

Back of this room and in full view of window are the Green Mountains of Vermont, and the surrounding country looks very elegant.

An interesting sidelight on the visitors may be gained from her letter of August 18th:

Out of hundreds in this village, but few are disposed to pass an hour in divine service. The pleasure parties and balls every evening in this village engross the attention of the old and young, sick and well, and this village place I fear will prepare more souls for destruction than these efficacious waters will ever heal infirm bodies.

Unfortunately, though her visit to Saratoga may have prolonged her life, it did not save it. Almira died in 1831.

The following journal of a tour to Saratoga Springs was written by Elihu Hoyt in August 1827. Hoyt was an influential citizen of Deerfield, Massachusetts, and was active in politics most of his life.

Monday, August 6th, 1827

Began to take the waters very soon after our arrival last night (moderately), this morning commenced a regular trial of them. Spent the day attending to the waters, and visiting various parts of the village, the various springs, and meeting many acquaintances from Massachusetts, particularly from Boston.

We begin to see the fashionable world as it displays itself at this place. We see here some of every condition in life. One would suppose that we should find everybody here on the sick list but it is far from the case. Many of the visitors come here probably in good sound health, for amusement and for the sake of spending a week or two among the fashionable to see and to be seen. Here we see all the latest fashions of the cities intermixed with the more plain fashions of the country. We have fashionable balls, concerts, and all descriptions of amusements, which are calculated to take up the time and spend the money in our pockets. Many matches have been negotiated here which has eventuated in wedlock.

Tuesday, August 7th, 1827

Weather warm, as has been the case since we left Deerfield. The first of every day's work is to take freely of the Congress water, then walk among the multitudes until the breakfast bell summons us to our repast, after which, this day we chartered a barouche and too, a ride to Barhyte's, a Dutch farmer's, about two miles east of the springs. Here we can generally obtain a repast of fresh trout, but this day the good lady was engaged in preparing a trout dinner for a party of high blooded Jacksonians, at the head of whom was Martin Van Buren, a senator in the congress of the United States from the State of New York, celebrated for his decided opposition to the present administration of the United States, and considered by some as the head of the opposition, in point of zeal, if not title. I confess

View of Congress Park, circa 1850. This "Gem of Saratoga" consisted of a small hill in the shape of a horseshoe, covered with handsome trees and laid out in small walks encircling the low ground surrounding the springs

From engraving by P.R.B. Pearson, 1873

High Rock Spring showing a dipper boy

Dipper boy at High Rock Spring

From engraving by P. R. B. Pearson, 1873

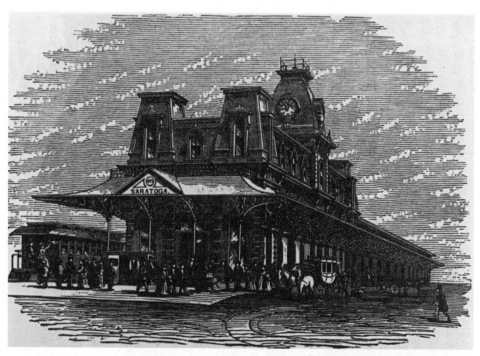

From engraving by P. R. B. Pearson, 1873

Passenger Depot, Saratoga. Elegant and tasteful, this depot faced an open square, adorned with fountain and shade trees. It was built of brick with elaborate iron trimmings and its interior was of black walnut.

Saratoga Club House, opened by John Morrisey in 1869 as a gambling casino

Congress Spring and Park, and Columbian Spring, 1873

Congress Spring Bottling House *From engraving by P. R. B. Pearson, 1873*

From engraving by P. R. B. Pearson, 1873

Scene in Congress Spring Bottling House
showing washing and filling

From engraving by P.R.B. Pearson, 1873

Packing Room at Congress Spring

From engraving by P.R.B. Pearson, 1873

*Grand Union Hotel. Located on the west side of Broadway,
its magnificent grounds embraced a space of seven acres. The
capacity of this hotel was greater than any other in the world*

Grand Union Ballroom   *From engraving by P. R. B. Pearson, 1873*

From engraving by P. R. B. Pearson, 1873

Lobby of Grand Union Hotel

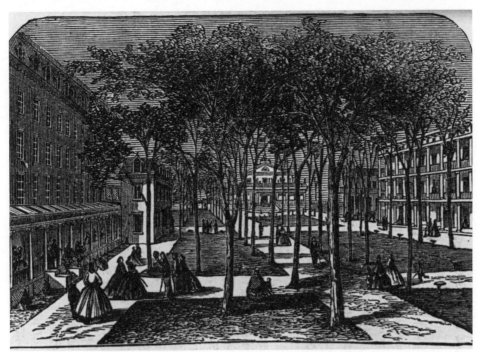

From engraving by P.R.B. Pearson, 1873

Grounds of the Grand Union Hotel, showing the Opera House in rear

From engraving by P.R.B. Pearson, 1873

Congress Hall. It occupied the site of the present Saratoga Springs Public Library on Broadway, reaching from Spring Street to Congress Street. It was erected in 1868 by H.H. Hathorn. The balls given here every Friday night with music of the famed Bernstein's orchestra surpassed all others that a preconceived view of him did not preposses my mind much in his favor.

Wednesday, August 8, 1827

I have met many acquaintances from Boston, and there is a brilliant display from New York, Philadelphia, and the southern and western cities. We have a great opportunity to see the fashionable. There seems to be a great similarity among the ladies in point of dress. I see very little difference in this respect between the ladies of Boston, those on the Connecticut, or at the Springs, except at the Springs the bonnet is gone.

No end to the balls, concerts and other exhibitions which are continually brought forward here to amuse and to pick your pockets. In the evening we stepped into Congress Hall to witness the brilliancy of the evening ball. Here was a full display of nearly all the flowers of beauty and elegance now assembled at the Springs; their dress was fashionable, and the ball, I presume, was managed in the bonton style. Yet I could not distinguish much difference between an elegant ball at Saratoga Springs and a ball on the banks of the Connecticut, except that it was more numerously attended, and by people of almost all ages. We stayed and danced a cotillion or two, and then left them to their own means. The music was probably good; I could distinguish but little difference from it and other music on similar occasions where I have had an opportunity to see it elsewhere. Men are singular animals (on general principles), meet with them when you will. They seem to find a time to dance, a time to sing, a time to eat, a time to cry, a time to be wise, and a time to act like fools; the latter time constitutes a very great proporton of the whole. We find it eminently so at the Springs.

Thursday, August 9, 1827

Took the waters freely this morning. We have spent the chief of our time about home today. The company has increased very much since we came in, and there has been more arrivals for two days than have left the Springs. The board houses are very much crowded so that it is difficult to get lodging in the principal houses.

It is time to be off, we have stayed out our proportion of the time allowed to us here. We shall be off to Schenectady tomorrow.

We passed in our walk this evening almost all kinds of amusements. At the Pavilion, Mr. and Mrs. Knight were giving a vocal and instrumental concert. At the United States Hotel there was a splendid fashionable ball. Opposite, Mr. Potter was displaying his powers of slight of hand and his art of ventriloquism, and somewhere else, Mr. Somebody was showing the wonderful qualities of his learned dog and the purring qualities of his tabby cat, while some few were rationally spending their time at the boarding house, but this number was small.

On Friday, August 10th, 1827, Mr. Elihu Hoyt left Saratoga Springs.

In 1822 a young Englishman from Yorkshire named John Clarke, came to Saratoga Springs. He had previously, in 1819, opened the country's first soda fountain in New York City. A lucrative business had resulted from this venture and he had become a successful and wealthy man. By the time he came to Saratoga Springs he was looking for new fields to explore. He found what he was looking for in Saratoga Springs. He was exactly the person to promote the mineral waters, experienced as he was with carbonated beverages.

He saw great potential in the Congress Spring as well as in the other springs. From the heirs of the late Henry and John Livingston he purchased property in the lower village which included the Congress Spring as well as the Columbian and Hamilton Springs.

Soon after, in 1823, he, with Thomas Lynch, built a bottling plant next to the Congress Spring and began to bottle the water and sell it all over the United States and the world. His experience with marketing paid off, and he realized a handsome income from this source.

Bottling was carried on only from November to June. John Clarke made the water available to the public free of charge, and, in order to insure an adequate supply, he did not bottle it during the summer months, the peak of the visitor's season, when there was a great demand for it. He had very decided opinions concerning the mineral water. One was that whatever spring a person drank of most freely, that he liked the best, was surely the one he needed most, and this he recommended most earnestly. Another was that the water should never be taken from the village except regularly in bottles; no barrels of "Spring water on draught."

Dr. John H. Steele, in his book, *An Analysis of the Mineral Waters of Saratoga and Ballston*, gives due credit to John Clarke for his handling of the Congress water as follows:

> The property of this fountain has, within a few years, passed into the hands of Dr. John Clarke, who is now the sole proprietor and owner of it. The gentleman has made it an object of his special care and attention, and it is to his liberality that the public are indebted for the convenient and cleanly manner in which the water is presented to them at the well, and for the improvements that have been made and are still being made in its immediate vicinity. He is likewise entitled to great credit for the water and preparing it for transportation. He is now the only person through whom it can be procured, and such has been the success of his exertions, and the public estimation of its value, that it has been introduced into almost every part of the world. There is scarcely a town in the United States of any magnitude that is not supplied with it; not a vessel destined to any distant port that does not enumerate the Congress water in the list of her sea stores of freight.

Clarke, like Gideon Putnam, was a very public-spirited man. He retubed his springs, made their surroundings attractive, and provided free public access to them. Over the Congress Spring he had constructed a classical Doric pavilion, and over the Columbian Spring a pretty Grecian Temple.

He carried on from where Gideon Putnam left off in planning and laying out the village. He planned and named Circular Street. On it, opposite Congress Park, he built a magnificent Greek Revival home, which remains to this day an outstanding example of Victorian architecture in Saratoga Springs.

With a generous spirit and good taste he increased the beauty of Congress Park. South and east of the Congress Spring he made a beautiful crescent lawn by reclaiming the ground from the deep mud swamp of the area by means of underground drains. The *Saratoga Sentinel* of June 22, 1829 commented that John Clarke had "converted the impossible marsh into an attractive park site."

He laid out the park with gardens, fountains and attractive paths with benches for the comfort of visitors. He built a bandstand and engaged Johnson's band for many seasons to play morning and evening in the Congress Park grounds.

Clarke was instrumental in having a law enacted which remitted to any landowner for every tree planted in front of his premises, a rebate of the highway tax of sixty-two and a half cents per tree. Many trees, mostly elms and maples, have been planted as a result of this law. This accounts for the uniqueness of Saratoga Springs in having such beautiful tree-lined streets.

In 1829 John Clarke went to Europe. While there, he purchased the famous Thorvalden vases, entitled "Day and Night." These handsome and valuable art treasures may be seen in Congress Park.

A letter published in the *Saratoga Sentinel* in the 1840's points out clearly the transformation in Congress Park which took place through John Clarke's efforts:

> In your late interesting reminiscences of Saratoga in the past, you refer to the condition of those grounds when you first saw them. Now I think I can go a little farther back, say 1817, and I can scarcely even imagine such a complete metamorphosis were possible to have occurred, and it must be still more astonishing to those of the present day to think, or believe, after having enjoyed a stroll through the present unsurpassed beautiful park, with its lakes, gushing fountains, shady promenades, listening to the strains of music filling the air and delighting the senses, that this park, one of Saratoga's main attractions, was once a dark dismal swamp, filled with huge treacherous bogs and quagmires, rendering it hazardous for man or beast to venture into unless frozen over. Grand primeval forest trees occupied large portions of these grounds, many of which are now standing, adding much to the picturesqueness of the park. There were no buildings for miles east, west or north of the Congress Spring, the grounds being densely covered by lofty pines and underbrush. The music by which visitors were regaled consisted of the caw of the crow, the croak of the bullfrog, the screech of the owl, the chirp of the cricket and katydid; the illumination consisting of the firefly, and the Jack-with-the-lantern, or ignis fatuus! No Bernstein's

and other crack bands in those days. And, above all, no Saratoga trunks.

This swamp extended north as far as the High Rock Spring, but was not so formidable as that of the Congress grounds. At that there was not a dwelling of any sort east of the swamp, from the High Rock to the Congress. In certain seasons of the year on the grounds on the flats, about the spring, vast flocks of wild pigeons gathered to partake of the mineral water as it oozed out and ran in various directions. I have often stood upon the high cliffs, near the spring and seen thousands of these birds taken in nets and shot down with guns. The late Dr. John H. Steele stated that these birds possessed a remarkable penchant for these mineral waters, and for a great number of years regularly visited their favorite watering place. It is supposed that the cause of their withdrawing their patronage in later years, Saratoga was getting "too big" for them, and, like the poor Indians, they were driven from their "fair hunting," or "drinking grounds."

It cost an immense outlay of money as well as a large amount of hard and very difficult labor, to redeem these once wild, unsightly Congress grounds and to finally cause them to "bud and blossom like a rose," and to the public spirit and liberality of the late Clarke and White, are the citizens of Saratoga, nay, the public at large, indebted for the accomplishment of this grand work. Bless their memory, say we.

(signed) An Old Albanian

John Clarke extended his purchase of real estate from time to time so that at the period of his decease he owned about a thousand acres of land contiguous to the Congress Spring. He died May 6, 1846 at the age of seventy-three.

Another benefactor of Saratoga Springs was Dr. John H. Steele, who was born in Leicester, Massachusetts in 1780, and came to the Saratoga Springs area at an early age. He read medicine with Dr. Daniel Bull who lived east of Saratoga Lake at Dean's Corners, and in 1800, received his diploma in medicine. He distinguished himself as a physician and was elected a member of many famous societies, not only medical but also historical and scientific in the United States, Canada and Europe. He was widely known as a distinguished physician and surgeon and also as a chemist, geologist and scientist. His treatise on the mineral waters of Saratoga Springs was the first thorough work of its kind. He received an honorary M.D. degree in 1830. Over his years in Saratoga Springs he gained valuable experience on the medical use of the mineral waters. He published this information in his book, *An Analysis of the Mineral Waters of Saratoga and Ballston with Practical Remarks on their Medicinal Properties*, the last edition of which was published posthumously in 1838. He died April 23, 1838 at the age of fifty-seven years.

Dr. Richard L. Allen was born in Greenfield in 1808. In 1833 he became a resident of Saratoga Springs and medical practice associate of Dr. Steele's. Dr. Allen was an active medical practitioner in Saratoga Springs for many years and acquired great knowledge of the waters and their therapeutic use. He published his analysis of the waters in 1844 under the title, *Historical, Chemical and Therapeutical Analysis of the Principal Mineral Fountains of Saratoga Springs*.

Another medical practitioner of Saratoga Springs of the early period was M. L. North, M.D. He published a valuable treatise on the waters in 1843 entitled, *Saratoga Waters or the Invalid at Saratoga*.

There were several other fine physicians who practiced medicine during the nineteenth century in Saratoga Springs. Some of them operated sanatoriums where the use of the mineral waters was stressed. Probably the most noted of these was Dr. Strong whose sanatorium stood on Circular Street near Spring Street where Father's Hall of Skidmore now stands. A notice in the *New York Tribune* in 1888 described his establishment:

DR. STRONG'S SANATORIUM
SARATOGA SPRINGS, NEW YORK

A popular resort for health, change, rest or recreation of the year. Elevator, electric bells, steam, open fireplaces, sun parlor and promenade on the roof, croquet, lawn tennis. Massage, Turkish, Russian, Roman, electric thermal, all baths and related remedial appliances.

In one of the brochures issued by the Sanatorium, it was noted that daily family prayers were conducted for the guests, "at no additional charge."

A great vogue for spas began to develop in America during the nineteenth century due to people's confidence in the curative powers of mineral waters, a confidence derived from the inhabitants of their native countries and from Europeans in general, and also from the long-standing faith of the Indians in the miraculous healing powers of the mineral waters.

After over a hundred years in this country, many colonial families had established themselves and produced moderate wealth. A certain aristocracy came into being which possessed a class consciousness, and which had the desire to communicate and come to know and to intermarry with the gentry of the other colonies. Sojourns at spas afforded an ideal way of accomplishing this end, and of maintaining and restoring health, and at the same time of exhibiting one's wealth to the best advantage.

Travel conditions had improved markedly since the early days of the colonies. More and better roads had been built, and many stage lines had been established between important centers. The river steamboat had come into important use, and the railroad, then in its infancy, was taking hold.

The custom among the affluent of taking an annual vacation at the seashore, the mountains, or a spa, developed along with the improvement in transportation. Bostonians and other New Englanders vacationed at Stafford Springs, as well as at certain other springs which had been discovered and developed in that part of the country. Warm Springs in Berkely County, Virginia was a very popular place. The springs had been given to the State of

Piazza of Congress Hall, 20 feet wide and 240 feet long afforded a beautiful promenade for elegantly dressed guests

From engraving by P. R. B. Pearson, 187

CONGRESS SPRING and PARK, SARATOGA

VIEW FROM THE GRAND HOTEL

From engraving by P.R.B. Pearson, 1

View of Congress Park from the veranda of Grand Hotel. The Congress Spring and Columbian Spring may be seen in the background

From engraving by P.R.B. Pearson, 1873

Grand Hotel, Congress Park

From engraving by P.R.B. Pearson, 1873

The Clarendon Hotel. Situated on South Broadway, this hotel was patronized by a very aristocratic and select class of guests

From engraving by P.R.B. Pearson, 1873

Recreative Garden in Clarendon Park, 1840

From engraving by P.R.B. Pearson, 1873

The Old United States Hotel. Built in 1823, it burned down in 1865. It had the reputation of being excellent and fashionable, as it was one of the most capacious establishments of its kind in the country

From engraving by P.R.B. Pearson, 1873

The New United States Hotel. Built of brick and stone, it contained 768 sleeping rooms in addition to 65 suites, each parlor of which had from 1 to 7 bedrooms. Street frontage was 900 feet. It opened June 1, 1874

Virginia by Lord Fairfax with the stipulation that they be kept forever free to the public. George Washington sought treatment for rheumatism there, and Martha Washington spent much time there while her husband was engaged with the Revolutionary War. A spring popular with Quakers and others of the Philadelphia area was Yellow Springs, located in Chester County about thirty miles west of Philadelphia. After the Battle of Brandywine in September 1777, the wounded of the Continental Army were treated there. Thus this spring, like the High Rock Spring of Saratoga Springs, played a role in the rehabilitation of the wounded soldiers of the Continental Army.

During the nineteenth century Saratoga Springs entertained more distinguished people than any other place of its kind. Governors, senators, congressmen and others in public life whose number included DeWitt Clinton, Martin VanBuren, Stephen Douglas, Daniel Webster, Millard Fillmore, James Buchanan and others are known to have been guests at the springs. Authors enjoyed Saratoga Springs. For many seasons Washington Irving occupied a cottage at the United States Hotel. He seldom missed a morning visit to the Congress Spring. The list of visiting authors also included Edgar Allen Poe, Nathaniel Hawthorne, James Fenimore Cooper, William James and William Dean Howells.

Among the celebrities of the early Victorian era who spent time in Saratoga Springs was Madame Jumel, one-time wife of a wealthy New York wine merchant, and divorced wife of Aaron Burr, former Vice President of the United States. She came every season from 1828 until 1849 to her Greek Revival home on Circular Street which she named "Les Tuileries." A strikingly beautiful woman, she cut an impressive figure when she drove down Broadway every afternoon in her gorgeous coach and four.

By 1870 Saratoga Springs had grown to a population of some nine thousand, with double or triple that number in the active summer season. It had the largest, costliest and most elegant hotels in the world which, along with the lesser hotels and the many boarding houses in the village, could accommodate about fifteen thousand visitors at once.

Congress Hall, rebuilt by H. H. Hathorn following its complete destruction by fire in 1866 and reopening in 1868, was an architectural masterpiece. It extended from Spring Street to Congress Street with a piazza 240 feet long and 20 feet wide on its 416-foot front. Its side wings extended back some 300 feet. A promenade on top of the hotel afforded a charming view. The guest rooms, dining halls, parlors and ballrooms were attractive and elegant. The finest elevator in the country carried guests to their rooms on the upper floors. The social events given here surpassed all others. Music for the Friday evening balls was furnished by Bernstein's famous orchestra.

The Grand Union Hotel, located on the west side of Broadway opposite Congress Hall and Congress Park, covered seven acres of ground. It was a brick structure with a street frontage of 1,364 feet. Within the spacious grounds were several elegant cottages which were greatly sought after by the elite. It boasted "a vertical railway" which rendered the six stories easily accessible. The largest hotel in the world, it could accommodate 1,200 people at one time. Its tremendous size may be seen by the following statistics recorded in *Saratoga Illustrated* by Dearborn:

> Length of piazzas, one mile; halls, two miles; carpeting, twelve acres; marble tiling, one acre; number of rooms, eight hundred and twenty-five; doors, one thousand, four hundred and seventy-four; windows, one thousand, eight hundred and ninety-one. The dining room was two hundred and fifty feet by fifty-three feet and twenty feet high, and accommodated at one time twelve hundred people.

There was music on the lawn every day at 9 a.m. and at 3:30 p.m. by Professor J.M. Sanders' celebrated orchestra, and in the evening "hops" were enjoyable social events.

The Grand Hotel on the east side of Broadway overlooking Congress Park, was managed by W.W. Leland, an "inn keeper" famous for his hospitality. It was a five-story structure, outstanding in its architecture and beauty, with a French roof, having a street frontage on East Congress Street of 550 feet. Wings on either side enclosed a beautifully landscaped park. In its basement were 25 stores in which could be purchased all sorts of rare and exotic treasures from all over the world. Its fine appointments were unequaled by any other hotel.

The United States Hotel burned to the ground in 1865 and was rebuilt on the same site and opened in 1874. It was a five-story fireproof brick building covering seven acres of ground. Its front which extended 900 feet on Broadway and its side wing enclosed a three acre park, beautifully laid out and landscaped, containing a bandstand where fine bands played daily. In addition to its 1,100 rooms were separate cottages to accommodate guests desiring that sort of privacy. The hotel catered to a most discriminating clientele with service remarkable for its efficiency. An example of this type of service is exemplified in the following extract from an account given in a travel book of the time:

> The great event of the day at the Springs is dinner which is taken at half past three. This, at the United States Hotel, is a tremendous undertaking. Conceive sitting down in an enormous saloon, or rather four saloons, at right angles to each other, with some six hundred guests, waited upon by one hundred and fifty negroes, commanded by a black maitre d'hotel. The operation of finding places for such a multitude—in itself no trifling task—being over, the waiters, dressed in spotless white jackets, extend their hands over the covers, and, at a signal from their chief, stationed in the center of the saloons, remove them simultaneously. Then arises a clatter of knives, plates and forks perfectly bewildering in the sharp rattling fire of which conversation is drowned, and confusion seems established. But a glance at the commander-in-chief shows that, although his black troops are rushing hither and thither in hot haste, at the bidding of impetuous Southerners and less irascible Northerners,

he has not lost his authority. At a clap of his hands they fall into their places, and at another all the dishes are removed. Bearing them dexterously on their extended arms, they march in step to the side doors, through which they disappear. Scarcely, however, are they out of sight, when, like harlequin in the pantomime, in they come again, each with three fresh dishes, with which they march to their appointed places. Then, with their eye on their commander, they hold a dish over the table, and pop it down at the first signal. With clap two the second dish descends; and at the third signal the tables are covered. So through the dinner; for even in the changing of the knives, forks and spoons, the same regularity is observed. The whole thing is excessively entertaining; and, what between looking at the various maneuvers, and at the ladies' dresses, I fared badly in the way of eating. The fault, however, lay entirely with myself, for the abundance of dishes was overpowering. This admirable organization is, of course, a great economy of time; for although no counting houses are near, the guests, without any display of quick eating, were evidently desirous not to remain longer at table than necessary; and in less than an hour the rooms were deserted.

The ritual of drinking the mineral water is an experience unique to Saratoga Springs. A vivid picture of this amusing routine is given in the following article published in *Leslie's Weekly* of September 6, 1871:

And if we really want to see the fun begin we must rise with the lark; for the professional water drinker here is an early bird who wets his whistle with the health-giving beverage before the more fashionable of the town has got fairly into his morning nap. An hour or so before early breakfast time the stream of drinkers begins to flow, and, standing just inside the round-arched building roofed but resting only upon pillars which shelter the Congress Spring, we can see all that goes on. In the middle of the strong floor a dry rectangular "well" is sunk, some six feet deep; and set in a wooden curb at the exact center of this well, bubbles the precious liquid. I used to think as I looked at the small circumference of the orifice, that it did not need a very lively fancy to feel the likeness between this little circular rim of the fisherman's bottle in the Arabian Nights, and to imagine all the fine hotels and well-dressed visitors and attendant donkeys as springing out of its narrow confines and spreading themselves over the face of the earth. This, as I said just now, is the hour for the old stagers to take their morning draughts. These are they who drink by rules derived from a physician, or, more likely, traceable to some obscure local tradition; a half dozen glasses of the Congress before breakfast, three of the Empire before dinner, and five of the Star just before going to bed - if it happens to be a man, or just before "retiring" if it happens to be a lady.

The little boy at the bottom of the well jumps briskly up and down the single step like a large-sized dingy canary, dips the wooden stick, set with wire cases holding three glasses in the fashion of a cruet stand, in the spring, and reaches them up all dripping to the eager hands outstretched to grasp them; and at this hour he can scarcely work fast enough to supply the demands of his customers, most of whom swallow the water as toplers swallow their daily drams. But an hour later, things assume a different aspect. The novices begin to gather, coming timidly and reluctantly up to the moist counter and waiting their turn for a glass as men await the peculiar delight of the dentist's chair. Many of them are young girls arrayed in fresh and spotless morning robes and very pretty they look until they begin to drink; but as they stand with their backs to the odious spring lifting their skirts with their left hand that the moist floor may not soil the hems of their garments, and craning their necks forward that no drop may fall upon the precious lawn or cambrick, they present spectacles rather more comical than pleasing in spite of the liberally bestowed glimpses of neat little bronze slippers. And their faces! What treasure house of expressions might this little aqueous temple become to an artist, where every phase of feeling, from mild dislike to the broad woe and wretchedness which trembles on the very verge of nausea, incessantly repeats itself. There is a sprinkling of men, young and old, always less numerous as well as less interesting than the girls - and many little children wander about with glasses in their hands slopping the water over themselves and others.

The following excerpt from a letter on "The American Spa" published in the *London Times* on December 9th, 1887, gives an English opinion of "The American Spa."

Everybody who is anybody comes to Saratoga, because here can be found an aggregation of people of a character to be met nowhere else.

The throng is essentially cosmopolitan, and comes from all parts of the country, besides many who cross the Atlantic. It embraces all kinds of people, and generally includes the leaders of every set. Not only the representatives of wealth are here, millionaires of every degree, and the most opulent of the money kings, great merchants, bankers, and railway princes, but also the grand dames of society, the heiresses, and the gilded youth of the land.

The most noted preachers come to fill the pulpits of the churches. The sporting fraternity from all parts of the country unite to make the Saratoga races the finest of the season. The Wall Street stock operators desert New York for Saratoga, yet they have at hand their brokers' offices and private wires, and can manipulate the market as readily as if the Stock Exchange were only across the street.

The boulevards display fine equipages, which drive out Broadway northward to Woodlawn Park, where the trees and greensward, and Judge Hilton's rural home are very attractive, or else they take the favorite route southward to Saratoga Lake, where "Moon's" is visited for indulgence in elaborate fish and game dinners at high prices, and to get the "Saratoga chips," which give the hostelry its greatest fame. The drive goes around the lake, and on either hand are favorite resorts.

Saratoga is the place in America to see diamonds. Their glitter dazzles the eye at every turn, as they sparkle under the brilliant electric lights illuminating the evening scene. Millions upon millions of money are invested in the diamonds that are exhibited at Saratoga, and it has been suggested that if the Grand Union Hotel should happen to perish in the height of the season, with all it contains, the future explorer who might delve in its ruins would come upon the rarest diamond mine the world ever knew.

Literary entertainments are provided for the intellectual. The most skillful and famous orchestras furnish the choicest selections of music almost all day and evening on the hotel piazzas and in the parks and gardens. The place is almost perpetually en fete. Balls and garden parties are given for the younger generation, and some of these Saratoga "hops," as they are called, are the most gorgeous known.

Saratoga has become in these later days a favorite location for holding all kinds of conventions. This is aided by the enormous lodging capacity of the town. The lawyers always have an annual convention in Saratoga, and listen to learned discourses upon legal questions, and the discussion of proposed improvements in legal procedure. The bankers of the United States also have an annual Saratoga convention, and similar meetings are convened by physicians, railway managers, scientists, and I know not how many other bodies; and all of them like to meet at Saratoga. The politicians, it will thus be seen, by no means have a monopoly of the business of holding conventions in the great Republic, though even they have a liking for the noted watering-place, for this year the New York Republicans and Democrats have both held their annual conventions at Saratoga. Thus the surroundings of these wonderful springs have become a kaleidoscope, and there is nothing else to be found like it on the American continent.

The latter half of the nineteenth century saw gambling flourish in Saratoga Springs. In 1861 John Morrissey, an Irishman from Troy, New York, the heavyweight boxing champion of America and a United States Senator who had operated gambling houses in New York City, moved into Saratoga Springs and began operations. He withstood local resistance to his activities by contributing generously to charities and in general by being a good citizen. In 1863 Morrissey, with three wealthy horse lovers, formed a racing association and ran a few races on a track they had constructed. The following year, they opened a large track and ran more races, among them " The Travers," named for a member of the association. With this meet, racing as it is known today in Saratoga Springs was born.

On an acre of land adjoining the Congress Spring property, which he purchased from the heirs of John Clarke, Morrissey built a substantial red brick building on a foundation supported by steel piles which had been sunk in the quicksand of the site. He called the place "The Club House" and in 1869 he opened it as a gambling casino where, for several years, he conducted a very lucrative business. After Morrissey's death in 1878, the business was purchased by Albert Spencer and Charles Reed who carried on the gambling until 1893. It was then purchased by Richard Canfield for $250,000 and, after refurbishing it, continued its use as a gambling house which he called "The Casino."

Canfield, unlike Morrissey, was a man of self-attained culture. He read voraciously and acquainted himself with the best literature. He also developed a genuine interest in art, spending whatever time he could in art galleries in the United States and Europe. In 1901 he became acquainted with the great American painter, James McNeil Whistler, who painted his portrait entitled "His Reverence" because of Canfield's immaculate and cultured appearance.

In 1902 Canfield was able to purchase the land northeast of the Casino where the Napanock Indians returned every summer to camp and sell the wares they had made during the winter. On this land, Canfield laid out a beautiful Italian garden which was enclosed in a carefully kept hemlock hedge. At the entrance were placed two columns of Carrara marble, replicas of those designed by the famous Renaissance architect, Vignola, the successor of Michelangelo, an architect at St. Peter's in Rome. The focal point of the garden was a beautiful fountain at either end of which has a Triton holding a conch shell in the form of a trumpet through which he blew water at his counterpart. About the garden were placed marble statues and seats. This garden has been restored and is considered one of Saratoga Springs' finest treasures.

To the existing building of the Casino, Canfield added a wing which includes a kitchen and a huge dining room with a vaulted ceiling containing priceless stained glass windows.

With the success of gambling experienced in the Casino, other gambling houses, at least a dozen, thrived in Saratoga Springs. However, law enforcement officials exerted pressure on all of these establishments from time to time. Finally in 1907, after a particularly strenuous attack, Canfield closed his Casino and put it up for sale. In 1911 it was sold to the village of Saratoga Springs for $150,000, one fifth of its value, as part of an arrangement with the Saratoga Springs commission to spend $250,000 to secure and maintain Congress and High Rock Parks.

The Victorian era was certainly the most glamorous period in the history of Saratoga Springs. In the early part of the era when there were but few hotels, people began to frequent Saratoga Springs to drink the waters and to participate in the luxury and comfort and entertainment offered there. When the price of cotton was high, many southern families spent the season at the Spa to enjoy the pleasures of social life, and, some in hopes of finding desirable husbands for their daughters. As the railroad reached Saratoga Springs in 1833 and more luxurious hotels were built, interest in Saratoga Springs increased and the village basked in splendor. The Civil War hit Saratoga Springs hard as it did the whole country. The valuable Southern clientele was lost and the village needed more patrons to replace the loss. It was about that time that John Morrissey appeared and opened his gaming house and built the race track. At this point, the emphasis in the village shifted somewhat from the mineral waters to gambling. However, interest in the waters was not lost.

Toward the end of the century there was a decline in American spas. Saratoga suffered some but not nearly as much as many others. As the automobile was introduced habits of people changed, and instead of spending a season at one place, most people of means were most likely to travel. As with all resorts, Saratoga Springs felt the impact of this change in life style. However, it survived and will continue to do so.

11

The Glass Factory

"From labor, health;
from health contentment springs."
—Beattie

Interest in Saratoga mineral waters spread beyond the confines of Saratoga Springs and people throughout the country and Europe became aware of the waters' value. It was clear that there was a market beyond Saratoga that would purchase and consume them at a rate that would make it profitable for any entrepreneur who had the business acumen to make the waters available.

Over the years mineral waters from many of the springs, probably as many as thirty or more, were bottled and sold. Among the first to venture into this area on a large scale was John Clarke, who had retired to the Springs around 1820. He purchased a plot of land which included the Congress Spring. Having had experience with merchandising in his successful soda fountain business in New York City, he saw the potential in Congress Spring water. In 1823 in partnership with Thomas Lynch, he built a bottling plant next to the Congress and proceeded to bottle the water. He purchased the bottles from the Mt. Vernon Glass Factory in Vernon, in Oneida County. The venture was an almost immediate success. The water was distributed throughout the United States and most of Europe, and it has been said that in the middle of the nineteenth century there was no hotel of any prominence nor any reputable ocean liner that did not serve Congress water. Dr. Clarke still made the Congress water available free of charge to patrons at the spring, and its use continued to be an important ritual in the life of the people who came to Saratoga Springs. At the spring, the water was served by dipper boys who used a long handle dipper which contained four glasses. With each dip four people could be served. Though the water was free, it was customary to tip the dipper boys.

As more and more spring owners bottled their waters, the supply of bottles for this purpose became an important consideration. There were many glass factories operating at that time in this part of the country; some in the New England states and New Jersey as well as in New York. Each produced bottles with characteristics distinctive of their area so they were not too difficult to identify. Of all the glass manufacturers who supplied these bottles for the Saratoga waters, the Mt. Vernon Glass Company was probably the leader. For this reason the history of that company forms an important chapter in the history of Saratoga Springs.

The history of the Mt. Vernon Glass factory and the history of the Granger family are intimately related. Nathan Granger, a native of Connecticut, came to Greenfield in Saratoga County sometime after the Revolutionary War. Here he married Hannah Monroe and had a family of six children. Three girls died in early childhood and three boys, Charles, Oscar and Gideon, survived. In 1832 he moved with his family to Vernon, New York where his three sons became apprentices in the glass blowing trade and finally became master glass blowers. Charles, the eldest, eventually became owner of the Mt. Vernon Glass works.

In the early 1840's it became apparent that the supply of wood necessary to stoke the fires of the glass furnaces would soon be exhausted in the Vernon area. This presented a very important problem since the business could not survive without an adequate supply of wood. At about the same time Dr. Clarke, owner of the Congress Spring, expressed his willingness to enter into a twenty-five year contract with the company for the supply of spring water bottles for his business, but with the stipulation that the bottles be produced nearer to Saratoga Springs so to diminish the expense of transportation over such a long distance and the resulting breakage.

The Grangers realized that if their glass business was to survive it would have to be moved to a place nearer a source of the essential materials used in glass blowing: firewood, sand and potash. Oscar Granger set out to find such a place. His quest took him to the township of Greenfield in Saratoga County where his family had previously lived. In the northwest corner of this township he came upon an area that in all respects seemed to be ideal for the establishment of his glass factory. It was a deeply wooded area on Kayaderosseras Mountain not far from Lake Desolation. The wood supply was assured by the vast woodland on the mountain, and the topsoil of the area consisted of sand of the type peculiarly suited for the making of fine glassware. While in Greenfield he came in contact with a very successful banker named John W. James. Mr. James owned a bank in the village of Jamesville (later Middle Grove). After a short acquaintance, Oscar Granger and John James developed a mutual respect making it possible for them to negotiate a business deal. Mr. James arranged for Oscar Granger to purchase 1,400 acres of land on Kayaderosseras Mountain and promised to help the Grangers to establish their business. He was to furnish the capital for the enterprise and the Grangers were to furnish the expertise. Shortly thereafter, a third member was added to the group, a carpenter named Walter Todd, whose experience in construction proved most valuable.

Once a new location was decided upon for the Granger glass factory, it was necessary to make plans to move to the new site. This was by no means an easy procedure. The old plant had to be gradually phased out while the new one was being built. The whole process covered a period of about two years.

It was somewhere around 1845 that Oscar Granger and his nephew Henry Granger, Charles' son, with their families moved to the new site on the mountain in Greenfield which they named Mount Pleasant. Charles and Gideon Granger and their families remained in Vernon to phase out the old plant.

With Oscar and Henry went most of the employees and their families together with all of their household belongings. All of the factory equipment had to be moved. Both people and possessions were loaded on to barges on the Erie Canal and transported to Schenectady and then moved by railroad to Saratoga Springs. The journey from Saratoga Springs to their destination at Mt. Pleasant was a rugged one over sandy roads in horse-drawn and oxen-drawn carts.

On arrival at their destination these enterprising people established a community in the wilderness. Trees were felled and roads constructed. Work, which had been started earlier was continued, and, to the twenty or so houses which had been built for the employees and their families were added other buildings and improvements. Three white frame houses were constructed for the three Granger families. A hotel, known as Temperance House was built to house unmarried men. They also built a blacksmith shop, a store with a post office, a sawmill, a gristmill, a box factory to make boxes in which to store bottles, barns and stables for horses and oxen, storehouses and, finally, a combination church and schoolhouse. Aware of the importance of educating the children of the community, Mr. Granger hired a teacher from the Normal School in Albany to come to Mt. Pleasant to instruct them.

The glass factory, the most important building in the community, was built much like the one at Vernon. It was a large round building approximately seventy feet in diameter with a high smoke stack in the center over the fire chamber. The fire in the fire chamber was fed at intervals by stokers who, working in six hour shifts, fed ten cords of wood to it every twenty-four hours. Wood driers, who were responsible for the wood supply, worked in twelve hour shifts drying the wood and cutting it into three foot lengths. The fire chamber was surrounded by a fireproof wall about three inches thick which was marked off into individual work areas. Each of these areas had a shelf in the wall which held individual firepots containing the molten glass. There were six pots in all, each two and a half feet in height and diameter and two inches thick. Two blowers worked at each pot. A glass batch was made up of twelve measures of sand, which had been previously washed and dried, five

Saratoga mineral water bottles

*ccasional Pieces. Produced by glass
owers at the Mt. Pleasant glass factory
Kayaderosseras Mountain circa 1850*

Collection of the Author

*Occasional Pieces. Produced by glass blowers
at the Mt. Pleasant glass factory on Kayaderosseras Mountain circa 1850*

measures of soda, three measures of lime and ten measures of ashes. In the pots the glass mix was heated to 2,400 degrees Fahrenheit and then cooled to 1,800 degrees Fahrenheit, the working temperature. At each workplace there was a direct opening to the fire chamber in the wall surrounding it. Through this opening the glass blower pushed his four-foot-long blow pipe. With a rolling motion he collected sufficient molten glass from the pot to make a bottle. This he brought out and rolled on an anvil to a satisfactory shape at which point he opened a two piece clam shell mould and, after closing it, he blew through the pipe until the bottle was formed. Then opening the mould, removed the bottle and broke off the blow pipe from it. The bottle was then finished by hand. Boys carried the finished bottles to the tempering oven where they remained several days before being packed for shipment. Many types of bottles in addition to the Saratoga Springs water bottles were made at this factory.

The problem of transporting the mineral water bottles from Mt. Pleasant to Saratoga Springs over rough hardpan roads was one which called for a practical solution. This challenge was met by the construction of an eleven-mile plank toll road between the two places. The project took over a year to complete. It necessitated the construction of four saw mills along the route to supply the 3,000,000 board feet of lumber required. Four toll booths were placed at intervals on the road. Three cents per vehicle was charged at each place. Over this road two wagonloads were transported daily from Mt. Pleasant to Saratoga Springs.

Soon after the community at Mt. Pleasant on Glass Factory Mountain had been established, several professional glass blowers were added to the work force. Among these was Samuel Archer, born in England and trained in glass blowing there. He was smuggled into the United States and soon thereafter found his way to Glass Factory Mountain in Saratoga County where he became a highly respected and valuable member of the community. Another foreign-born glass blower to come to the community was Louis Comanginger, born in France and trained in the art of glass blowing there. In addition, there were several master glass blowers who drifted to the mountain from other glass factories in this country.

For the purpose of finding more people to train for work in the factory, Oscar Granger made a trip to Ireland. At the time of his visit, Ireland was in the throes of the tragic potato famine which was having a devastating effect on that country. Mr. Granger arranged for a number of men and their families to come to America to Mt. Pleasant to be employed at the glass works. Many of the descendants of these families are to be found in the Saratoga area to this day.

Another infusion of foreign blood came to the mountain when Canadian woodsmen were employed to cut and prepare wood for the furnaces.

Oscar Granger was a many faceted man. His vocational skill was demonstrated by the fact that he had been successfully trained as a glass blower and had arrived at the top of that ladder as a master in the art. His business ability showed itself in his planning and implementing the building of a successful business at Mt. Pleasant. The 1850 Federal census attested to this fact by the following listing:

GRANGER COMPANY — GLASS MANUFACTURER

Capital invested in real and personal property	$20,000
Cord wood, 4000 cords	$6,000
Average number of hands employed	45
Average monthly cost of male labor	$35
Annual product, 7,200,000 bottles	$18,000

In this mountain community of approximately two hundred people Oscar Granger was somewhat of a patriarch. He felt a keen sense of responsibility for all his employees, both for their moral and physical well-being. To this end he formulated rules and regulations for behavior which he enforced rigidly. Total abstinence was on the top of the list. No drinking whatsoever was tolerated. He even sponsored a talk by Henry Ward Beecher, then running for president on the Temperance ticket. This speech was given on the front steps of Temperance House, the hotel which had been built to house the single men of the community.

This rule of temperence proved to be a real hardship on many of the Irish at Mt. Pleasant who had been brought up on Guiness and other alcoholic beverages in their homeland. They found it necessary to make occasional trips to the village to satisfy an unquenchable thirst, and they were even known to smuggle a quart or so into Mt. Pleasant on occasion.

Church attendance was required on the mountain. Most of the social activities were religious in nature. This was not unusual, as at that stage in the social history of this country, that was the typical situation.

The pledge that had to be signed by an indentured apprentice reveals the strict discipline imposed on young men.

APPRENTICE INDENTURE

This indenture, made the seventeenth day of September in the year of our Lord, one thousand eight hundred and fifty-one, witnesseth that Ezra W. Drake, son of Richard W. Drake, aged sixteen years, three months and one day, by and with the consent of Richard W. Drake, his father, and of his own free will, hath placed and bound himself as an apprentice to Oscar Granger, Henry C. Granger and Samuel Archer of Mt. Pleasant, in the Town of Greenfield, County of Saratoga, and State of New York to learn the art and trade of blowing glass and with them, as an apprentice, to dwell continuous and serve from the day of the date hereof until the said Ezra W. Drake shall have attained the full age of twenty-one years which will be on the sixteenth day of June in the Year of our Lord, one thousand eight hundred and fifty-six, during all of which term, the said apprentice, his said Masters will well and faithfully serve, their secrets keep, their lawful commands gladly do and obey. Hurts to his said Masters he shall not do, nor willfully suffer it to be done by others but of the same, to the utmost of his power, he shall forthwith give notice to his said Masters. The goods of his said Masters he shall not embezzle or waste nor them lend to any without the said Masters' consent. At cards or dice or any other unlawful games he shall not play. Taverns, ale houses and tippling houses he shall not frequent. Fornications he shall not commit. Matrimony he shall not contract. From the service of his said Masters, he shall not at any time depart or absent himself without his said Masters' leave, but in all things as a good and faithful servant shall and will demean and behave himself toward his said Masters during the said term and the said Masters, in the said art and trade of blowing glass which they now use, with all things thereunto belonging, shall or will teach and instruct or cause to be well and sufficiently taught and instructed after the best way and manner they can and shall and will also find and allow unto the said apprentice his meat, drink, washing, lodging, and the necessaries fit and convenient for such apprentice during the term aforesaid and the sum of fifty dollars, at the end of each and every year pay him toward and for the purpose of clothing him and in addition thereto, to pay for his services from the time that he shall become eighteen years of age until he shall become nineteen years and six months, one eighth of the regular wages of other workmen when engaged in blowing glass and for the next year and six months, one fourth of the regular wages to be paid at the end of each year. When the Glass Factory of the said Oscar Granger, H.D. Granger and Samuel Archer shall not be in operation said Ezra W. Drake is to do such other work as shall be required of him and during first year from the date above mentioned, the said Ezra W. Drake is not to be employed in blowing glass while the factory of said Oscar Granger, H.C. Granger and Samuel Archer is in operation but at such other work in said factory as may be directed by the said Oscar Granger, H.C. Granger and Samuel Archer.

In witness whereof the parties to these Presents have set their hands and seal the day and year first above mentioned.

Signed, Sealed and   Richard W. Drake (L.S.)
delivered in presence of   Ezra W. Drake (L.S.)
Truman Brown   Oscar Granger (L.S.)
                                      Henry C. Granger (L.S.)
                                      Samuel Archer (L.S.)

As Oscar Granger aged and others gradually took over the management of the business, he was able to indulge in some of his hobbies, one of which was horses. He had time to take part in county fairs and to act as judge on various occasions. He imported Merino sheep from Spain and enjoyed the challenge of improving the breed. He developed a dairy business and supplied hotels in Saratoga Springs with milk. In 1870 he passed away and was greatly mourned by all.

In the late 1850's the Mt. Pleasant Glass business was sold to the Congress and Empire Spring Company who eventually moved it to Saratoga Springs. In 1871 they located it on Congress Avenue not far from the present Saratoga Spa. The area came to be known as Congressville.

Many of the houses of the workers were moved to this place from the mountain and may still be seen there today.

Meanwhile on the mountain the few remaining inhabitants, being deprived of the glass business, turned to dairying and to the manufacture of boxes and crates for shipping spring water bottles.

Thus for about a half century the business of producing mineral water bottles thrived in the Saratoga area. Eventually, however, the hand-blown bottles came to be replaced by less expensive, machine-produced ones, and so a flourishing industry died out.

Though today practically all traces of the thriving community of the mid-nineteenth century at Mt. Pleasant on Kayaderosseras Mountain have disappeared, interest in their product lives on. The beautiful handblown bottles used for shipping mineral water are avidly sought after by bottle collectors. So popular has this hobby become that it is now the third-ranking one in the country being surpassed only by stamp and coin collecting.

The Saratoga-type bottle is found in a variety of colors, ranging from a dark olive green to a light olive amber with many graduations between. The shape is straight sided cylindrical with rounded shoulder and short cylindrical neck. On today's antique market these bottles are bringing increasingly greater prices.

Of special interest are those glass pieces known as "occasional pieces." These were produced by the glass blowers at the end of a run when there was a small amount of mix left in the pot. They were allowed to use this to blow small pieces for their wives and children. Great artistic ability and imagination was shown in many of these pieces. Such things as pitchers, sugar bowls, candlesticks, animals, flowers, birds and many other interesting items were produced. Many of these pieces have survived, the prized possession and heirlooms of the families of the makers. These pieces are in great demand today but are hard to come by because they are carefully guarded by the families that possess them. When they do come into the market they bring extremely high prices.

It seems ironic that the bottles that were produced by the glass blowers of the last century should become the prized collector's items that they are today. If these glass blowers, who were paid thirty-five dollars a month for their labors, could see the price these bottles are bringing in the present day antique market it would be, to say the least, a real revelation and shock to them.

12

The Era of the Gas Companies

"O, What may man within him hide,
Though angel on the outward side!"
—Shakespeare, *Measure for Measure*
Act III, Scene 2

During the closing decade of the nineteenth century it was found that carbonic acid gas existed in a free state in many of the springs in Saratoga. The discovery of the "dry gas," as it was called, was purely accidental. It was first discovered while boring for mineral water a short distance south of the center of the village. The drill used in the boring entered a pocket, or stratum, of pure carbonic acid gas in which the pressure was so great that the drilling tools and large quantities of gravel and stone were hurled into the air with great force. This was followed by a blast of carbonic acid gas which emitted a great roar as it burst forth. Since this finding was entirely unexpected, no provision had been made to collect the gas. The result was that several days elapsed before the escaping gas was controlled. The gas obtained from the pocket was in a pure state. It was dry, clear and free from any foreign matter and was, therefore, greatly preferred over gas obtained by decomposition or chemical process, the method in use at that time. The gas was ideally suited for use as an additive to food or drink for human consumption. Soda fountains were very popular during the Victorian era. Carbonic acid gas was in great demand because it was the ingredient used in making the artificially carbonated water used in ice cream sodas. The gas also found an important use in refrigeration.

Earlier in the century some carbonic acid gas had been extracted from the Saratoga carbonated mineral waters, but it had never been done on a very great scale. With the discovery of the dry gas it was realized that a new source of wealth had been discovered, since it would be possible to collect the gas, liquify it, and sell it commercially. Immediately companies were formed for this purpose, and one after another they began boring wells, collecting and marketing the gas for commercial use. The industry, thus started, very nearly struck the death knell of the famous carbonated mineral springs at Saratoga.

In the beginning the gas companies obtained the carbonic acid gas from "dry wells" or pockets in the springs. Later, as the demand for it rose, they extracted it from the mineral water itself as it flowed naturally from the ground. Still later it was found that a much larger amount of mineral water could be forced from the ground by pumping, thereby increasing the yield of carbonic acid gas. This resulted in the installation by the gas companies of pumping plants in the area of what is now Geyser Park and in the Lincoln and Washington bath house areas on South Broadway. Such springs as Champion, Lincoln, Vichy, Geyser, Arondack and many others were victims of this devastating practice.

The ceaseless operation of powerful deep well pumps operated by steam power extracted a tremendous amount of mineral water from the well, many times that which natural flow would have yielded. A very marked decrease in gas pressure and a lessening of the flow of water was noted in all of the natural springs and wells and there was a complete disappearance of some of the springs. It appeared that continued pumping at such an exorbitant rate would result in the destruction of the natural springs.

Up to the time the commercial gas companies began pumping mineral water for the purpose of increasing the flow, the Saratoga mineral waters had been used as they emerged from the ground. No attempt had ever been made to alter them in any way, either by the addition or extraction of any substance. The springs were all privately owned. Each spring had its own peculiar qualities for which specific reason it became famous. Though all of the springs contained the same minerals and all were charged with carbonic acid gas, each one differed from the others in the concentration and proportion of the various minerals and in the amount of carbonic acid gas it contained. Some springs, because of a greater content of certain minerals, had become famous as cathartic waters; others with a lighter concentration were widely used as table waters; and still others, because of a high content of iron, had been found to be effective in the treatment of anemia.

Each owner was content with his spring, regarding it as an independent property having no direct relation to the other springs in the area. This tradition was upset when, in July 1907, Mr. Frank H. Hathorn, owner of the famous Hathorn Spring located at the corner of Spring and Putnam Streets in Saratoga Springs, brought suit against Dr. Strong, who owned and operated a sanatorium on Circular Street about two blocks east of the Hathorn spring. Mr. Hathorn charged that excessive draft from the spring located on the Strong property, which was used in connection with the sanatorium, had adversely affected the water in the Hathorn Spring.

At the conclusion of the litigation which resulted from this suit, the opinion of the Supreme Court was issued by Mr. Justice Spencer in July 1907 as follows:

> Among the witnesses are a number, possessing worldwide fame as specialists in the departments of chemistry and geology, who have made the springs of Saratoga objects of special study and whose opinions are entitled to the gravest considerations. . . . From this and the other testimony in the case, I am of the view . . . that all the mineral springs and wells of Saratoga have a common source, consisting of a stratum of mineral rock of comparatively limited area and located far down in the earth. We may, however, leave to the domain of speculation the question of whether such stratum is the remains of an extinct volcano, as claimed by some, or a remnant of the ancient Silurian ocean, as contended by others. Nevertheless, the fact of the existence is sufficiently demonstrated by its productions. The same may be said of the fact that surface waters percolate in this stratum; that chemical action takes place, forming gas, and that the latter impregnates the water and forces it to the surface by the easiest and most direct route. . . .
>
> The history of the springs divides itself into three periods. During the first, only springs were known and these found their way to the surface by means of the geological fault. In some instances the natural vents were supplemented by adjacent borings; but no pumps were employed, except to dislodge temporary obstructions or to remove surface water which occasionally found its way into the vents and by its weight held back the water charged with gas. It was during this period that the springs acquired their fame because of their medicinal virtues, and, in consequence, a considerable village with large and expensive hotels was built in their neighbor-hood, and multitudes resorted thither to partake of the healing waters. All these springs flowed by reason of their gas pressure. Their flow was generous and substantially continuous. . . .
>
> The second period is marked by extensive boring of wells. The popularity of the waters created a great demand, not only at the springs but throughout the country, and large quantities were bottled and sold for use elsewhere. This occasioned a quest for additional means of supply, and deep borings were resorted to. It was found that the mineral stratum lay along the east side of the fault and that borings along that line pierced the stratum and relieved the gas and water. In this manner wells, producing great volumes of water and strong forces, were produced. In some instances the water spouted to a height of thirty feet above the surface; and, in others, only gas was discharged. It seemed as if the supply was inexhaustable; and, in one case, a spouting spring was left to flow for spectacular effect alone. I think the evidence indicates that, during this period, there was a diminution observed in the force of gas and flow of water throughout the entire system. I cannot affirm, but it is probable, that, had such borings been continued and sufficiently increased in number, they might have exhausted the supply; but events

Gas Company Plant in Geyser Park

Plant of the Natural Carbonic Gas Company on South Broadway. The building was converted to the Lincoln Bath House soon after the state purchased the property in 1911

were not permitted to take that course. The business of extracting
gas from the water and compressing it into steel cylinders for market
had then assumed large proportions and became profitable. The
demand for larger supplies of water for this purpose called for
another and more effectual force to bring the water to the surface
than that of the gas itself.

This demand brings us to the third and present period, which
begins with the installation of powerful deep well pumps in many of
the wells and their ceaseless operation by steam power. That serious
consequences would result should have been anticipated. I think the
evidence leads to the conclusion that, since the general inauguration
of pumps, there has been a marked depreciation of gas pressure in
all the springs and wells and a lessening of the flow of water, and
that, in many instances, both have disappeared entirely; that, if
such pumping be continued it will result in the destruction of all the
natural springs and wells, that is, all that flow by virtue of their gas
pressure alone. It may be noted here that two methods of pumping
are employed, one by the use of a plunger far down in the well,
drawing the water thereto by powerful suction and raising it to the
surface, and the other by forcing gas far down into the earth where it
is released into the well, and, by its lifting power, forces the water
up. Both methods are equally fatal to wells and springs where no
pumping takes place.

I think from this outline of the history of the springs, in connection with the teachings of the men of science who have been called,
we may safely say that all the Saratoga mineral waters come from a
common source and are held in the earth in a state of percolation
and that pumping upon one may seriously affect the force of gas and
flow of water in another . . . I cannot escape the conclusion that
pumping at any one of the wells, which reaches the line of mineral
stratum producing the gas, operates by lessening the force of gas
and flow of water in all other wells and springs which draw their
supply from that stratum.

This verdict judiciously established the fact that pumping on one spring
could materially affect the flow and character of another spring, thereby alter-
ing its properties.

Over the years following their formation, the gas companies continued their
excessive pumping of the springs with a devastating effect on the waters.
Many conservation-minded citizens became very alarmed. They recognized
this excessive and reckless pumping of the waters as a threat to the survival of
the springs as a natural resource. After the verdict was given in the case of
Hathorn vs. Strong, a committee of concerned citizens was formed with
Willard Lester as chairman. Their purpose was to protect and preserve the
mineral springs of Saratoga for posterity. They wished to restore the springs
and the prestige of Saratoga Springs as a natural health resort and sought to
accomplish their purpose through legislation. Through their influence a bill
was introduced in the New York State Legislature by Assemblyman George H.

Whitney. It passed, and on February 10, 1908 was signed into law by Governor Charles Evans Hughes. It was known as the Anti-pumping Act of 1908 and among other things, declared unlawful:

> Pumping or otherwise drawing by artificial appliance from any well made by boring or drilling into the rock, that class of mineral waters holding in solution natural mineral salts and excess of carbonic acid gas, or pumping, or by any artificial contrivance whatsoever in any manner producing an unnatural flow of carbonic acid gas issuing free or contained in any well made by boring or drilling into the rock, for the purpose of extracting, collecting, compressing, liquifying or vending such gas as a commodity otherwise than in connection with the mineral water and the other mineral ingredients with which it was associated.

Such regulative laws had been in effect for some time in many countries of the world. However, this was the first law of its kind to be enacted in New York State. It was to have a very marked effect on operations of the commercial companies which pumped the mineral water from springs for the purpose of extracting carbonic acid gas and selling it commercially.

Immediately after the passage of the bill a stockholder and bondholder of one of the gas companies whose operations were threatened by the act brought suit against the officers of the State and all others to enjoin them from enforcing the provisions of the act on the ground that it was unconstitutional. This suit, which began in June 1908, was long drawn out, finally ending in the U.S. Supreme Court. A decision was not finally rendered until March 1911, when the Court affirmed the constitutionality of the act.

The group of concerned citizens followed their success in having the Anti-pumping law passed putting pressure on the gas companies to discontinue pumping. They supported Frank H. Hathorn, owner of the famous Hathorn Spring, in bringing suit against the Natural Carbonic Gas Company to restrain that company from excessive pumping in violation of the Anti-pumping Act of 1908. The group also was influential in having the New York State Attorney General bring suit in the name of the people against six other gas companies for the same purpose.

This action was possible since the author of the Act of 1908 in his remarkable wisdom had anticipated the possibility that the gas companies might not voluntarily stop pumping the waters and would have to be forced by further legal action to do so. Included in the bill was the following provision: "The Attorney General may at any time, in the exercise of his discretion, bring and maintain an action in the name of the people of New York State, to restrain any person or corporation from any of the unlawful acts specified in section one of this act. It shall be the duty of the Attorney General to institute and prosecute such an action, upon the written request of ten citizens of this state who are assessed for taxes therein and whose aggregate assessments amount to not less than ten thousand dollars."

The suits were vigorously defended by the gas companies who had retained as their lawyer Senator Edgar Truman Brackett, who had been defeated in 1906 in his bid for re-election to the Senate. The companies maintained that the flow of water from the springs was a property and that that property included the right to accelerate that flow of their own springs as they saw fit, whether or not it resulted in injury to other springs. They further claimed that the injunction did not prevent their pumping if they did not extract to sell the gas or make any profit from their pumping, but merely let it run to waste on the ground. Preliminary injunctions against excessive pumping were granted in all of these suits pending further judgments.

These injunctions were not respected by the gas companies. They continued their pumping, although not, as they said, in order to sell any product, but for sheer waste which they claimed to be within their right of private ownership. The constitutional prohibition of the Act of 1908 and the prohibition of the injunction were, so they insisted, directed against pumping only in case the water or gas extracted from it was sold for use off from the premises. Though the companies were within the technical letter of the law they certainly put law and order to derision.

The continued pumping for whatever cause, whether for business profit by sale of the gas or for sheer waste, had a value to the companies in their ability to inflict damage on other properties, thereby making them less valuable and enhancing the companies' property value. This would make it possible for them to exact a higher price for their properties in case they were to be sold.

In preparing the Act of 1908, prohibiting excessive pumping for the purpose of extracting gas for profit, no one of the legislators, even in their wildest moments, would have ever conceived of anyone going to the pain and expense of artificially pumping the mineral waters for the purpose of wasting them. But in actual fact this is exactly what happened. Pumping continued undiminished. The quantity of mineral water pumped was at least ten times the natural flow of all the springs in Saratoga put together.

A critical period in the history of the Saratoga mineral waters had been reached. To rescue the springs from possible extinction, drastic action was called for, and called for immediately.

13

Establishment of the State Reservation at Saratoga Springs

"The heights by great men reached and kept
Were not attained by sudden flight
But they, while their companions slept
Were toiling upward in the night."
　　　　　　　—Henry Wadsworth Longfellow

The realization that the gas companies could prolong litigation on their violation of the Anti-pumping law of 1908 by delays and appeals, while the springs were rapidly becoming depleted, made it apparent that the only salvation for the springs would be control of the entire group by a single ownership sufficiently powerful to act with the authority to control the situation. It was obvious that the state should be the single owner which would give this harmonious unity of administration.

At this critical time in its history Saratoga was fortunate to have Spencer Trask as a resident. An active member of the Citizens Committee, he was a successful financier and businessman who had decided to devote the final years of his life to the development of Saratoga Springs as a health resort.

Trask had purchased the property of Jacobus Barhyte in 1881. Barhyte was a soldier who had fought in the Revolution under General Gates in the Battles of Bemis Heights and Saratoga in the Saratoga Campaign of 1777. It was shortly after these battles that he discovered the beautiful site which had a magnificent view of Bemis Heights. After the war he purchased about two hundred acres in the area and settled there. In time the place became famous for the trout dinners which he prepared for guests from the trout caught in Barhyte Lake on the property.

On this land Spencer Trask built an imposing Victorian mansion. In 1926, the estate was to become the realization of his dream: a retreat where artists, musicians and others could work in an atmosphere conducive to the creation of works of art, music and literature.

Mr. Trask, being a man of influence, interested Governor Hughes and members of the Legislature in the idea of state ownership of the springs. Senator Brackett, a resident of Saratoga Springs, who, in the election of 1908, had been successful in regaining his seat in the Senate, responded to the recommendations of Mr. Trask and the Committee of Concerned Citizens. He, together with Assemblyman Whitney, who had sponsored the Anti-pumping bill of 1908, introduced a bill in the Legislature which would make the springs of Saratoga a State Reservation.

The bill authorized "the selection, location and appropriation of certain lands in the town of Saratoga Springs for a state reservation . . . for the purpose of the preservation of the natural mineral springs therein located." It made an appropriation for that purpose and authorized an issue of bonds to pay such appropriation. It provided for the appointment by the governor, with the consent of the Senate, of three commissioners to constitute a board under the name of "The Commissioners of the State Reservation at Saratoga Springs." They were given the power "to select and locate such lands in the town of Saratoga Springs, in the county of Saratoga, and any rights, easements, or interest upon or in any lands in said town, as it shall deem proper and necessary to be taken for the purpose of establishing a state reservation, of preserving the natural mineral springs in said town of Saratoga Springs, and of restoring said springs to their former natural condition, and for that purpose to acquire any rights, easements, or interest in any property, the whole of which it shall not acquire, for the purpose of protecting the springs or mineral water rights upon any lands it shall acquire."

The Board was given the authority to determine, with the owners, the value of the various properties, and request the agreed upon sum to be paid by the State Treasurer. In case of disagreement between the Board and an owner of the land, such owner could recover judgment for the value of the land thereof in the Court of Claims as a claim against the state. The land so acquired was to be kept and remain and be known as part of the "State Reservation at Saratoga Springs." The care, custody and control of the Reservation and of all the mineral springs, wells, mineral water and natural carbonic acid gas therein, thereon and thereunder was assigned to the Board.

This bill, to establish a reservation with the purpose of protecting the springs had phenomenal support throughout the entire state and seemed from the beginning to be assured of passage by the Legislature. The idea that the mineral springs of Saratoga are a national monument and their preservation a state duty was generally accepted. Their acquisition appeared to be a logical step for the state to take. The state had already demonstrated its interest in the springs with the passage of the Anti-pumping bill of 1908.

For the state to acquire a natural resource for the purpose of preserving it for posterity had already been set as a precedent several times. Some years previously the state had purchased the land on the American side of Niagara

Falls at a cost of three million dollars and had made it into a state reservation. It had spent very large sums of money in reservations in the Adirondacks and the Catskills. It had purchased Watkins Glen and made it a state park, and had done the same thing with the Palisades. The Federal government had likewise established itself as guardian of natural resources when it nationalized "The Hot Springs of Arkansas."

To be sure, New York State, in acquiring the springs at Saratoga, was following the example of foreign states in guarding their springs. There are examples closely parallel to Saratoga in the European spas. These are practically all under public control as visitors to Carlsbad, Vichy, Hamburg, Bath, Baden Baden and other places of the kind can testify.

In an editorial in the *New York Journal of Medicine* March 1909, Dr. Algernon Thomas Bristow prints the following in discussing the situation at Saratoga Springs:

> If the state is to conserve its resources it must control them. Why should our citizens go to distant Carlsbad when we have a spa of our own, situated among scenes of great natural beauty?
>
> If Germany has found it necessary and of advantage to exercise state control over certain of her natural springs of healing, why should we in America, in view of our natural tendencies, not take similar measures to secure for all time to the people of this state the advantages which are known to accrue from such resorts?
>
> The United States exercises a certain control over the Hot Springs of Arkansas, to prevent their exploitation at private hands and to render it possible for people of moderate means, or even no means at all, to avail themselves of the curative properties of these springs.
>
> The State of New York may well consider whether it would not be of advantage to its people if it exercises control over the waters of Saratoga by making the region a state reservation.

The press of the state was unanimous in its enthusiastic support of the project. The following excerpts from a few of the many editorials published throughout the state illustrate this support.

The *Poughkeepsie News-Press* of March 12, 1909 under the headline "State Should Save Springs" presents the case as follows:

> The plea of the people of Saratoga Springs for the bringing about of State ownership of the springs there, seems to have every merit necessary to commend it to the state at large. The state finds itself obliged, at times, to acquire reservations, and the like, in order to safeguard the public benefit, and the other. Here is a proposition which, if accepted, bids fair to contribute largely to the growth of a great city, which, because of its public advantages, will probably attract people from over the world, and certainly from all over the United States.
>
> The private ownership of the springs at Saratoga has greatly narrowed the popularity of the place as a resort. That the waters there

are counted among the best in the world is not questioned. State ownership will mean preservation of the springs. It will mean improvements and widespread popularity, which cannot fail to result in great benefit to the whole state. It will bring thousands of strangers into the state, and it will mean the spending of money in great quantities on the railroads, in the hotels, and, in every way shall benefits come which inevitably follow the spending of money in quest of health and pleasure.

If for none other than these reasons, the State should save Saratoga Springs. The health-giving properties of the waters constitute alone sufficient reason for the action of the state in heeding the quest of the people of the place.

The *Wall Street Journal* presents a strong argument in favor of state ownership of the springs in the following editorial of March 6, 1909 under the title "A Strong Case for State Ownership":

Government is largely a matter of compromise, and, although the strict rules of morality obtain there as much as in the conduct of the private individual, questions of policy cannot be laid down with anything like the same certainty. It is easy to say, and the statement is broadly sound, that the individual is debilitated rather than helped when the state does that for him which he should do for himself. In actual practice, however, the executive power has to consider all the individuals in the state and their collective good as well as their individual good.

The medicinal spring district of Saratoga is unique in its way. The curative qualities of its waters are unquestioned and they have a demonstrated ameliorating effect on many diseases of a chronic character. The springs are owned by private individuals and there is no question that private ownership has not been a success. The pumping of gas is no doubt in the main responsible for the exhaustion of a number of the springs, but also individual greed must have put many springs out of commission by demanding more than their fair flow of water.

It has now been laid down by the Court of Appeals that the pumping of the gas from the subterranean reservoir which must lie below the whole district, in order to sell it for the manufacture of aerated waters, is illegal, on the ground that individual property cannot be developed at the expense of the whole community. The largest pumps are now restrained from the extraction of gas for commercial purposes, but the rivalry of the local spring owners continues and we are doing in Saratoga what we have done with some of the finest resources of this continent. It looks in fact, as if individual selfishness would finally leave the medicinal spring as extinct as the buffalo.

It will be seen that there is a strong case for state ownership. The United States owns a formation closely related in the Yellowstone Park. Perhaps New Zealand is hardly a fair parallel, but the state is the only landlord in the hot springs district of Rotorus, only second in importance to our own wonderful geyser formation. There are other examples closely parallel to Saratoga in the European spas. These are practically all under public control.

State ownership seems the least of two evils in this case, and it must be admitted at once that it is an evil. A condition of private commercial morality which should safeguard the springs district is quite conceivable. In this case, however, the greatest number must be considered. Private ownership has its limits, and no owner has a right to destroy one of these springs, any more than the owner of a painting by Raphael is morally entitled to burn it. What will of course be necessary is to see that the state buys springs which are really active, and does not invest the public's money in a number of holes in the ground which certain disinterested villagers of Saratoga would doubtless be willing enough to sell.

The *Daily Saratogian* of February 23, 1909 under the heading "What State Control Would Mean" states:

> The Saratoga mineral springs are God given—the result of a geological fault in the rock—and permanent save for man's interference. Private competition, bitterness and bickering, misuse, lack of intelligent, scientific care, no power to remedy such evils, little money - all prevent these natural, medicinal healing waters from achieving all the good nature intended. They were meant for all mankind, but under present conditions they fail largely to accomplish that end.
>
> The Brackett-Whitney Bill in the Legislature to "Preserve the Natural Mineral Springs in the Town of Saratoga Springs" by "Creating a State Reservation," is the one method under which these natural resources of the State may fulfill their usefulness.
>
> This bill provides for State acquisition and control - that the springs shall hereafter be forever free, under control of three commissioners appointed by the Governor. State ownership would be a guarantee of every analysis. It could enter upon any land in order to retube old bores, cut off the wasting of water and gas, prevent surface water from entering into the bore and, by communicating under the earth, weaken other springs. All this no private ownership could accomplish.
>
> Scientific, intelligent handling of the mineral wells would maintain all of the present active, strong springs, and would permit the temporarily exhausted wells to recuperate.
>
> State control would immediately attract to the state and this locality thousands of health seekers. Saratoga Springs is ready to follow state control with a kurtage, a casino, park, walks, sanitoriums and the enforcement of a proper regimen—diet, rest, etc. Thus are the foreign spas conducted, and only thus can they be thoroughly effective. These things can only be accomplished by state control.
>
> State control abroad amasses great wealth for the state, and it

would do the same thing for New York, besides adding fame to the old Empire commonwealth.

Will New York State preserve its own - the people's rights - these medicinal springs? Are not these neglected resources to be protected, nurtured and scientifically handled by the rightful owner - the state?

The state has assumed the proper protection to Niagara, the Palisades, Watkins Glen, the Adirondacks - why not these Saratoga Springs?

The government blazed the way at Hot Springs, Arkansas, which yields a revenue of $195,000 from the baths yearly.

The original and more lasting foundation of this village was recognized, and the seal of approval set by the Legislature in its enactments last year for the protection of the springs.

The next natural thing for the State to do is to create this "State Reservation."

The present state reservations were all acquired by purchase and continue as an expense each year. A state reservation at Saratoga Springs would return a large sum for the bath houses and shipping concession, estimated at from $30,000 to $40,000 a year.

Plainly this is a duty the state owes to itself and to posterity.

It would reap the renown and added wealth.

In no particular is it a local matter or one of politics.

It should become a law.

The bill was passed by the Legislature and signed by Governor Hughes in May 1909. It became chapter 569 of the laws of 1909 of New York State.

The passage of this bill which created the State Reservation, enabling the State to make available and keep forever what is undoubtedly the most remarkable and medicinally valuable group of mineral springs in the world, was celebrated in Saratoga Springs with the ringing of bells and the firing of a 21 gun salute. A new day had dawned and with it the promise of a bright future in which the mineral springs could fulfill their destiny as a source of health benefits for the people of New York State and the world.

14

The First Commission of the
State Reservation at Saratoga Springs

"Nothing is ever achieved without enthusiasm."
—Ralph Waldo Emerson

Immediately after the passage of the bill providing for the establishment of a state reservation at Saratoga Springs, Governor Hughes, as provided in the law, appointed three Commissioners: Spencer Trask, a resident of Saratoga Springs and distinguished financier, Edward M. Shepard, an outstanding member of the New York State Bar, and Frank N. Godfrey, Master of the State Grange. Mr. Trask was made chairman of the Commission.

The Commission began at once to investigate the matters which, under the law, were left to their judgment. Their investigation was threefold. First it involved a study of the mineral springs, their past and present condition, the status of spring rights and the uncertainties over the legal rights of owners and the effect upon such rights of Chapter 429 of the Anti-pumping laws of 1908. Secondly, they studied the experience of the United States Government and of foreign governments in dealing with similar problems. Mr. L. McH. Howe, under instructions given by Mr. Trask, was commissioned to go to Europe to make a study of the methods that foreign governments used in the operation of their spas. Thirdly, they studied the bearing of future policies of the State of New York on these and similar matters so that they might advise the Legislature on their future policies.

The members of the Commission found it advisable to include the village of Saratoga Springs in the planning and operation of the Reservation. In this matter they had the wholehearted cooperation of the village through the Park

Commissioner, the Honorable William W. Allerdice.

It was proposed that the village cooperate with the Commission in its municipal functioning in such areas as the arrangement of its water and sewage systems, in the care of its streets and buildings, in its safety and sanitary regulations and other related matters. It was further proposed that the village expend the sum of $250,000 to acquire the Congress Park and the block immediately adjoining it known as the Canfield Park property. This latter property contained the famous Canfield Casino.

The commission requested that an act be submitted to the Legislature to amend Chapter 569 of the Laws of 1909 (the law establishing the Reservation). This act was to contain several recommendations, including one that would make the president of the village of Saratoga Springs an additional, ex officio Commissioner and member of the Board if and when the agreement between the Board and the village of Saratoga Springs (i.e. to cooperate with the Commission and to expend $250,000) should be approved by the electors of the village.

The Commissioners felt that they could not justifiably commit the state to expenditures for the purpose of the springs until the validity or effect of the Anti-pumping Act of 1908 was settled. The value of the properties could not properly be assessed while the unlawful pumping continued since the apparent value and output of some of the properties were artificially and unlawfully diminished, while others were increased by the pumping.

However, since the state had an interest in finding a speedy solution of the problem of unlawful pumping, they made an exception to the overall policy of not acquiring any mineral springs until the question of legal rights should be determined by making a small part of their permanent acquisition of spring properties possible immediately. In that way they could, as owners test the proprietary rights of spring owners and test the practical efficiency of the Act of 1908, a thing for which none of the individual owners of the other springs found himself able, or at any rate, inclined to assume, considering the heavy burden of litigation involved.

After obtaining the approval of the Governor, they acquired for $20,000 a one-tenth part of the Hathorn Spring property in the center of the village on which was located a fine mineral spring. Later they acquired for the sum of $6,250 a one-quarter interest in the Champion Spring property. The Champion is a spring in the area south of the village known as The Geysers. The owernship of these enabled the State Attorney General to bring suit in the name of the people of the state, as owners of both Hathorn and Champion Springs, against the gas companies to force them to obey the anti-pumping laws.

These items were included in the 1910 report of the Commission of the State Reservation at Saratoga Springs to the Legislature. The report was completed and signed and ready for final printing on December 30, 1909. Early on the morning of December 31st Spencer Trask left his home at Yaddo, Saratoga Springs for New York City carrying the report so that, under his personal

*Spencer Trask Memorial entitled the "Spirit of Life." The statue is the
work of Daniel Chester French, architectural setting by Henry Bacon*

supervision, a few corrections could be made in the printer's proof and then the printed copies could be sent to the Legislature in Albany without delay that afternoon. He boarded the Montreal express which was to take him to New York City. At Croton-on-Hudson there was a violent collision when a freight train from the west struck the rear of the express train. The rear car of the express train in which Mr. Trask was riding was practically demolished. However, he was the only person to lose his life in the accident. This generous public-spirited man had lost his life while on a mission for the Reservation.

There was great consternation and deep mourning throughout the whole country that morning when the news was flashed of the tragic accident.

People in all walks of life paid tribute to Mr. Trask for by his kindnesses and benefactions he had endeared himself to many. The following tribute published in the *Saratoga Sun* is typical of the warm feelings expressed by the press throughout the country.

> Spencer Trask had planned to spend the remaining years of his life as a Saratogian, working with the object of making Saratoga the greatest health resort in the world. Of the truth of this statement there is not the slightest doubt. It is, to Saratogians, the cause of most profound regret that this noble ideal of service should have been cut short by the tragic event of Friday morning last.
>
> No other living man was so well equipped as Mr. Trask for the special services to Saratoga Springs, to the state, and to humanity. He had a profound and comprehensive knowledge of the whole mineral spring question. He had repeatedly visited all the great mineral springs resorts in Europe. He had studied their conditions, development, management, and especially their methods of achieving financial success. He had investigated their medical and sanitary regulations, their attractions and amusements, their social accessories, their parks and architecture, and possessed much valuable data on these subjects.
>
> He also knew thoroughly all the facts regarding the mineral springs of Saratoga Springs. He had studied the subject for years, both practically and scientifically . . . He was a Saratogian by choice, having founded here a magnificent estate.
>
> Mr. Trask was not simply a shrewd financier and able business man. He was an idealist as well, being moved by profound impulses to make the world better and more beautiful. He had strong imagination, and the mystic power of vision, although his dreams were characterized by direct insight into the possibilities of future accomplishment. When to such a spiritual foundation was added a powerful and untiring physique and a magnificent mental equipment, his success in the business world is quite understandable. Such would be the man to finance an Edison, as he did; a great newspsper; a book publishing house; to found a noble country estate; to love art and nature with passion; and, when retired from active business, to take up such work as developing Saratoga Springs as a great health resort.

Hard and absorbing work was instinctive with Mr. Trask. Having formed the idea of giving the closing years of his life to the developing and protection of Saratoga Springs, he took hold of the work with enthusiasm and energy. He became treasurer of the Citizen's Committee. He contributed to and aided by his influence the fight for mineral spring protection. When the Saratoga Reservation law was proposed, he supported it with utmost zeal and enthusiasm. He served on committees, got up meetings, made addresses, and in every public and private way urged on the good work. The passage of the law through the Legislature and its approval by Governor Hughes were largely due to his influence and efforts. His appointment by Governor Hughes as chairman of the Reservation Commission placed him at last in a position to press forward toward the success of his plan for the great Saratoga health resort.

How hard and devoted was his unrewarded work on the Saratoga Reservation Commission only those who were close to or associated with him can know. It was unselfish work, and he had large capacity and large means for doing it well. That he did it well will appear in due time. It may need a giant to start a great boulder rolling down a mountainside; when it is started the law of gravitation will do the rest. . . . With the proof sheets of the report of the Saratoga Reservation Commisssion, Mr. Trask was on his way to a meeting of his associates, for its final consideration when he met his death.

The loss Saratoga mourns today is indeed a great and grievous one. In some respects, and important ones, it is irreparable.

In Congress Park may be seen a beautiful and artistic memorial fountain erected by Mrs. Trask in memory of her husband. The statue, "The Spirit of Life," is the work of the dean of American sculptors, Daniel Chester French. It is considered to be his finest work, even surpassing his great and much loved piece "The Seated Lincoln" in the Lincoln Memorial in Washington, D.C. and ranking above his almost as famous "Minute Man" in Lexington, Massachusetts. The architectural setting of the statue was designed by Henry Bacon, the architect who worked with French on the setting of the Lincoln Memorial in Washington, D.C. These great works of art were created at about the same time.

The bronze figure of "The Spirit of Life" surmounts a pedestal of granite from which gushes a stream of living water. In one uplifted hand there is a bowl of water signifying the medicinal mineral waters of Saratoga Springs. The other hand holds a pine branch emblematic of the salubrious climate of the area.

Above the statue words written of Spencer Trask by Governor Hughes are carved: "His Chief Aim Was to Do Good and to Serve His Fellow Men."

On the base of the monument is carved the Motto: "For a Man's Life Consisteth Not In the Abundance of the Things Which He Possesseth."

This motto, tattered and torn, was found in Spencer Trask's pocketbook on his death, and it is said by his intimate friends to have been carried by him from his early manhood as a constant and continuous reminder to him as to the real value and obligations of wealth. That he accepted this as true and lived in accordance with its teachings is exemplified by the fact that, instead of having a tremendous estate to leave in his will as might be expected from the magnitude of the benefactions bestowed during his lifetime, it was found that his possessions aggregated a very modest sum as fortunes are ranked today. He enjoyed life because he thought of others, and gave freely and generously while he was alive to individuals and public charities.

Governor Martin H. Glynn gave the eulogy at the dedication of the memorial in Congress Park on July 14, 1914. Daniel Chester French, a close friend of Mr. Trask's, was present at the ceremonies. Judge Charles Lester spoke for the citizens of Saratoga Springs to whom Mr. Trask had been a beloved benefactor.

15

The State Reservation   1910 - 1916

"It does good alike to the poor and the rich."
—Horace, I Epist. 1.25

Following the tragic death of Spencer Trask, Governor Hughes appointed Mr. Trask's business partner, George Foster Peabody, to head the Commission of the State Reservation at Saratoga Springs. At the same time Commissioner Edward M. Shepard was replaced by Benjamin F. Tracy. It was found that Mr. Shepard could no longer hold the position of Commissioner since it was legally inconsistent with his holding the position of trustee and chairman of the College of the City of New York. Mr. Frank N. Godfrey remained the only original member of the Commission.

The new Commission carried on the work of the development of the Reservation with the same interest and dedication as had their predecessors. Their goal was to restore the mineral springs to their original state and to make Saratoga Springs a world-famous health resort. To this end they devoted a large part of their valuable time. Mr. Peabody purchased a home in Saratoga Springs so that his presence as a member of the community, might, as in the case of his predecessor, Spencer Trask, facilitate the work of developing the Reservation.

Before his death Mr. Trask had commissioned Mr. L. McH. Howe to go to Europe as a representative of the Saratoga Springs Reservation Commission. He was to visit the various spas of the Continent and England to study the methods the foreign governments used in dealing with their spas. His report on the European spas on his return convinced the members of the Commission that the plan for the acquisition of the mineral springs of Saratoga by the State of New York was entirely feasible and that, based on the experience of European countries, they could look forward to a very beautiful and highly successful spa at Saratoga.

Mr. Howe reported that the mineral water springs in all of the countries visited were recognized by their governments as a very valuable natural resource. They were protected by special laws over and beyond those which applied to plain water wells and streams. Most governments had invested large sums of money in their mineral springs. Many, including France, Germany, Spain and Italy, had constructed fine military hospitals on these sites where thousands of government employees and members of the armed forces could receive treatment at state expense. Also, large investments were made in bath houses and recreational facilities. It was found that the latter investments paid off handsomely. Mr. Howe compared Saratoga to Vichy where the water is like that of Saratoga and is suited for bottling as well as bathing. He noted that Vichy is owned by the government of France and is leased to a private company under government supervision. The Vichy Company made an initial investment in permanent improvements. Subsequently it has realized an annual profit after paying rent to the government and a subsidy to the village of Vichy. In addition it has been able to set aside exceedingly liberal funds and allowances for depreciation, and to pay 16% to its stockholders on its total capitalization. Aix-les-Bains, another mineral water spa owned by the French government, has also proved profitable under similar circumtances. The Grand Duchy of Hesse in which the health resort of Nauheim is located, and the municipality of Carlsbad have had similar experiences, as did the municipalities of Harrogate, Bath and Buxton in England.

The commission concluded from the report of Mr. Howe that the experience of foreign spas fully confirmed the wisdom of the action of the New York Legislature in passing the Bill of 1909 establishing a state-owned spa in New York State, and that the work of restoring and preserving the mineral springs was entirely feasible since it would "make available and keep forever what is undoubtably the most remarkable and medicinally valuable group of springs in the world." They were gratified to learn that the large financial expenditures on the development of spas had proved not to be a burden on the government, but had in reality become a source of perpetual revenue by enabling the spas to be exceedingly profitable as a business enterprise. Upon receipt of this very favorable report, the New York State Legislature increased the appropriation for the Reservation to $950,000, the limit of bonds available under the Constitution.

The task of restoring the mineral springs to their original state was a very difficult one to accomplish. For a period of years the springs had been deteriorating because of irresponsible, reckless and wanton treatment until they had almost reached a point of no return. To restore the springs it was necessary to place all of them under unified ownership, namely the State of New York, so that the amount of water taken from them could be controlled. Since

Hathorn Drink Hall, Putnam Street side

Fountain inside of the Hathorn Drink Hall

Collection of George Bolster

Scene inside Hathorn Drink Hall

Gathering at Lincoln Spring area, circa 1912

Avenue of Pines soon after planting, circa 1912

Scene in Geyser Park, circa 1915. Note rustic bridge

it had been determined by experts in the field of geology and accepted by a court of law that the mineral waters have a common source and that, therefore, abuse by excessive pumping of any one of the springs could adversely affect all of the springs, the logical solution to maintaining them in a state of maximum efficiency was to have them all under the control of one authority. This would make it possible to regulate the supply of the water by allowing only those springs to run which would collectively supply the amount of water required to maintain the system in a state of equilibrium. Under private ownership it was found that certain owners would draw an unreasonable amount of water, as in the case of the gas companies, thereby lowering the water level in other springs, even those at a distance from where the water was drawn. Individuals could do nothing about controlling other owners' springs. A single owner controlling all of the springs, on the other hand, would be in a position to shut off one or more springs as necessary to maintain a desirable level of water in the mineral water basin. When necessary, springs could be stopped from running entirely by capping them.

The Commission proceeded under a very carefully devised plan to carry out their objective of placing all of the springs under the unified ownership of the State of New York. They worked under the mandate which stated: "The state to proceed to acquire all the spring rights with such surface land as may be incidently necessary or convenient within the proper area in the springs valley running through Saratoga Village together with whatever rights of any character or whatsoever situate, may be necessary or proper to protect such springs and spring rights, with the intention that, when the state's acquisition shall be complete, there shall be no outstanding ownership which can impair or jeopardize the value of the holdings."

The Commission filed the necessary surveys, maps and certificates required for the acquisition by the state of the various springs properties for the Reservation. They then began the systematic purchase of the springs together with the lands necessary for complete control of the waters.

In July 1911, a corps of engineers was organized to make observations and secure data on the waters and the condition of the Saratoga mineral water basin. At about the same time the state acquired the properties of two of the largest gas companies operating in the South Broadway and Geyser Park areas, namely the Natural Carbonic Gas and the General Carbonic Companies. These companies and other gas pumping companies were largely responsible for the depleted state of the Saratoga mineral waters.

The corps of engineers made careful observations of the springs and acquired some very valuable data. They recorded the water levels in the various springs, the amount of water and gas flowing from each, the temperature of the water and the pressure of the gas. In addition, a record was made of the daily and monthly rainfall and many other related details. Frequent chemical analyses were made of the waters from the various springs by the State Department of Health.

Observations were made to determine the effect of pumping on the water, not only of neighboring wells, but also on those outside of the area where the pumping was carried on. It was noted that, with the cessation of pumping, there was a marked increase in the water levels of all of the springs and some springs which had ceased were again running under their own natural gas pressures. Wells formerly pumped which had never flowed now burst forth as natural spouting springs. The Island Spouter in Geyser Park began to overflow with mineral water for the first time in its history. During the era of pumping, this well had been a large producer of the so-called dry gas. The large production of gas was made possible by keeping the water level in the well low by heavy pumping in adjacent wells. Two days after the pumps were stopped, the level of the water in the Island Spouter well had risen to a point where it sealed off the gas vein and the well ceased to yield gas and overflowed with mineral water.

By 1915 the state had acquired 600 acres of land with approximately 110 mineral springs as well as mineral rights on seventy-two acres of land on which were located approximately forty-five springs. Thus with 155 springs, the state had sufficient control of the mineral waters to prevent such a crisis from ever happening again.

Of all the springs under state control, only eighteen were left running. Some had spontaneously ceased running; others were capped and sealed. The springs which were left running were carefully cleaned and retubed where necessary. The waters were analyzed and periodically examined bacteriologically to ensure their safety. Many springs were topped with glass domes so that the water could be seen bubbling as it left the spring. Most of these flowing springs were covered with pavilions or shelters making a pleasant environment for the ritual of drinking the waters.

A market demand for a pure, non-carbonated, non-mineral spring water was met by the development of such a water from a spring on the Reservation by Herbert Ant, chemist of the Reservation, and Professor Charles G. Anthony, consultant engineer. Because of a double hydraulic system in the Saratoga plateau, it was possible to find fresh water springs in the same area mineral springs were found. The mineral waters come from a level deep within the earth, while the fresh spring water is found at a more superficial level. The superficial level of fresh ground waters and the deeper system of mineral waters are not connected. This is due to the presence of a heavy deposit of clay, quite impervious to water, at a depth of about fifty feet below the surface. This sustains the upper ground waters and prevents their passing down into the lower strata where the mineral waters are found. It also confines the mineral waters in the lower strata and prevents their mingling with the upper fresh ground waters.

Extensive tests were made on numerous fresh water springs on the Reservation. Samples of fifteen different springs were analyzed in the Reservation laboratory. From all of these, a spring located in a very beautiful ravine near the Willow Gate of Geyser Park was chosen for development. The content of total solids of the water of this spring was so low that it approached that of distilled water. The water was bottled and sold under the name "Saratoga Soft Sweet Spring Water." It had a strong taste appeal, and was of medical value when use of such a pure water was indicated.

The total plan of the Commission for development of the Reservation included the development of four different areas as parks. The areas designated were High Rock Park, Congress Park, Lincoln Park and Geyser Park.

HIGH ROCK PARK

This park derived its name from the dominant spring in the area, the High Rock, which was the first spring known to the early settlers of Saratoga Springs. The area lay at the north end of the village, three quarters of a mile north of the Congress Spring. It covered an area of 3.57 acres which included not only the High Rock Spring property, but also several other properties on which springs were located.

The Star Spring property adjoined the High Rock on the north. On it were located two springs, namely, the Star, a mild saline cathartic water, and the Governor, a chalybeate (iron) water.

The Seltzer Spring property adjoined the High Rock on the south. On it were located two springs, the Seltzer and the Emperor.

The Magnetic-Peerless Spring property lay across Spring Avenue (the present High Rock Avenue) from the other springs in High Rock Park. On it were two springs, the Magnetic, a spring of relatively low mineral content, which had acquired its name from the fact that the tube through which the water came to the surface was found to be highly magnetized. This is not an unusual occurrence in mineral springs. The tubings of many of the springs have been found to be so strongly magnetized that steel tapes could not be used in measuring their depth. Also on this property was the Peerless Spring, a saline water of moderate strength, which flowed freely from the ground next to the Magnetic.

The Red Spring Property lay north of the High Rock property. Though it was not contiguous, it was so near the High Rock that it was considered to belong to the same group. On the property were two springs, the original Old Red Spring, which was discovered in 1785 and had over the years acquired a reputation for its effectiveness in the treatment of skin diseases, and the New Red Spring which was discovered in 1870 when the owners were excavating around the Old Red Spring preparatory to tubing it.

Interesting landmarks on the High Rock property which the Commission planned to enhance and carefully preserve were the High Rock Spring, which had been one of the landmarks from which the early surveys of the area originated, and the escarpment of the Saratoga fault. The calcareous cone of the High Rock Spring, which resembled a small volcano, had been moved by a former owner of the property when he attempted without success to improve the output of the spring. The cone was restored to its original site over the spring and the swampy ground around the spring, which at times resembled a lake, was filled in and raised to a level where it could be planted. An attractive shelter was erected over the spring to serve as protection in inclement weather.

The cliff on the west side of the park formed by the calcareous sandstone escarpment of the geologic fault through which the mineral waters emerge was overgrown with weeds and was covered with debris and garbage. On its summit were tenement houses in bad repair, the refuse and drainage from which provided a serious source of pollution to the springs. The Commission had the houses razed and the debris and garbage removed from the wall of the cliff. This enabled the face of the escarpment, an area of magnificent rock 30 feet high and 300 feet long, to be exposed to view, making a suitable backdrop for historic High Rock Park. The northern slope of the area was planted with grass seed and, with the rest of the park, was landscaped with trees and shrubs. A sewer which ran across the tract was removed by the village at the request of the commissioners.

Located at the Red Spring at the time the property was purchased was a bath house in such poor repair that it had to be demolished. The water in the Red Spring was found to be contaminated, but after retubing was again suitable for drinking. A glass bowl was placed over the spring and the water was dispensed free of charge to visitors.

The bath house of the Magnetic Baths was improved and prepared for use. The water of the Magnetic Spring was supplemented by the waters of the Emperor and Peerless Springs as a source of supply for the baths. The Peerless Spring, like the Red Spring, was covered with a glass bowl and the water was dispensed to the public. The Governor, Star and Seltzer Springs had ceased to run when the land was acquired by the state.

CONGRESS PARK

This park, a 3.081 acre plot, located in the center of the village of Saratoga Springs, included several spring properties as well as the present Congress Park.

The nucleus of the park was formed in 1910 when an act was passed by the Legislature to amend Chapter 569 of the Laws of New York State. As discussed previously, it was by this act that the Legislature authorized the formation of The State Reservation including arrangements for ex-officio representation on the Commission by the village president as well as financial and maintenance obligations to be borne by the village.

On February 24, 1911, not long after the creation of the State Reservation, the properties between Broadway and Circular Street and from Spring Street south to the southern end of Congress Park were purchased by the village. These properties included, with Congress and Columbian Springs, the original Congress Park. On April 20, 1911 the village of Saratoga Springs purchased the casino and its park from Richard Canfield for $150,000, one fifth

Geyser Lake and Geyser Falls

Geyser Bottling Plant showing Geyser Lake

Visitors enjoying spring water at the bottling plant in Geyser Park

Magnetic Spring Baths. Later remodeled and named the High Rock Bath House, it was condemned and demolished in 1918

Kayaderosseras Bath House on Phila Street, also known as Saratoga Baths. Condemned by state architect in 1925 and closed. Putnam Bath House occupied this site earlier

Old Lincoln Bath House. This converted gas plant was used as a bath house until 1929 when it burned to the ground

Rear view of tenements on Maple Avenue as seen from High Rock Avenue. These houses were on top of fault which later served as backdrop to High Rock Park

of its value. The commissioners planned to use the casino as a kursal, or treatment area, to enhance the attractiveness of the proposed health resort.

In 1913 old Congress Hall was razed. This building which stood on the northwest corner of the park on the corner of Broadway and Spring Street, where the Saratoga Springs Library now stands, had been purchased by the village in 1912. The village obtained permission, through an act of the Legislature, to close Congress Street, which had previously run through the park from Broadway to what is now known as Union Avenue. This united the Congress Park properties into a single area. With the fine stand of giant trees and the natural fountains, the potential for a very beautiful park existed. The state purchased the mineral rights of the Congress and Columbian Springs, so the land belonged to the village and the mineral rights were owned by the state.

Also included in the Reservation's Congress Park, in addition to the city Congress Park, were several nearby spring properties:

The *Hathorn Spring* property was a plot of approximately .7 of an acre on the northwest corner of Spring and Putnam Streets, diagonally opposite the Canfield property. On this property was a large building used for bottling and drinking the waters.

The *Patterson Spring* property was an area on Phila Street adjoining the Hathorn property on the north. The mineral rights to this spring were purchased in 1911 and the spring was purchased later.

The *Levengston Spring* property, also called the Putnam Spring, was a plot north of the Patterson Spring on the opposite side of Phila Street. The property included a bath house in addition to the spring. Mineral rights were purchased in 1911 and the spring purchased later.

The *Favorite Spring* property was an area containing three artesian wells located on the west side of Broadway opposite the Columbian Spring. The land was later leased by the state to the Hudson Valley Railroad who built a trolley station on it in 1915. This attractive building was designed by New York architects Ludlow and Peabody.

Congress Park was carefully graded and laid out in walks and driveways. It was beautifully landscaped and planted with flowers, shrubs and trees to make a pleasing and picturesque park.

The state, having mineral water rights, retubed the Congress and Columbian springs. The restoration of the Congress Spring was considered to be one of the most important accomplishments of the Commission. This spring, the most important and best known of the springs of Saratoga, was acknowledged to be the foundation of Saratoga's reputation as the principal watering place in America. In order to recover the spring, it was necessary to penetrate to a depth of 300 feet through hard rock. This spring was restored by the use of the newest scientific methods then available. Samples of rock from each of the different strata encountered were taken and a complete analysis made of each. The water of the well was tested every five feet for both mineral and gas content. The best vein, which was believed to be the old original Congress vein, was selected for tubing. In the beginning the flow of water was only three quarts per minute. However, after several months it suddenly increased to seven gallons per minute and then decreased to five gallons per minute where it remained. A bowl was excavated about the spring to a level of fourteen feet below the surface of Congress Park. This was of sufficient depth to afford access to the spring at a point low enough to obtain a flow of water under the influence of the natural hydraulic head or pressure of the spring itself so that it was not necessary to pump the water. The bottom of the bowl was several feet below the level of the adjacent ground water course. The problem of seepage of ground water into the well was overcome by the installation of two automatically operated pumps capable of discharging eight hundred gallons of water a minute. The area surrounding the bowl was made into a sunken garden covered with grass and flowers. Red Roman stone steps led down to the spring.

By this new arrangement the public could go down the steps to a point where the water of the spring flowed naturally into a bowl where it could be dipped and served. Previously, the spring had flowed at a level below the floor of the building in which it was enclosed and the spring could not be seen, the water being brought up on a lift and served to visitors by boys who dipped it with long handled dippers.

The requirement of having a drink hall where all of the mineral waters could be dispensed to the public was met by remodeling the Hathorn building which stood near the Hathorn #1 Spring on Spring Street. The building was painted inside and out in white trimmed with green. A large multiple drinking fountain thirty-four feet in diameter and four feet high was installed. It was designed so that a number of people at a time could fill their glasses with different mineral waters. It was capable of serving twenty-four people a minute. A warming table was installed so that mineral waters could be served warm on doctor's prescription. About the hall were tables and chairs to accommodate a hundred people at a time. A fee of five cents was charged for admission to the hall. The Hathorn #1 water was served from a double fountain; one side of which supplied water inside the drink hall; the other side, separated by an ornamental partition, supplied the water free of charge to people outside at the spring.

LINCOLN PARK

Located on the west side of South Broadway at the southerly limit of the village of Saratoga Springs, about a mile south of Congress Spring, this park consisted of approximately forty-five acres of land in addition to mineral water rights throughout. The park included considerable area adjacent to the fault through which the mineral springs make their appearance. The mineral rights had little or no commercial value but their ownership enabled the state to make suitable plans for the permanent future protection of the springs on the

Saratoga plateau. It was in this area that the discovery of dry gas on the property of the Lincoln Spring Company very nearly tolled the death knell of the mineral springs. On this land the gas companies drilled between fifty and one hundred artesian wells and carried on extensive pumping, depleting the mineral water head in some wells to a level of as much as 180 feet below the surface of the ground. The Natural Carbonic Gas Company had pumped more water and sold more gas than any other gas company. Following acquisition of this land, the Commission learned that over 200,000 gallons of water had been pumped daily by this company from the ground on the property, gas being extracted and water thrown on the ground. At times, double this amount had been pumped, which equaled seven times the estimated flow of all of the natural springs in Saratoga at the time of their greatest activity. Though after the cessation of pumping, the water level in the wells had recovered to a level of approximately forty feet below the surface, by the time the state took over the property in 1912, there was still some distance to go before complete recovery was accomplished.

The famous Lincoln Springs on this property yield mineral water of the highest content of carbon dioxide gas of any water in the world, making it ideal for use in mineral baths. Since acquisition of the property, these wells have supplied the mineral water for all of the bath houses in Lincoln and Geyser Parks.

There were no naturally running springs on this land at the time it was acquired so there was little public interest in it. The Natural Carbonic Gas Company building was leased to the Saratoga Wood Craftsmen, Inc., makers of fancy cabinet furniture.

Plans were made to lay out walks and drives on this property which would connect with the streets of Saratoga Springs on the east and with Geyser Park on the west. An "Avenue of Pines," sixty feet wide and one mile long, planted with four rows of white pines to be reserved for pedestrians and wheel chairs, was laid out connecting Lincoln Park with Geyser Park.

GEYSER PARK

This largest park of the Reservation comprised over 250 acres, acquired by purchasing the land of several gas companies and bottling plants as well as other land as necessary to ensure the protection of the natural springs in the area. Located about two miles southwest of the village of Saratoga Springs, it contained within its borders a seventy-five foot ravine, the gently sloping banks of which included many species of trees having attained great height. Through its valley ran a picturesque stream of fresh water, Geyser Creek, which added greatly to its natural beauty.

It was in this area, as well as the Lincoln Park area, that the gas companies pumped exorbitant amounts of water from the wells, nearly depleting the mineral water basin. It was in this park area also that the first spouting geyser was drilled in 1870. Since then, many others have been drilled, the most famous of which was so spectacular that it was allowed to run for the enjoyment of passengers on the Delaware and Hudson train which passed the site daily. The springs in the region were found to have the largest flow of water and gas of any of the springs of Saratoga. They varied in mineralization and gas content from a mild table water to the most powerful medicinal water. Such springs as Carlsbad, Hathorn #2, Hathorn #3, Coesa, Hayes, Victoria, Orenda and Karista were among those that were famous. As many as 200 wells were drilled in the Geyser and Lincoln Parks in all, many of which were never named.

While the excessive pumping was going on at the Geysers, when the land was still in the possession of the gas companies, no representatives of the state were allowed on the premises to make observations on the waters. Since it was important to have information of the effect of pumping, it was decided, after the gas company properties had been acquired by the state, to allow pumping to continue in order that observations could be made by qualified people and information could be acquired on the effect of the pumping on the mineral water springs.

Pumping was continued for a time under state auspices and careful records were kept. The gas was put up by the gas companies in their own cylinders. A royalty was paid to the state on the gas sold. Thus it was possible to obtain the desired scientific data and to secure considerable revenue at the same time. The pumping was gradually stopped and the wells were allowed to recover. It would take approximately eight years for complete recovery.

Three springs on the west side of Geyser Park were made available to the public. These were Hathorn #2, Hathorn #3 and Coesa Springs. They were covered by pavilions which provided shelter from the elements, and glass domes were placed over the water as it bubbled from the springs. A "Reservation Stop" on the Schenectady and Hudson Valley trolley car route at the Coesa Spring offered very easy access to the springs from the village.

All of the gas and bottling companies' buildings were demolished with the exception of one brick building at Geyser Spring which was restored as a bottling plant.

A ten-acre area of land in this park was set aside for a forest tree nursery under control of the State Conservation Commission. Millions of trees to be used for reforestation of the State of New York were grown here.

Dr. Simon Baruch, professor of Balneology at the College of Physicians and Surgeons of Columbia University, a well-known authority on hydro-therapy, was very interested in the development of Saratoga as a health spa. Born in Europe, he was familiar with spas and spa therapy. He volunteered to make an intensive study of the important European spas and make recommendations on the development of a spa at Saratoga. In 1913, at the request of the Spa Commission, he visited the spas at Bath and Harrogate in England, Vichy in France, Baden-Baden, Hamburg, Wiesbaden, Kissingen, Nauheim and Briehevan in Germany, and Karlsbad, Marienbad and Franzenbad in

Austria-Hungary.

While at Bad Kissingen he was impressed with the ability of the director, Paul Haertl, PhD., who appeared to be a genius in construction, organization and management of the spa. Dr. Baruch suggested that Dr. Haertl come to the Saratoga Reservation as a consultant on the development of a spa, if the necessary arrangements could be made with the Bavarian Government. The Commission lost no time addressing a communication on behalf of the State of New York to the Royal Bavarian Government, which was seconded by the United States Department of State. A leave of absence was requested for Dr. Haertl to visit Saratoga Springs to inspect the property of the State Reservation and give counsel to the Commission. When the request was granted, Dr. Haertl came to Saratoga with instruments, equipment and charts from Bad Kissingen and made a complete survey of the situation. As a result of his visit the Commission obtained a vast amount of information and advice which was to prove of inestimable value in the future management of the spa.

On his return from Europe, Dr. Baruch brought with him interesting observations on all of the spas he visited. The information proved very valuable to the Commission as they planned the future of the spa at Saratoga.

In 1913 the Commission engaged Dr. Albert Warren Ferris, Senior Resident Physician at the Glen Springs Sanitarium at Watkins Glen, New York, as medical expert, advisor and superintending director. He was needed to perform those duties at the Reservation which they, as a voluntary group, found it impossible to perform. Dr. Ferris was to visit the various mineral springs of the United States to study their methods of operation. He was also to make a complete study of the Saratoga mineral waters to determine their most effective utilization in connection with the comprehensive plan for development of the Reservation. The Commission intended to submit his report to the 1915 session of the Legislature, making it possible for that body to justify to the taxpayers the appropriation of sufficient funds to put Saratoga Springs on its proper basis as a great spa.

During their tenure from 1910 to 1915, the accomplishments of the Commission of the State Reservation at Saratoga Springs were very creditable. In fact, the Commission fully achieved what it set out to do, namely to restore the reputation of Saratoga as a health resort and to save and restore the mineral springs by having them placed under the unified control of the State of New York. Over its period of control, the Commission secured over 150 mineral springs and approximately 300 acres of land necessary to control the springs. As a result of these purchases, the frantic pumping was stopped, making possible the springs' recovery until, at the time the reservation was turned over to the Conservation Commission in 1916, they had very nearly reached their normal state.

With extraordinary vision and foresight, the Commission planned and developed four beautiful parks where mineral waters were used for the benefit of the public. Three of these, High Rock, Lincoln and Geyser Parks were on Reservation property. The fourth, Congress Park, was owned and maintained by the village of Saratoga Springs, while the state owned mineral rights on the spring properties.

Under lease to the Hathorn Spring Water Company, the mineral waters were bottled and sold. A non-carbonated, non-mineral water was developed and marketed. The waters of the reservation were served to the public at the Hathorn Drink Hall on Spring Street and were provided free of charge at the various springs on the Reservation. Two bath houses, the Magnetic and the Saratoga, provided mineral water baths and other forms of therapy.

This dedicated Commission left behind a record of achievement of which they and the whole State of New York could be proud.

16

The Reservation Under the
Conservation Commission 1916 - 1930

*"A healthy body is the guest chamber of the soul;
a sick one its prison."*

—Francis Bacon

According to Chapter 296 of the Laws of New York State, the Conservation Commission was, on April 21, 1916, vested with the jurisdiction of the State Reservation at Saratoga Springs. A special division of this Commission was established for the purpose of administering this important property. Since its establishment in 1910, the Reservation had been administered by the Commissioners of the State Reservation at Saratoga Springs.

The Legislature considered this transfer of jurisdiction to be a wise move. The Conservation Department, created in 1911, had proven itself to be very efficient in its undertakings. It had done a very creditable job in purifying water, in breeding and protecting game, in hatching and distributing fish, in forestry, in conservation of water power, drainage and reclamation. It was, in fact, nationally regarded as one of the most effective and progressive departments of conservation in the country.

At the suggestion of Governor Whitman, the Legislature made George D. Pratt, Conservation Commissioner, a member of the Commission of the State Reservation at Saratoga Springs, along with the other appointees to that Commission, Frederick W. Cameron, chairman, Frank N. Godfrey and George C. Van Tuyl, Jr.

To make it possible for the Conservation Commission to put the affairs of the Reservation on a business basis and enable it to realize a profit on its operations, the Legislature passed a bill appropriating $158,000. The bill was promptly signed by Governor Whitman.

In its first annual report to the Legislature after the Reservation had been transferred to it, the Conservation Commission noted that "The prediction of several years ago with regard to the growth of Saratoga Springs as a health resort is being fully realized with greater rapidity than even the most optimistic dared hope. The conclusion of the season of 1916 has brought more forcibly home to us than ever before the realization that there are unlimited resources stored up in the earth under Saratoga Springs, and that all that is needed is a proper scientific development of these natural resources to make the establishment of the State Reservation one of the most important acts of conservation ever undertaken by the State of New York."

One of the matters high on the priority list of the Conservation Commission was the bottling and sale of the Saratoga mineral waters. At the beginning of this administration there were two separate mineral water bottling plants on the reservation: one at Geyser Spring and one at the Hathorn #2 Spring. As both were antiquated and inefficient, they were consolidated into one plant at the Geysers, and plans were made for construction of a new up-to-date plant.

Careful research was carried on to determine the best methods for bottling the waters to preserve their natural qualities. To this end, very efficient and sophisticated machinery was developed and installed at the Geyser bottling plant. In order to preserve the total carbon dioxide content of the water, the air in the bottles was replaced with carbon dioxide gas. The bottles were then filled with mineral water directly from the spring so that the water was not at any time exposed to light or air. When full the bottles were immediately capped. Maintaining the total content of carbon dioxide gas in the water in this way prevented the minerals dissolved in the water from settling out as sediment. The end result was a clear sparkling water with no turbidity. Everything in the plant was handled automatically from the time the water left the spring until the bottles were labeled and placed in the case for shipment.

The research and development on bottling procedures which was carried on over a period of four years resulted in such increase in efficiency that the capacity of the bottling plant was increased to one hundred cases of two dozen pints an hour, more than thirteen times the capacity of the earlier plants.

The fresh spring water of the Ferndell Spring, which was bottled and sold under the name "Saratoga Soft Sweet Spring Water," was bottled in a plant built in 1914 on the east side of Geyser Park next to the spring. The bottling was continued with modifications to the plant so that, like the mineral waters, there was no exposure to light or air as the water was carried directly from the spring to the bottle.

The name Saratoga Soft Sweet Spring Water, which had been given to the water by the previous Commission, was found to be too cumbersome for advertising and all practical purposes. It was, therefore, changed by the Conservation Commission to "Ferndell Spring Water." The rise in sales which followed the name change could be explained in no other way than that the new name was more acceptable than the old one. The water became very popular. It was furnished to all the state departments in Albany, and had a very lively sale in the market. During the influenza epidemic of 1918 it was provided to hospitals free of charge.

About a month before control of the Saratoga Springs Reservation passed to the Conservation Commission, the Commission had negotiated a lease with the Saratoga State Waters Company giving it the right to bottle and sell the mineral and fresh spring waters of the Saratoga Reservation. The lease was for a term of five years beginning May 1, 1916, renewable for four five-year terms, making the total life of the lease twenty-five years. The terms of the lease stipulated that the Saratoga Springs Reservation Commission was required to "make all major repairs and replacements to buildings, machinery and equipment, to maintain tubing, seals and pumps for the various springs and pipe lines from springs to bottling plants, and to maintain chemical and bacteriological control and make analyses of the waters as delivered to bottling plants and bottled by the corporation." The corporation was to pay the state a royalty on water sold.

Mr. George D. Pratt, Conservation Commissioner, after carefully studying the provisions of the lease, determined that it was not in the best interest of the state and probably was not legal, so on advice of the Attorney General and the State Comptroller, cancelled it. Fortunately it had not yet gone into effect. The Saratoga Waters Corporation then brought suit for damages against both the Conservation Commission and George D. Pratt as an individual. On motion of the Attorney General, they were required to sue one or the other but not both. They elected to sue Mr. Pratt. The Supreme Court rendered a decision in favor of the plaintiff in January 1918. Mr. Pratt immediately appealed the case. In September of 1918, the Appellate Division reversed the decision of the trial court. The plaintiff then appealed the case and, in 1920, the Court of Appeals handed down the final decision giving the Saratoga State Waters Corporation the right to bottle and sell the mineral and fresh waters on the State Reservation at Saratoga Springs under the original lease.

Accordingly, after a delay of four years during which time the Conservation Commission had prevented occupation of the bottling plants by the Saratoga State Waters Corporation, the Commission was forced by law to turn over the bottling business to the new operators and, much against their better judgment, to abide by the terms of the lease which seemed very unfair to the State Reservation. Under the terms of the lease, the Conservation Commission turned over the Hathorn #2, Coesa, Geyser, Orenda, and Ferndell Springs, the Geyser bottling plant, the Ferndell bottling plant, the warehouse at the Geysers, the Hathorn Drink Hall and water department offices, and land surrounding the springs and buildings. Thus in March 1920, the Saratoga State Waters Corporation assumed control of the bottling and sale of the Saratoga waters.

There were three bath houses in use in 1916 when the Reservation was taken over by the Conservation Commission; all were antiquated and in poor repair. The High Rock on High Rock Avenue opposite the High Rock Spring was the

Congress Spring as it appeared in 1920, ten years before it was buried due to contamination

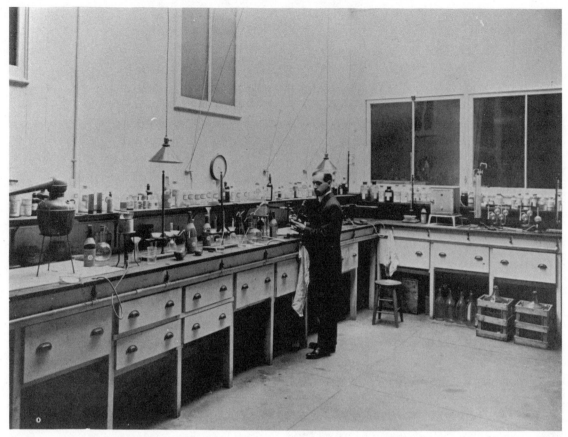

*Herbert (Doc) Ant in early Reservation Laboratory
in Hathorn Building*

Washington Bath House, built in 1920

View of rotunda, Washington Bath House, looking west

Taking the "Sun Cure," west terrace, Washington Bath House

The new Lincoln Bath House, built in 1929

remodeled Magnetic Bath House and could accommodate only a very limited number of people. The Kayaderosseras, or the Saratoga as it was called, was located on Phila Street. It also was limited in the number of people it could accommodate. The Lincoln Bath House was the remodeled gas company building.

With this inadequate set-up, the Saratoga Springs Commission carried on the mineral bath business. The popularity of the mineral baths increased year by year. During 1916, the first year of control by the Conservation Commission, there was an increase of fifteen percent over 1915 in the number of treatments given in the bath houses. The increase accelerated as time went on. There was a constant struggle at the Reservation to keep ahead of the demand for accommodations.

In 1918 the High Rock Bath House was condemned and had to be demolished. The following year work was begun on the new Washington Bath House and it was opened for use in 1920. Here an appointment system was instituted, where, for a somewhat higher fee, patrons could enjoy the luxury of a semi-private or a full private room, and could be assured of being promptly accommodated. This was a great improvement over the tiresome long wait these people were subjected to when the lines for admission began to form at 5:30 a.m. for a seven o'clock bath house opening.

In 1921, when there had been a 58% increase in business in one year, the facilities at the Lincoln Bath House were doubled in capacity by construction of a two-story addition. In 1925, the Saratoga Bath House was condemned by the State Architect and was closed. Again, the Lincoln was increased in size by the addition of a third two-story wing and the Washington was rearranged to increase its capacity. The treatments given at the bath houses had increased to 107,299 in 1927 as compared to 21,959 in 1916.

On the morning of March 15, 1928 the Lincoln Bath House burned to the ground. The fire was discovered at 4:00 a.m. by the night watchman who immediately telephoned the fire department. They responded at once, but because of the complete lack of water pressure, efforts to control the blaze were severely hampered. Two hours after the fire had been discovered there was nothing left standing above the foundation walls.

By a stroke of phenomenal luck, it happened that the Legislature was still in session when the fire occurred. By request, they met in emergency session and made an appropriation of $775,000 to replace the Lincoln building and its equipment. The bill was signed by the governor on March 23, eight days after the fire, and work was begun promptly on what would prove to be the largest and finest bath house in the world.

As planned, the new Lincoln Bath House was to be of white stucco with buff trim. It was to have three wings on either side of a lobby, each extending 240 feet in a north-south direction. The central part of the structure, which included the wings and the central lobby, was to be two stories in height. At the extreme outside ends of the wings would be a connecting arcade one story in height in which would be placed cots where patrons could rest after the bath.

This structure would give the building a rectangular appearance. At the rear of the lobby beyond the wings would be a section planned for semi-private accommodations and special treatments. In this area would be a stairway leading to the second floor as well as to the basement. The construction was to be entirely of fireproof material, consisting of a concrete foundation with hollow tile walls to be covered with white stucco. All window frames, doors and interior partitions were to be made of metal. The roof was to be gravel, and the trim terra cotta, an exception to be at the entrance to the building where marble would be used.

The front of the building would be impressive with large columns of Tennessee marble supporting an entablature bearing the coat of arms of the State of New York and the name of the building, "Lincoln Baths." There would be four marble steps leading up to a veranda the width of the building. Three double doorways with beautiful fan-shaped transoms would lead into the ivory tile lobby, where on the right would be the cashier and ticket offices and on the left, the check room. Three broad steps would lead from this level to another part of the lobby/lounge where a fountain spouting Lincoln water would run constantly. Leading from either side of this lobby would be the wings where baths would be given; on the right were three wings for men, on the left, three wings for women. Between the wings on either side of the lobby would be courts, open to the sky, beautifully planted with flowering plants and shrubs. The arcades with rest areas connecting the wings would serve to completely enclose the courts.

Access to the second floor would be by a beautiful wide stairway on either side of the lobby just beyond the section where the ticket and cashiers' office and the checking counter would be. The floor of the lobby as well as those of the rest rooms would be polished terrazzo, while those in bath sections would be red quarry tile laid on concrete floor slabs. The walls of the bath wings would be of ivory and white terra cotta tile reaching to the height of the partition between the bath rooms. Above this the walls would be white plaster. The partitions would be made of aluminum which is resistant to corrosion from contact with mineral water. Partitions between dressing rooms and hall would be of white-finished steel. When completed, the new Lincoln Bath House would have facilities for giving as many as 4,500 baths daily and would be the largest such facility in the United States, and probably the world.

One wing of the new Lincoln Bath House was opened for business in 1929. The formal opening and dedication took place on June 3, 1930 with Governor Herbert H. Lehman giving the main address. Later the same year the whole building was opened for use.

Special attention was given to the grounds of the spa. Roads were repaired, regraded and resurfaced. Some, with the cooperation of the State Highway Department, were widened to relieve traffic congestion caused by cars stopping along the highway at the springs. Driveways from Route 50 leading to the Hathorn #1 and the Coesa Springs were increased from ten to twelve feet in width. New Tennessee marble fountains were installed at both of these springs.

Here the water was served, with drinking cups provided by the girls in charge.

Extensive improvements were made throughout Geyser Park. Old bridges were replaced and new ones built. New landscaping with thousands of trees and shrubs enhanced the natural beauty of the park. Benches of an attractive design were placed about the park for the convenience of the public. Old abandoned trolley tracks and the trestle over the ravine were removed. Recreation facilities were increased. New picnic areas and camping grounds with fireplaces and tables were built.

At High Rock Park a new concrete stairway replaced the old wooden one. A new concrete fountain was placed in the Peerless Springs pavilion.

Many springs throughout all of the parks provided mineral water free of charge. The waters provided included the water of the Old Red Spring, the Emperor and Peerless Springs in High Rock Park, the Hathorn #1 Spring by the Hathorn Drink Hall on Spring Street, the Hathorn #2, Coesa, Hayes, Polaris and Ferndell Springs in Geyser Park. Four service drinking fountains provided Lincoln water.

The Pine Promenade, a mile long gravel walk, running from Lincoln Park to Geyser Park, originally designed to accommodate wheel chairs and pedestrians, was enlarged and paved and opened as a parkway for automobiles. Two rows of pine trees had been planted along either side of this promenade several years before and had grown to considerable size so the parkway was appropriately renamed "The Avenue of Pines." Buildings on the Reservation were painted in the Reservation colors of white trimmed with green.

The great popularity of the park was evidenced by the ever increasing number of visitors who patronized it. The traffic along Route 50 in the vicinity of the free service springs, Hathorn #2 and Coesa, increased several hundred percent over the years. Two members of the state police force were required to handle the traffic during the busy season. A check of the traffic for a twelve hour period made by the State Highway Department in 1923 showed that 5,870 vehicles passed by their checking point, or one every 7-1/3 seconds. There were only three or four points in the whole state of New York where the highway census showed greater volume of traffic.

With the United States' declaration of war in April 1917, the use of the therapeutic facilities of the Saratoga Spa were offered to the United States Surgeon General for the treatment of wounded service men.

With the advent of World War I, the spa at Saratoga was brought into the limelight position to which it had not previously been exposed. The war made trips to Europe for spa "kur" treatment for wealthy Americans very difficult in the case of many spas, and, in the case of German and Austrian spas, impossible. Those who were in the habit of takng the "kur" at such European resorts as Nauheim, Kissingen, Weisbaden, Vichy or Harrogate would now have no choice, if they desired the "kur," but to visit an American spa. Since Saratoga ranked highest among American spas, it was hoped by the administration at Saratoga that their spa would be the choice of these Americans.

At Saratoga they would find mineral waters equal or superior to any or all of those of the spas of Europe, the facilities the most modern, the medical care the most professional and knowledgeable and the environment and recreational facilities possibly superior to any in Europe. It was hoped also that Europeans would be attracted to American spas because of the pressures and unrest in Europe. This was realized only to a minimal degree.

In accordance with an act passed in 1924 by the New York State Legislature, Governor Alfred E. Smith appointed a Commission to investigate possible future development of the State Reservation at Saratoga. Appointed to the Commission were: George Foster Peabody, George D. Pratt, Robert Tremain, Bernard Baruch and Jefferson DeMont Thompson.

The Commission authorized the superintendent of the Reservation to visit American spas in the eastern United States to gather information on the status of American spas. The spas visited were Glen Spring at Watkins Glen and Mt. Clemens in New York, Battle Creek in Michigan, Martinsville, West Baden and French Lick in Indiana and Hot Springs in Virginia.

The Commission invited two foreign experts, Gustav Toepfer, M.D., of Carlsbad, and Paul Haertl, M.D. of Bad Kissingen to make a survey of the situation at Saratoga Springs and make recommendations as to further development of the spa. Both men were very favorably impressed with the spa to that time. They prophesied that Saratoga would be, with proper development, the outstanding spa of the world. The Commission reported the results of their investigation to the Governor who in turn submitted this information to the Legislature.

Appointments to the Reservation staff during the years of Conservation Commission jurisdiction included Cyrus B. Elmore, who was appointed to succeed Thomas R. Kneil as secretary. Mr. Elmore had been assistant engineer at the Reservation since his graduation from Union College in 1914. John Jones was continued on as superintendent and Herbert Ant as chemist.

In 1921 the term of Conservation Commissioner, George D. Pratt expired. Ellis J. Staley was then appointed Commissioner serving for about a year until he was elected Justice of the Supreme Court. In 1922 Alexander McDonald was appointed to succeed him. Mr. McDonald had previously served as Deputy Commissioner under two former Commissioners.

The improvements at the Saratoga Spa after fifteen years of Conservation Commission jurisdiction were very impressive. The land had been increased from approximately 350 acres in 1916 to over 1,100 acres in 1930. The acquisition of the land had been planned in such a way that all of the springs were protected. The springs had been well cared and were all in good condition. All had been cleaned and retubed as necessary. Some had been shut off to protect the flow in others. The mineral water in all of the springs had returned to normal concentration of minerals and carbon dioxide gas from the depleted condition it had been in when the irresponsible pumping of the waters to extract the gas had finally stopped. The fountains where the mineral waters were available to the public were attractive and accessible. A new drink hall on

Broadway in Saratoga Springs had been provided where all of the waters could be enjoyed in a leisurely manner. Income from the sales of mineral water had increased from approximately $32,000 to over $250,000. Bottling of the mineral waters had been centralized in the Geyser bottling plant. Two magnificent bath houses had been built where mineral baths were available to people of all ranges of income and even to those who could not afford to pay. Certainly the Conservation Commission could be proud of their record.

17

The Temporary Commission of 1929 and the Baruch Report

"Better to hunt in fields for health unbought,
Than fee the doctor for a nauseous draught.
The wise, for cure on exercise depend;
God never made His work for men to mend."
—Epistle to John Dryden of Chesterton

From the beginning, Franklin Delano Roosevelt was an ardent supporter of the Saratoga Spa. When he became Governor of New York State in 1929, F.D.R. worked actively and diligently for the Spa's development. He visited Saratoga and personally inspected the springs and the bath houses. In his first report to the Legislature, submitted in 1929, he made an urgent plea for the development of the Saratoga Reservation.

> The State has during recent years acquired one of the greatest gifts of nature in the whole world - the mineral springs at Saratoga. I am not satisfied that the program for that development in the past has taken sufficient account of the great benefits to mankind that can be derived from them as medicinal and therapeutic agents. We in this country are far behind Europe in the internal and external use of natural mineral springs for health purposes.
>
> The springs at Saratoga should be developed primarily for health purposes under far more careful medical supervision than we have hitherto attempted. The physical development of the State properties at Saratoga must proceed and I ask you to authorize the appointment of a temporary commission of scientific and medical experts, in order that a careful plan may be worked out under their advice.

He asked for an appropriation of $50,000 for this preliminary study.

Unfortunately there was great controversy in the Legislature over appropriations for the Saratoga Spa. Some of the legislators were of the opinion that the state's money could be spent more advantageously elsewhere. They were also concerned about appointments and patronage. On February 19, 1929, the entire sum of $50,000 for a commission to make a preliminary study at the spa was eliminated from the budget by the legislative committee, without comment. On February 20th a bill requesting the appointment of a temporary commission to study the feasibility of a spa at Saratoga was defeated because the Governor had not yet appointed a commission. Later when the Governor did appoint a commission there was controversy with the Republican leaders over the appointment. It seemed that there was little hope of getting a bill passed that would make possible the development of a spa at Saratoga.

When a fourth Saratoga Bill was finally introduced on March 18th, Governor Roosevelt personally called members of the Legislature on the phone urging them to vote favorably on the bill. He induced Bernard Baruch to do the same. The result was that the bill passed both houses of the Legislature. This Saratoga Survey bill (the Brown-Esmond Bill) was promptly signed by the Governor and became law April 16, 1929.

The Commission was to make a comprehensive study and survey of the springs at Saratoga to determine the advisability of their further development for health purposes. They were to make recommendations as to the extent and character of such development which might be practicable. They were to receive no compensation for their services, but allowance was to be made for expenses incurred in the perfomance of their duties. A report was to be made on or before March 1, 1930 with recommendations.

In accordance with the provision of the act (Chapter 668 of the laws of 1929), the following members were appointed to the Commission: Senator Thomas E. Brown, Senator John Knight, Assemblyman F.L. Porter, Assemblyman Joseph McGinnies, Bernard Baruch, Thomas Cochrane, and Robert Goelet. Mr. Baruch was appointed chairman.

The members of the Commission wasted no time in attacking the colossal task before them. With the cooperation of the New York Academy of Medicine, they appointed a committee of distinguished physicians, who served without compensation, to make an intensive investigation of the springs at Saratoga, and of the outstanding spas of Europe. They hoped to find sound medical justification for establishing a similar program at Saratoga.

They engaged Dr. Paul Haertl, for twenty years head of the Staatslaboratorium at Bad Kissengen and balneotechnician in charge of all the mineral springs of Bavaria, to come to Saratoga to make a survey of the springs and make recommendations for the development of the spa.

Professor R.J. Colony of Columbia University was engaged to make a geological study of the springs paying special attention to the supply of the waters, a consideration which was considered to be of prime importance.

W.P. Beazell, assistant to Mr. Baruch, was to make a comparative study of the principal spas of the eastern United States.

When finally submitted, the reports of the various committees studying the feasibility of establishing a spa at Saratoga were most encouraging. The committee of physicians, in a long comprehensive report included the following statement:

> The spas of Europe provide desirable and effective means for the treatment and relief of many chronic ailments. The fact that constantly increasing numbers of patients patronize the spas must be taken as an indication that hundreds of thousands of people consider the effects of the treatments at the spas beneficial. The clinical testimony is overwhelming in amount and variety. Whatever be the physiological or biochemical action of the waters, the fact remains that the regimen at the spas, taken as a whole, exercise a beneficial effect on thousands of sufferers.
>
> The committee believes that something of the type of the conservative spas of Europe should be developed in connection with Saratoga Springs, in view of the existence there of springs whose chemical composition is considered suitable for the treatment of certain conditions.

Dr. Haertl, concluding his report, said, "What I have seen on this third visit has strengthened my previous conviction that Saratoga Springs is most fortunate in having all the natural requisites of a first class spa, and that it is within the power of the State of New York to develop there an institution of incalcuable value to suffering humanity."

Professor Colony's report included a very complete geological survey of the Saratoga area. His conclusion regarding the supply of the Saratoga waters was that the problem of water supply offered no insurmountable obstacle to continued development.

Mr. W. P. Beazell, in making a comparative study of the principal spas of eastern United States, concentrated on nine which are comparable with the Saratoga Spa in the scope and character of the treatments given at them. These included Clifton Springs, Glen Springs and Watkins Glen, New York; Mount Clemens, Michigan; West Baden, Indiana; French Lick Springs, Indiana; Hot Springs, Arkansas; Bedford Springs, Pennsylvania; White Sulphur Springs, West Virginia; and Hot Springs, Virginia. He concluded from his study that the "kurs" of the United States as a major industry bear an interesting relation to the $100,000,000 that was spent this year by the 100,000 Americans who took the "kur" in Europe.

Based on the information contained in these reports, the Commission submitted to the Legislature a seven year program for development of a spa at Saratoga. The program was contained in a 216-page report to the Legislature (later known as the Baruch report). In it were also included the complete report of the committee of physicians, Dr. Haertl's report, and the reports of Mr. Beazell and Professor Colony.

According to the plan proposed for the development of the spa, the springs,

Aerial view of the Saratoga Reservation, circa 1929, showing Lincoln Bath House on left, and Washington Bath House on right. Avenue of Pines is seen behind Washington Bath House. It was later rerouted to join Route 9 south of the Lincoln Bath House

Franklin D. Roosevelt as Governor of New York. He was influential in the creation of the "New Spa" at Saratoga

the buildings and the Reservation surrounding them were to be taken from the jurisdiction of the Conservation Department and placed under the control of a temporary commission. To be known as the Saratoga Springs Commission, it was to administer, for a period of seven years, the maintenance, operation and development of the project in keeping with the recommendations of the report. The Saratoga Springs Commission should consist of seven members to be appointed by the Governor with the consent of the Senate. Commission members should serve without pay and hold office for the seven years, direction and control should again be vested in the Conservation Department, the Saratoga Springs Commission being continued as a division of that department.

The Commission was to be directed to bring the mineral waters at Saratoga under strict medical control and supervision. To accomplish this they were to appoint a medical and scientific director under whom would lie the supervision of the baths, the drink hall and pavilions and reserach laboratories.

Provision was made in the plan for the construction of several buildings including a new bottling plant, a new drink hall (to be called "The Hall of Springs" having in connection with it a concert hall, promenade, and facilities for the drinking of the mineral waters), a recreation center and an administration building containing a research laboratory.

In the plan the Commission recommended the establishment of privately financed sanatoriums preferably located in the Vale of Springs. These sites would be leased by the State at nominal rental. Also recommended was the establishment of small hotels and the equivalent of European pensions to be built and managed privately.

Also included in the plan was provision for landscaping the various parks included in the spa in keeping with the health aims of the spa. This would include walks scientifically laid out as to length, grade and paving so they might be used as part of the system of treatment; also pavilions approached by inviting walks where refreshments would be served, and areas barred to traffic to serve as playgrounds.

On April 3, 1930, a bill (the Brown-Porter Bill), which included the recommendations proposed by the commission and which called for the appropriation of $1,000,000, was introduced in the Legislature. At the time of its introduction even the most optimistic supporters believed there was little chance of its passage in original form because there was so much opposition to it. The Conservation Department's opposition was so strong that it was felt in Albany that if any bill was passed, Senator Brown would be forced to accept an amendment leaving the Conservation Department in control of the bulk of the patronage at Saratoga. The fight for its passage was bitter to the very end. However, Senator Brown and Assemblyman Porter fought vigorously and refused to accept any change or amendment diminishing the bill.

The deciding stroke came when, during the final hours of the legislative session, a message came from Governor Roosevelt, a true friend and loyal supporter of the bill from the beginning. He had followed the bill closely during its stormy course in the Legislature. When he saw that it was doomed to failure he sent a plea for its passage which read as follows:

> In this, probably my final message to the Legislature on 1930, I want to make a heart-felt plea that your honorable bodies pass the legislation to appropriate $1,000,000 for the development of the Saratoga Spa as a great health agency for the people of the State of New York.
>
> For a quarter of a century effort after effort has been made toward this great objective. This year, under the leadership of a special commission, and with the enthusiastic cooperation of medicine and science, a definite plan has been submitted. This plan was approved in conference between the leaders of the legislature, the other members of the commission and myself. I feel that the moral obligation which rests on all of us whereby we agreed that $1,000,000 could and should be appropriated this year should be lived up to by us. The finances of the state can bear this charge at the present time, and the appropriation of a smaller amount means essentially that the carrying out of the great plan is deferred to some future year. It is my earnest plea that the full appropriation be made by your honorable bodies before you finally adjourn.

It was this message that decided the fate of the bill. This urgent request from the Governor resulted in the passage of the bill in its original form. By Chapter 866 of the Laws of 1930, this program became part of the public health policy of the state and, in accordance with provisions of the act, the Saratoga Commission was appointed by Governor Roosevelt for a term of seven years to undertake the task of carrying out the program. The sum of $1,000,000 was approriated for the first year's work.

18

The New Spa   1930 - 1936

"The reward of a thing well done is to have done it."
Ralph Waldo Emerson

The year 1930 marked the beginning of the new modern spa which was designed to make Saratoga a great health center. The new spa as planned, would be the largest, finest and best equipped in the world with a variety of naturally carbonated mineral waters equal, if not superior, to any in the world.

On May 17, 1930, the beautiful new $750,000 Lincoln Bath House, the largest in the world under one roof, having a capacity of 4,500 treatments a day, was opened with a formal ceremony at which Lieutenant Governor Herbert H. Lehman was the principal speaker. On that day merchants and other employers in Saratoga Springs allowed their employees an hour to visit and inspect the magnificent new building with its fine modern bath equipment and handsomely landscaped courts. On their return to work other employees were released to make a similar inspection. Buses were run between the city and the bath house to accommodate the visitors.

The new Saratoga Springs Commission, mandated by Chapter 866 of the Laws of 1930, was appointed by Governor Roosevelt early in 1930. The following members were appointed:

George Foster Peabody, of Saratoga Springs, a partner in Spencer Trask's brokerage firm who had become chairman of the original Saratoga Springs Reservation Commission upon Trask's death, and served until 1916, was appointed chairman.

Jerome D. Barnum, of Syracuse, well-known publisher of the *Syracuse Post Standard*.

Carl R. Comstock, M.D., of Saratoga Springs, a heart specialist and student of hydrotherapy both in this country and abroad.

L. Whittington Gorham, M.D., of Albany, Professor of Medicine at Albany Medical College, a member of the Saratoga Springs Commission who went abroad in 1929 to study the spas of Europe.

Henry Morganthau, of New York, authority on international relations and former ambassador to Turkey.

Pierpont B. Noyes, of Oneida, President of Oneida Ltd. since 1910.

Linsley R. Williams, M.D., of New York, formerly Deputy Commissioner of Health of New York State, since 1912 managing director of the National Tuberculosis Association.

Messrs. Morganthau and Williams found themselves unable to devote the necessary time to work and soon resigned. Edward H. Butler of Buffalo, a publisher, and Frederick H. Ecker, of New York, President of the Metropolitan Life Insurance Company were appointed in their places. Within a few months Mr. Peabody resigned. Mr. Morton L. Schwartz of New York was appointed a member in his place. Mr. Noyes was then appointed chairman of the Commission. The Commission as then constituted served throughout the seven-year term with no further changes in membership.

In June 1930 control of the Saratoga Springs Reservation was turned over to the newly appointed Commission by the Conservation Department. This control was to continue for a period of seven years to June 30, 1937, at which time the life of the Commission was to end. Control of the Reservation was again to be vested in the Conservation Commission with a Saratoga Springs Reservation Commission appointed to act as the head of the Division of the Saratoga Springs Reservation in the Conservation Department.

At the time the Commission took over the Reservation from the Conservation Department, the Reservation included 1,122.32 acres of land. A small part of this was in the city of Saratoga Springs, one tract surrounding the site of the famous High Rock Spring, another surrounding the Old Red Spring, and still another included the Congress and Columbian Springs in Congress Park and the land on which Hathorn #1 Spring and the Drink Hall were located. The remainder was in Lincoln and Geyser Parks on the southern edge of the city. There were 163 springs on the land, all of these but nineteen were shut off so that the flow of the mineral water might be controlled and the carbon dioxide gas content might be safeguarded. Those springs still being used were Hathorn #1, #2, and #3, Geyser, Coesa, six Lincoln wells, Peerless, Hayes, Karista, Old Red, Congress, Champion and two spouters.

The equipment of the Reservation consisted principally of three bath houses. Two of these, the new Lincoln, completed in 1930, and the Washington, were in Lincoln park on the Reservation on the southern edge of the city. The other, the Saratoga bath house was on Phila Street in the center of the city.

With the million dollar appropriation by the Legislature a reality, the Commission began work in earnest on plans for the development of the Saratoga Spa. One of the major items of the program as outlined in the Baruch report was "the bringing of all use of the waters of Saratoga under strict medical control and supervision, and the appointment of a medical director to this end." In recommending this provision in his report of 1930 to the Legislature, Bernard Baruch had said: "I will repeat what I have said before that I am opposed to any use of the springs here which does not include strict medical supervision and a regulated and closely watched diet: I believe that a patient taking the waters and baths here should be just as closely watched as one undergoing an operation."

To fill this position of medical director, the Commission chose Walter McClellan, M.D., a physician well qualified by training and experience to undertake the task of establishing an appropriate medical regime at the Saratoga Spa. He was commissioned to visit the various spas of Europe before assuming his duties at Saratoga. While in Europe he visited twenty-five spas in Germany, Czechoslovakia, Austria, Italy, France and Belgium.

An eminent architect, who was recommended by Mr. Baruch, was employed to lay out plans for the development of a spa in Geyser Park. He was James M. Friedlander, a graduate of Massachusetts Institute of Technology and Ecole des Beaux Arts of Paris, a man of wide reputation who had won a long list of prizes. He was sent to Europe to study health spas there and to confer with Mr. Baruch who was in Europe at the time.

On his return he laid out a plan for the development of Geyser Park designed to take advantage of the natural beauty of the area by retaining the existing picturesque vistas as much as possible. In the midst of the thousand acre wooded Geyser Park, an area of 140 acres was laid out on the east side of the beautiful Vale of Springs as a great open court or esplanade one-half mile in length running north and south and two hundred feet in width. On the norththwest corner would lie the Hall of Springs. Opposite of the northeast corner would lie the building housing a research laboratory and administrative offices. In the mall between these buildings would be a reflecting pool. On each of the two southern corners would be built a bath house. The four buildings surrounding the mall would be connected by arcades, 700 feet in their greater and 400 feet in their lesser lengths. This would allow passage from one building to another in any kind of weather, an essential feature in a year-round health resort. At the northern end of the esplanade a bandstand for open air concerts would be built and at the southern end would be a fountain symbolizing Saratoga and its waters.

A cross mall 200 feet in width would be built at right angles to the center mall. The west end of this cross mall would overlook the Vale of Springs with Geyser Brook tumbling through it. At the other end, 2,200 feet to the east, would lie the complex of recreation buildings surrounding a swimming pool and plaza. To the southeast would be built the first tee of a nine hole golf course. About 400 feet east of the cross mall would be a sanatorium-hotel.

Administration Building

Hall of Springs

Patrons drinking mineral water at the Hall of Springs

Roosevelt Bath House

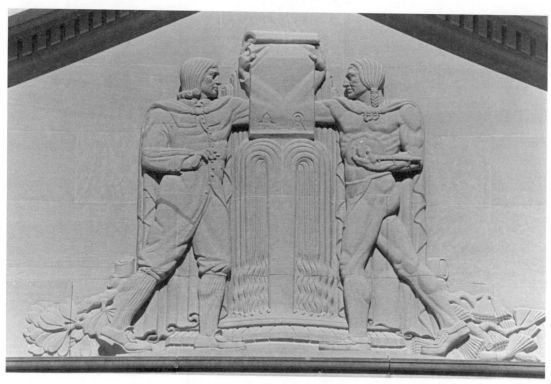

Pediment over the entrance to Hall of Springs

 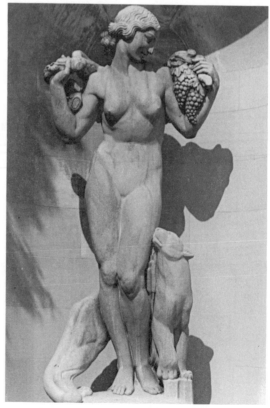

Statues in niches on the front of the Hall of Springs

Northwest near Geyser Creek a new bottling plant would be constructed.

In June of 1932 excavation for the first building of the new spa in Geyser Park was begun. It was a new drink hall to be known as The Hall of Springs. It was to include, in addition to facilities for the therapeutic use of the mineral water, a concert hall, a prominade, rest rooms, writing rooms, lounges and a restaurant.

On July 25th of that year there occurred at the Geysers at the site of excavation for the proposed Hall of Springs, an event which later became known as the Saratoga Gold Rush of 1932. It began in the afternoon of that date when several workmen, employees of the construction company which had the contract for the excavation, picked, from the excavated earth, several gold coins. An account carried in *The Saratogian* of July 26, 1932 ran as follows:

HUNDREDS JOIN "GOLD RUSH" TO GEYSERS
$1000 or More in Coin Unearthed at State Excavation

A genuine gold rush of amazing proportions overwhelmed Saratoga Springs last night and today. Early this morning hundreds of amateur, but none the less earnest, prospectors, armed with pick-axes, shovels and improvised sieves, had taken upwards of a thousand dollars in gold and silver coin from a mound of loosely piled earth a few feet south of the foundation site of the new Hall of Springs in Geyser Park.

The rush of the modern forty-niners started late yesterday afternoon after three workmen employed by the Lowe Construction Company of Schenectady, which has the contract for the excavation and foundation work for the Hall of Springs, picked up twenty-dollar gold pieces. The news quickly was noised about the city and the rush was on. Saturday a workman had found a five dollar gold piece but little importance was attached to the discovery at the time.

Richard O'Brien, state engineer in charge of construction work at the Geysers, said today that the earth which bore the pay load had already been turned over four times when the rush started. It was originally removed from the site of the Hall of Springs in excavating, dumped in a mound a few feet south of the location, brought to the original site for filling and finally returned to the spot where the prospectors were still feverishly digging and sifting this afternoon.

More than three hundred men and boys were working throughout the day and probably more than a thousand others came to see the fun. Many who came to watch stayed to dig for hardly a minute passed that someone did not make a discovery of the precious metal.

They came in automobiles, bicycles and on foot. They carried all varieties of digging instruments, shovels, scoops, pickaxes and even hatchets. Everyone it seemed had a sieve of some kind to sift the dirt in search of a strike. They worked singly and in pairs and even formed syndicates to recover the money from the ground. Sometimes as many as six or seven would join forces under an oral agreement to split the profit equitably.

The money was found in bottles, jars, tin cans and scattered in the soil. Three men who worked until one thirty o'clock this morning with the aid of lanterns and flashlights were reported to have collected more than four hundred dollars. One man found a jar which contained about three hundred dollars in gold coins. Others reported finding smaller amounts. The gold and silver pieces ranged from twenty dollars down to three cents. Many bore dates in the early eighties. The most recent coin found was marked 1890. All of the coins were legal tender of the United States.

"Happy days are here again" hummed the forty-niners as the sweat poured from their fevered brows in the heat of the merciless sun. But at noon today it appeared that the lode was almost exhausted although workers continued to pick up dimes, quarters, and occasionally half or silver dollars. Many, however, kept on grimly hopeful that another large strike might be unearthed. Some even expressed the opinion that the pay lode had hardly been touched as yet, and that much larger amounts would be found eventually. The "gold fever" was strong upon every man, woman and child who sought the money.

"There was no fooling about this Klondike fever," one of the searchers said. "When you are pouring over the dirt and something shines you start to tremble all over. It's worse than buck fever ever was."

It was well nigh impossible to secure the names of the lucky finders or to get them to divulge the amounts they had taken out of the earth. For it became immediately apparent that the question of legal ownership of the buried sums might prove disastrous to the interests of the prospectors.

Authorities of the Saratoga Springs Commission were today undecided whether the find rightfully belonged to the State of New York, which purchased the land about twenty years ago, or whether the old adage "finders keepers" would prove true in this case. In any event it seemed likely that it would be exceedingly difficult to recover any substantial amount from the discoverers for they have for the most part taken care to keep their identities as well as the amounts found secret.

Back in the early part of the century the land where the money was found was the property of Lyman F. and Harvey E. Pettes who lived at the Geysers and had extensive estates there. It was known that Mrs. Agatha W. Pettes, wife of Henry E. Pettes, former mayor, is contemplating legal steps to protect her possible interest.

Mrs. Agatha Quintora, niece of Mrs. Pettes, who resides with her at her North Broadway residence, recalled today that Mrs. Lyman F. Pettes, Harry E. Pettes' mother, used to be in the habit of hiding objects and even money around her house, and expressed the belief that possibly she had buried several hundred dollars in coins in vessels and jars in the cellar of her home years ago.

Pierpont B. Noyes, chairman of the Saratoga Springs Commission, today assigned Spencer B. Eddy, Commission council, the task of ascertaining the legal responsibility of the commission in regard to the money should it be claimed later by previous owners of the property.

"I have no personal objection to anybody digging as much as they please from the excavation at the Geysers," Mr. Noyes said, "but the commission may have a legal responsibility regarding it which it is my duty to safeguard until we know more about it."

Attorney General Bennett, when the matter was brought to his attention in Albany today, directed that the state put a stop to the mining operations on the ground that "the treasure found on the state property belongs either to the state or to the owner of the property prior to its acquisition by the state."

Following the exciting episode of the gold rush, work on the Hall of Springs proceeded uneventfully.

The cornerstone of the Hall of Springs was laid July 12, 1933. The event marked the beginning of the development of the new spa. The structure designed by Joseph Friedlander was the first of the handsome structures to be built in the program of development that was to make the Saratoga Spa the finest and most beautiful in the world, as well as the largest and most completely and modernly equipped.

The building was to be constructed of red Harvard brick with white Indiana limestone trim and a roof of black slate. Facing the mall would be a pillared portico opening off from which would be a foyer leading in to the 160 foot by 70 foot marble-floored main hall. In this great hall would be fountains surrounded by marble counters. From the fountains would flow the mineral waters - Hathorn, Coesa and Geyser, under the pressure of the carbon dioxide gas with which they are saturated. Around the hall would run a 12 foot mezzanine at the end of which, above the portico, would be a music room where orchestras would play while visitors strolled about and drank the waters. On both sides of the hall would be lounges 72 feet by 30 feet. Men's and women's retiring rooms would be placed on the main floor and would connect with similar rooms on the basement level. An elliptical-shaped foyer at the western end of the hall would have offices and large telephone rooms opening on to it, and on either side stairways leading to the mezzanine floor. Opening to the outside would be an automobile entrance.

The exterior of the building would be decorated with bas reliefs on either end: one of Gideon Putnam, the father and early architect of Saratoga Springs; the other of George Washington, the father of our country, who, after a visit to the High Rock Spring, tried unsuccessfully to purchase it. The outer walls and arcade would be ornamented with panels graved with passages from an epic of Saratoga written by Reuben Sears in 1919.

The celebration of the laying of the cornerstone of the Hall of Springs began with a community luncheon at the Rip Van Dam Hotel at noon sponsored by the Saratoga Springs Rotary Club, joined by the Saratoga Springs Lions Club and the Chamber of Commerce. The visiting dignitaries present for the laying of the cornerstone of the Hall of Springs at the Geysers were the honored guests.

The main exercises took place later at the Hall of Springs which was under construction at Geyser Park. Present were dignitaries from all walks of public and private life, along with visitors from all over the world and throngs of Saratogians. Pierport B. Noyes, chairman of the Commission, presided. After a short address in which he paid tribute to all those who had played a part in bringing to fruition the dream of a great spa at Saratoga, he introduced Governor Herbert H. Lehman, who gave the principal address. Speaking to the large gathering, the Governor expressed the belief that with the completion of the new spa, Saratoga would be able to offer the system of cardiac therapy given there to vastly greater numbers of people. He pointed out that heart disease has risen to first place in the list of diseases which cause death and, since there is no spa in the world that offers the advantages and treatment to be found at Saratoga, there could be no greater service to the people of the world than bringing the treatment of heart disease within the reach of all.

He spoke of dedicating the new Lincoln Bath House two years before and stated that his interest in the spa had grown steadily since that time. He paid tribute to such friends of the spa as George Foster Peabody, Bernard Baruch and Pierpont Noyes. He recalled that his first visit to the Saratoga Spa was when, at the age of six, he came with his parents who were taking the baths here.

After the Governor's speech, Mr. Bernard Baruch was introduced. He gave a few words of greeting and proceeded to preside over the laying of the cornerstone in a Masonic ritual ceremony similar to the one that had been used in the laying of the cornerstone of the Capitol in Washington, D.C.

By the time the 1933 Legislature convened the country was in the depth of the tragic Depression following the Stock Market Crash of 1929. Since the Legislature felt that they could not appropriate further money for the development of the Saratoga Spa when the finances of the state were in such dire straits, they authorized the Saratoga Springs Commission to borrow money from the Federal government through the Reconstruction Finanace Corporation, set up as part of President Roosevelt's New Deal. Accordingly, since the Commission as such was not empowered to borrow money, a corporation to be known as the Saratoga Springs Authority composed of the members of the Saratoga Springs Commission was created by Legislative enactment (Chapter 208 of the Laws of 1933) with provision to borrow up to $5,000,000 from the R.F.C.

Mr. Spencer Eddy, attorney for the Saratoga Springs Commission, proceeded with the formation of the Authority with the members of the Commission as directors.

On July 27, 1933 he contracted for the purchase at par of $3,200,000 of Saratoga Springs Authority 4½% bonds by the R.F.C., the proceeds to be used for the development of the Saratoga Spa project, which, according to agreement, was to be completed by January 1, 1936. For a period of three years after completion of construction work the Saratoga Springs Authority was to make interest payments only; the first payment of principal to be made in 1938; final maturity to be in 1954.

With the assurance of an adequate supply of money to complete the project, construction work was speeded up at the Saratoga Spa so that its completion by the January 1, 1936 deadline might be assured.

Two additional architects were employed and put to work on the buildings under the direction of Mr. Friedlander. Dwight Baum of New York City was assigned the work on the group of recreation buildings, which was to include a gymnasium, an outdoor swimming pool and a golf house.

Marcus T. Reynolds of Albany was assigned the work on plans for a sanatorium-hotel.

Mr. Friedlander himself concentrated on the completion of the laboratory and research building on the northeast and on the two new bath houses to be built at the southern end of the central complex around the main mall.

Dr. Franz M. Groedal of Bad Nauheim, Germany, an internationally famous heart specialist, who had been advisor to the Commission during preparation of the Hall of Springs and the research laboratory, was again retained by the Authority as consultant during the work to be done at the spa.

Ground was broken for the foundation of the research laboratory/administration building on February 3, 1933. The cornerstone was laid September 14, 1934 with appropriate ceremonies before a large gathering of spectators. Governor Lehman presided over the exercises. In a short address he announced that the building would be named the Simon Baruch Research Laboratory in honor of Dr. Simon Baruch, father of Bernard Baruch. Dr. Simon Baruch had worked out the system of cardiac therapy which has been so successful in the treatment of heart disease at the Saratoga Spa. He predicted that the Saratoga Spa would become one of the most famous watering places in the world. He then introduced Dr. John Wycoff, dean of New York University-Bellevue Medical College, the primary speaker of the day, who, in his powerful address, urged the founding of a medical school at the spa. He expressed the belief that here would be the ideal place to study the nature and course of chronic diseases, a subject which the medical profession had neglected in favor of studying and concentrating on the more demanding acute diseases of the time.

The cornerstone was laid by Dr. Herman Baruch, second son of Dr. Simon Baruch. The trowel used in the ceremony was handed by John H. Friedlander, the architect who designed the building, to Governor Lehman, who, in turn, handed it to Dr. Baruch. The ceremonies were concluded by the benediction given by the Reverend George A. Brock, pastor of the New England Congregational Church of Saratoga Springs.

The Baruch Research Laboratory building, the largest of the Spa buildings, contained, in addition to the laboratories for research on the mineral waters and related health subjects, many other facilities. These included administrative offices, offices for the medical director, a museum, meeting rooms and a theater.

The recreation center was designed by Dwight Baum with the idea of making scientific provision for play part of the Spa program. The center was comprised of four buildings in the Georgian mode of architecture, joined by arched and roofed walks, surrounding an interior court 150 by 220 feet in which there was a swimming pool 45 by 105 feet. The pool was lined with blue faience terra cotta and was submarine lighted, making night swimming possible. The water was filtered and heated. Surrounding the pool was a flagstone terrace 32 feet wide at the sides and 40 feet wide at the ends on which were set attractive tables and chairs shaded with varicolored umbrellas. Surrounding this terrace was a 20 foot border planted with shrubs and flowering plants.

These buildings were similar to the other buildings at the spa, being constructed of red Harvard brick and trimmed with Indiana sandstone.

The administration building of the complex was 100 feet in width and 40 feet in depth. It was placed at the eastern end of the cross mall facing west. Inside its pillared portico lay a vestibule, beyond which was a reception lobby 24 by 35 feet decorated in the classical Empire style. On the right of the lobby was a grill room 30 by 35 feet on one side of which was a grill for preparation of short order foods; on the opposite side was a soda-fountain and a buffet. The building also housed management offices and rest rooms.

On the east side of the court was a gymnasium, one side equipped for women and the other for men. Between the two were locker rooms, showers and offices for the instructors.

On the north side of the group was a bath house with a first aid room and a center lobby where valuables might be checked and swimsuits rented.

The south building was a golf house with locker rooms, showers, offices, a shop, and a large outside terrace overlooking the first tee on the golf course.

The therapeutic golf course, designed by Allen and Palmer, in consultation with the golf expert Seymour Dunn and the cardiologist Dr. Groedal, was unique in many respects. It was probably the only course in the country that was planned from a scientific and therapeutic viewpoint. Golf here was not just a sport; it had a definite place in the regimen of restoration and preservation of health. It was prescribed as cardiac therapy as well as for pure recreation. Even though the course had been designed with cardiac patients in view, it offered excellent possibilities for an average good test of golf.

The golf expert, Mr. Dunn, in a report to the Authority stated:

> Your course should bring out the skill of the more advanced player without being too penalizing to the mediocre one. The poorer player is further helped by virtually no carries from the tees and but little trapping to catch errant tee shots or shots through fairways.
>
> A checkup of the hole variety shows that all players will have opportunity to use every club in their bag when the prevailing winds are taken into consideration. I have no hesitation in saying that the course will offer an excellent test for all players and yet will not be in the least fatiguing to them.

Mr. Dunn stated that a real championship nine could be constructed on ground nearby set aside for that purpose.

The two new bath houses built at the south end of the main mall were designed by Mr. Friedlander in architectural harmony with the other buildings of the Spa. The bath house on the east contained twenty private mineral bath rooms, ten for men and ten for women. It also had provision for infrared, ultra violet and diathermy treatments as well as for mud packs, Vichy douches and massages. There were, in addition, steam rooms, hot rooms and electric light cabinet rooms.

The west house had forty private bath rooms. It had an inhalation department and a large mechanotherapy department.

The tubs in the bath rooms of the bath houses were carefully designed for maximum comfort. They were deeper than an average tub and were set six inches lower than the floor to allow easy access. The enamel was of a material impervious to carbon dioxide gas, and the fixtures were of polished stainless steel. In many ways these bath houses were the ultimate in bath house design.

The Spa hotel designed by Marcus T. Reynolds of Albany, was small in keeping with the custom established at spa hotels in Europe. It contained only eighty-seven guest rooms. The main portion of the building was 178 feet long and 94 feet wide with a kitchen wing 33 by 64 feet. On the first floor were the lobby and lounges, card rooms, writing rooms, a main dining room with beautiful murals of Saratoga scenes done by the famous English muralist, James Reynolds. Off of this main dining room was a smaller private dining room which was used for meetings.

There were three floors of guest rooms. On the south end of each floor were suites of two, three or four connecting rooms. On the top floor were servants' quarters.

To the back of the lobby on the south side of the building was a paved terrace 26 by 97 feet, commanding a beautiful vista looking toward the recreation center and the golf course.

The hotel was appropriately named The Gideon Putnam, after the man who built Congress Hall, the first real hotel in Saratoga Springs in 1812.

Mr. Edward C. Sweeney of Saratoga, owner of the famous New Worden Hotel there, was given a five-year lease with option of renewal, to operate the hotel on a year round basis, giving preference to Spa patients.

The bottling plant, the last building in the new Spa to be completed was built northwest of the main mall near Geyser Creek and a short distance from the three springs whose waters were bottled: Hathorn #3, Coesa and Geyser. It was 120 by 124 feet and was two stories in height. Architecturally it was in the same character as the recreation center and the other buildings in the reservation; Georgian in style, it was constructed of red Harvard brick with white limestone trim. Its main feature was the bottling room which contained a line of sophisticated machinery designed for great efficiency in bottling the waters.

A relief measure undertaken by the Federal government during the Depression was the organization of a service known as the Transient Division of the

Pediment over entrance to Spa Theater   Collection of the Saratoga Spa

Ethel Barrymore on the steps of the Spa Theater   Collection of Edwin J. LaDue

Architect's drawing of Recreation Center

Bottling Plant

Gideon Putnam Hotel

Collection of Edwin T. Ladue

Collection of the Saratoga Spa

Patrons at Lincoln Bath House in early morning waiting to purchase tickets

Temporary Emergency Relief Organization. It was organized to care for those men who, traveling from one place to another in search of employment, found themselves destitute and without resources. Camps to care for these men were set up throughout the country. Such a camp was built at the southern extremity of the Saratoga Springs Reservation well out of the park area proper, under agreement made March 16, 1934 between the Saratoga Springs Commission and the T.E.R.O. It housed between 100 and 200 men who would be employed in laboring activities and paid ninety cents a day for spending money in addition to their maintenance. Most of the men enrolled in the program allowed their money to accumulate until they left.

These men under the direction of the Saratoga Springs Commission carried out very important tasks that could not have been accomplished otherwise, since all of the money from the R.F.C. loan was allocated to the construction of the buildings. It was they who aided greatly in landscaping the grounds and grading and constructing the walks and drives.

The tremendous job of laying out the grounds and landscaping the Reservation was done under the direction of the landscape architect, A.F. Brinkerhoff. It entailed grading and seeding fifty acres of lawns, planting 3,000 shrubs, and transplanting 5,000 pines and 400 elm and oak trees from the previously reforested area on the State Reservation. Eight miles of roads and paths were constructed, and specially graded walks for use of heart patients and those who must limit their activity were laid out and built. Bridle paths were constructed for use of visitors who might enjoy riding as a form of recreation. One of the finest of these, comfortably carpeted with pine needles, ran along mile-long Avenue of Pines connecting the bath houses in the Lincoln Park area with the main mall area of Geyser Park.

The completion of the new Spa, as outlined in the 1930 Baruch report to the Legislature represented a colossal achievement. Incredibly, all of the pieces finally came together and, through the concerted effort of many dedicated people, the dream became reality. The Spa was ready for a formal opening in July 1935, several months before the deadline set by the R.F.C. when the loan was made in 1933. Interestingly enough, the completion of the Saratoga Spa was the first major program to be finished under the New Deal. It was particularly significant because of its social aspect, the $3,200,000 loan granted by the R.F.C. being the first one made for a purely social development. In announcing the fact Mr. Noyes, chairman of the Saratoga Springs Authority stated: "The spa will give health, happiness and increased years to persons who otherwise would not have had them." Jerome D. Barnum, Authority member, Syracuse publisher and president of the American Newspaper Publishers Association said: "The development has been carried to a point where it is possible to see how magnificent a gift to the nation New York State is making in the physical equipment for use of medicinal waters at Saratoga Springs."

The City of Saratoga Springs was understandably quite proud of the achievement since many of its citizens had played a very important role in its accomplishment. The whole city became very much involved in the celebration of the opening of the new Spa. They began their preparation weeks before the July date fixed for the event. They began in March with preview campaign meetings held in the casino where members of the Spa staff addressed large gatherings in an effort to educate them on various aspects of the Spa and spa therapy. William P. Beazell, managing director, Herbert Ant, chemist and Dr. Walter McClellan, medical director were among those who gave informative lectures.

In May they launched a "Know Your Spa" campaign for which an emblem picturing a spouter with the words "Know Your Spa" in front of it was extensively used. Members of the Junior Chamber of Commerce acted as guides to take Saratogians on inspection tours of the various buildings at the Reservation. All of the buildings of the development were visited by hundreds of people.

A clean-up campaign to get Saratoga homeowners to improve their property prior to the opening of the spa was planned by the Civic Improvement Committee of the Chamber of Commerce, assisted by the Women's Civic League. A luncheon opened the campaign, which ran for a week.

A festive atmosphere pervaded the city as the time for the exciting event drew near. The city appropriated $10,000 to finance an appropriate celebration. A huge banner was hung across Broadway and billboards leading to the city welcomed guests. Signs carrying the Seal of the State of New York in red with the spouting spring in the background were placed at entrances to the city. Mayor Schrade announced that there would be a half-day business holiday on the day of the opening.

A three-day program of community events attracted thousands of visitors. Saratoga Springs thronged with medical men, legislators and citizens gathered for the observances. The fesitval began on Thursday evening, July 25th, with open air dancing in Broadway. On Friday, July 26th, the formal opening ceremonies of America's first spa, in the European sense of the word, took place on the esplanade between the Hall of Springs and the Simon Baruch Institute. The program printed for the occasion contained the following information:

> The first of the 163 Saratoga springs was known to the Mohawk Indians in the fourteenth century as the "Medicine Spring of the Great Spirit."
>
> Throughout the early eighteen hundreds, in the years before the Civil War, Saratoga rapidly grew to be the first place among the ranking social resorts of the east. At the Grand Union Hotel is a register of The Union Tavern, on the yellow pages of which can be read the names of the aristocracy of the south, the political leaders of New York and Washington, the social elite of America and the Continent. They arrived in June to stay until September. Life centered about the springs and the walks and drives laid out about them.

1912 - all but a dozen of the 180 springs were purchased. Many were capped to prevent further flow and the important springs were made available to the public.

A motorcade of Saratogians left North Broadway at 3:00 p.m. and rode to the Spa to attend the exercises there at 4:00 p.m. Even before their arrival at the Spa, the reserved seat section which flanked the speakers stand was filled to overflowing with distinguished guests and the esplanade in front of the stand was alive with the excitement of thousands of enthusiastic guests.

The ceremonies were preceded by a band concert by the Saratoga City Band conducted by Charles E. Morris. The band played selections between addresses and at the end of the ceremony as well.

The theme of the opening ceremony was "Realization of the Dream of 1910." Pierpont B. Noyes, Chairman of the Saratoga Springs Authority, presided. After the invocation by the Right Reverend Thomas Frederick Davies, Episcopal Bishop of Western Massachusetts, he made a brief welcoming address to the distinguished guests and all the others who came to celebrate the occasion. He then introduced, in turn, Governor Herbert H. Lehman and Dr. Frederick E. Sondern, president of the Medical Society of the State of New York. Each gave a brief address. George Foster Peabody, the only surviving member of the original 1910 Saratoga Springs Commission, appointed by Governor Hughes and appointed again in 1929 by Governor Roosevelt, was then introduced. He noted that this opening was a very welcome gift for his 84th birthday which would come on the following day. He traced the history of the development of the Spa from its earliest days in 1910 to the present dedication of the world's finest spa, truly the realization of a dream. He recalled many interesting episodes which occurred during the long struggle.

The ceremonies ended with a Benediction by the Reverend Augustus Smith, C.S.E.R., rector of St. Clement's College and Church of Saratoga Springs.

The buildings remained open for inspection until 8:00 P.M.

Among the many people who extended congratulations on the opening of the Spa were U.S. Supreme Court Justice, Charles Evans Hughes, former New York Governor, who had signed the bill authorizing the creation of the State Spa. He stated: "I have followed with keen gratification the development of extraordinary opportunities which nature has furnished in this favored spot."

Mr. Bernard Baruch, another great supporter of the Spa, sent this message from Paris: "This is a particularly happy day for me as the dream of my father to have a place where the suffering could be healed and made better able to face their daily problems, comes true."

In the evening after the ceremony there was a street parade in town, a band concert and street dancing on Broadway again, as well as a professional boxing match in Convention Hall.

On the following day, July 27th, the Gideon Putnam Hotel opened. The first guest to register was Joseph H. Friedlander, the architect who designed the general layout of the development as well as several of its buildings. The day's program included a motorcade tour of the Saratoga Battlefield at 10 o'clock in the morning and a pageant in Congress Park in the afternoon. Two band concerts and fireworks in Congress Park were planned for the evening.

There was an open air church service for all the churches in the county held in Congress Park on Sunday morning, July 28th. In the afternoon Saratogians and their guests enjoyed a ball game at the Recreation Field or trips to points of interest in the vicinity. There was another fireworks display in the evening.

And so, with the completion and formal opening of the Spa, ended the 1930 - 1936 period of the realization of a great spa in America. It was probably the most eventful period in the history of the Spa; truly its golden age and high point.

19

The Saratoga Spa   1936 - 1950

"Come ye who suffer, and lose your pain;
From beds of languishing rise again;
Drink these waters for you unsealed,
Partake of the fountain by nature revealed.
O children of earth; to you they are given
And the fairy's skill is the blessing of heaven."
—From a sign in Congress Park, 1867

The era of the 1930's at the Saratoga Spa was climaxed in 1935 by the opening to the public of the new development which consisted of ten buildings forming "the most complete government health unit in the United States." It was indeed an exciting period in the history of the Spa which portended great promise for the future.

On June 30, 1937, the term of the temporary Commission came to an end and control of the Saratoga Spa Reservation reverted to the New York State Conservation Department. A new Saratoga Springs Commission was then appointed to act as head of the Division of the Saratoga Spa Reservation under this department.

The year following the opening of the new Spa was a memorable one. There was an increase in patronage over the previous year. Treatments at the bath houses increased 24%, including the baths and other treatments given free of charge to the people who could not afford to pay for them. This provision was mandated in the law of 1930 when it made the recommendations contained in the Baruch Report part of the State's public health policy. Admissions to the drink halls were up 60%, and 42% more bottles of mineral water were sold than in 1936. The figures seemed to indicate a real appreciation of the waters by the people.

Pierpont Noyes, as chairman of the Saratoga Springs Commission, made the following statement in the 1937 report to the Legislature:

The commission wishes to bring especially to attention the fact that the spa is for all the people. It is possible to take a three weeks course of treatments at the spa (identical in character with those given at any price) for as little as $110.00, the cost of the treatments, living expenses and physician's fees all being included. In addition, during the past year, fifteen out of every one hundred treatments were given without cost to those able to show that they "do not possess and cannot obtain means with which to pay for these treatments," as the regulations laid down for the operation of the spa require.

One of the most popular attractions at the Saratoga Spa was the free-flowing mineral springs whose waters were available free of charge to the public. These springs were to be found from one end of the Reservation to the other. They included, starting from the north end of Saratoga running to the southern end of the Reservation on Route 50, the Old Red, the Peerless, Hathorn #1, the Congress, the Lincoln, the Orenda, the Karista, the Hayes and the Hathorn #3 Springs. It was estimated that 750,000 people visited these springs annually. With this increase in the number of visitors came a real problem for management. It was found necessary to post state police at certain springs to ensure proper sanitary conditions and also to protect the public from indiscriminate use of the waters. Some patrons were found to be drinking excessive amounts and some were mixing the waters of the various springs indiscriminately. It is very important that these waters be used wisely and with knowledge of their effects on the human body. Casual drinking of any of the waters is beneficial for anyone, but intensive prolonged use for specific medical conditions should be undertaken only under the supervision of a physician.

A positive step was taken by the Commission when they regained bottling rights. It was found to be impossible to modify the lease in such a way as to ensure an adequate supply of mineral waters for the new drink hall. After much negotiation, the Commission purchased the lease for a sum considerably less than the anticipated profit to the bottling corporation during the remaining fifteen years of the lease.

Under Dr. McClellan, the Spa's medical department was active in educating both the general public and the medical profession. Exhibits illustrating Spa activities, the benefits of spa therapy and the value of the mineral waters were shown at both lay and scientific meetings. Scientific literature on the waters and on spa therapy were sent to physicians on request.

Dr. McClellan was appointed a member of the faculty of Albany Medical College as associate professor of medicine. Each year, the senior class of the medical school was invited to spend a day at the Saratoga Spa where the students were able to experience first hand the mineral bath, massage and other forms of therapy, to tour the Spa and to take part in discussions on spa therapy. Since American colleges do not offer courses in balneotherapy (spa treatment), as do all European medical schools, this proved to be an opportunity to provide some knowledge of spa therapy to at least a small number of future doctors.

Dr. McClellan also lectured at other medical schools and at medical conventions, and in many ways spread knowledge of the Saratoga Spa and its facilities. Through his efforts as a member of the Committee on American Health Resorts of the American Medical Association and as chairman of the Committee on Spas and Health Resorts of the American Congress of Physical Therapy the Saratoga Spa was recognized as the American pattern for health resort activities.

In 1937 a volunteer attending medical staff for the Spa was organized. This staff was composed of thirty-eight physicians of Saratoga Springs and vicinity who, at scheduled times, assisted without fee in the care of charity patients.

Also in 1937 new forms of treatment were introduced. The use of mud packs was begun and proved to be a very effective treatment for arthritis. Mud from the area of the Karista Spring, very rich in iron, was used for the packs. The same year inhalation therapy was initiated using mineral water in addition to other medications. This proved to be of value in the treatment of various respiratory diseases.

Research on the mineral waters was carried on at the Spa, both in the research laboratory by chemists and in the bath houses by the medical staff. In addition, studies of the waters were carried on elsewhere. One such study was done in 1937 by Dr. Charles I. Singer of Long Beach, California. In an investigation on the use of the Saratoga mineral waters, he studied the response to the internal use of Geyser water by children spending the summer at a beach camp on the seashore. He observed a group of children who received Geyser water and compared the results with another group of children who were living under the same conditions, but who did not receive the water. His conclusions reached in this study are summarized as follows:

> 1. In the group of children studied, some of whom had taken the mineral water before, it was noted that 40% of the children liked it at first taste and 60% refused it after the first taste. This latter group took the water when raspberry juice was added. At the end of the first week nearly all of the children reverted to the use of the mineral water without flavoring.
>
> 2. Changes in the nutritional index which depends on the changes in height, weight and chest expansion, showed in general that those children who were above or below normal values approached the normal values during the course of the summer on the beach. The underweight children who received the mineral water showed a more rapid approach to the normal index value than did a similar group who did not receive the water. With overweight children, no evident variation from the control group was noted.
>
> 3. The occurrence of heat cramps in the beach camps had been

noted during the previous seasons. During the summer of 1939 when the mineral waters were used by certain groups it was noted that no heat cramps or heat exhaustion developed in the children who received the mineral waters, while the usual occurrence of this condition was evident in the group of children who did not receive the water.

4. Technical observation of the children included the use of the Muck test. This test in general shows variations in the body response as a result of acclimatization on the shore. The seashore climate and bathing are stimulating. A comparison of the tests at the beginning and end of the summer showed that the children who received the mineral water apparently reacted in a normal healthy way to the test, while those who had not received the mineral water over-reacted, possibly as the result of an excessive amount of climate stimulation resulting from the exposure to the seashore.

The conclusions presented by Dr. Singer represent the result of a vast amount of observation and detail and suggest that the waters have a definite place in the field of nutrition, particularly of the growing child. Their value in combating the ill effects of exposure to heat is well known.

In 1939, as in all succeeding years, the Saratoga Spa began to experience drastic cuts in its appropriation by the Legislature. This necessitated changes in its operating procedures. Advertising and promotional work had to be curtailed to a minimum. This resulted in reduced patronage since the public was not being informed about the Spa. Experience over the years has shown that the amount of advertising and promotional work that was done bears a direct relationship to the amount of business experienced. It was pointed out to the Legislature by the Commission that reducing the appropriation for the Spa to the point where publicity and advertising has to be cut is false economy since it results in fewer people visiting the Spa. It was noted that the state has an investment in Saratoga in land, buildings and equipment of approximately $8,800,000; $5,600,000 of this was paid for by state appropriaton and $3,200,000 by an R.F.C. loan. If the number of people visiting the Spa drops, then only a small minority of the people are getting the benefit of the baths and the waters.

The Commission stated that operations at the Spa cannot produce a profit because "expenses involved in maintaining the Reseravtion as a public recreation area, together with maintenance of free service at the springs and giving the thousands of free baths to indigent persons, seems certain to absorb any profit from other Spa activities." For this reason it is absolutely necessary that the Spa be helped by adequate appropriations of the Legislature.

In 1940 the old Hathorn Drink Hall on Spring Street, which had become antiquated, was demolished and the land was cleared, graded and planted to make an attractive setting for the Hathorn #1 Spring which had always been popular with the general public. The spring which had previously flowed inside the Hathorn Drink Hall was now diverted to flow in an open pavilion on

SARATOGA SPRINGS RESERVATION
SARATOGA SPA STATE PARK AND SARATOGA SPA

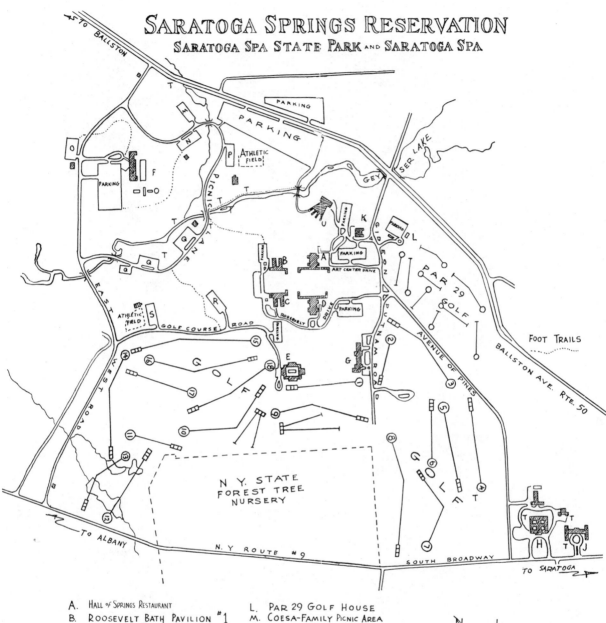

N. Y. STATE FOREST TREE NURSERY

TO ALBANY

N. Y ROUTE #9

SOUTH BROADWAY

TO SARATOGA

FOOT TRAILS

BALLSTON AVE. RTE. 50

A.	Hall of Springs Restaurant
B.	Roosevelt Bath Pavilion #1
C.	Roosevelt #2 and Park Adm.
D.	General Adm. Bldg. & Theatre
E.	Golf House & Victoria Pool
F.	Peerless Pool
G.	Gideon Putnam Hotel
H.	Lincoln Bath Pavilion
J.	Washington Bath Pavilion
K.	Bottling Plant
L.	Par 29 Golf House
M.	Coesa-Family Picnic Area
N.	Hathorn-Family Picnic Area
O.	Carlsbad-Family Picnic Area
P.	Orenda-Group Picnic Area [Reservation Required]
Q.	Geyser-Family Picnic Areas
R.	Ferndell-Family Picnic Area
S.	Columbia-Group Picnic Area [Reservation Required]
T.	Natural Mineral Springs
U.	Performing Arts Center

C. H. Chapman 65

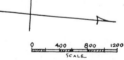

N

0   400   800   1200
SCALE

Broadway Drink Hall. Designed by Charles S. Peabody and built in 1915 as a trolley station for the interurban railroad. At termination of lease it was remodeled as a drink hall

Bath House of Victoria Pool in Recreation Complex

Victoria Pool

Saratoga beauties at Victoria Pool   Collection of Edwin T. Ladue

Spa Theater   Collection of Edwin T. Ladue

Walter S. McClellan, M.D.
Medical Director, Saratoga Spa, 1931-1953

Oskar Baudisch, PhD.
Director of Research, Saratoga Spa, 1939-1950

the one-quarter acre area which was approached by a promenade with attractive landscaping. The demolition saddened many Saratogians. This feeling was expressed by Saratoga's beloved humorist, Frank Sullivan, by the following lament published in the *Saratogian* on February 12, 1941:

AN ERA PASSES

Passing the old Hathorn Spring building will bring a sigh from The Dipper Boy Alumni. A good many of us entered the business world by way of the glass bowl in the spring pavilion, from which flowed the bubbling waters. We stood at the bowl for long hours, pouring the water into glasses held in the outstretched hands of patrons or other boys who served the customers at the tables around the big room.

We recall serving Chauncey M. Depew and Tom Platt when the State Republican convention was being held here. We well recall the beauteous lady who once gave us a quarter tip. We recall, too, the summer when, in order to keep two jobs, we faced the task of leaving the Hathorn building and arriving at the old High School building on Lake Avenue on one and the same second.

After all we are sorry the old spring building is to go the way of the wind. We had a secret hope that some day throngs of pilgrims from regions far remote might throng the old drink hall to view with reverential gaze a plaque bearing the inscription: "Here a great editor got his start in life."

Well, there's to be no plaque, no pilgrims, and, truth to tell, no great editor. There now only remains to some of us the pleasant recollection of another era now far remote and mostly forgotten.

A new city drink hall was provided by remodeling the Albany, Schenectady, Saratoga Interurban trolley station which was located on Broadway opposite Congress Park. This was made possible by the reversion of the property to the State of New York at the termination of a lease made in 1915 for rental of the ground on which the station was located.

The trolley station which was built in 1915 was outstanding architecturally. It was designed by Charles S. Peabody of the firm Ludlow and Peabody Architects of New York and Paris. Its transformation into a drink hall was carried on by forces of the Saratoga Spa Authority, supplemented by labor from the W.P.A. work camp in Geyser Park, under an appropriation of the Legislature to cover the cost of materials. The result was most pleasing. The train shed was made into an outdoor pavilion furnished with tables and chairs so that the waters could be drunk in the open air. The inside of the building was redesigned to provide a large lobby where the waters could be dispensed and patrons accommodated. Ample storage and refrigeration facilities were provided. It was opened to the public February 13, 1941. During 1941 there was an increase of 200% in the patronage over that of the old Hathorn Drink Hall.

During the years following the United States' entry into the second World War, activities at the Spa were changed to accommodate the war effort. Some of the buildings were closed to save fuel, bus schedules were changed to conserve gasoline, and construction and repairs, where possible, were postponed because manpower had been diverted to the armed forces and war industries.

The spectrochemical laboratory of the research department of the Spa was able to make a significant contribution to the technical resources of the nation which proved of great value in the war effort. This laboratory, with its excellent optical equipment, aided in exploring new domestic sources of urgently needed strategic metals. The research radiographer was given the highly responsible task of examining hundred of samples of metals urgently needed in aircraft production. The spectrographic techniques used were similar to those employed in the study of the process by which a rare metal is picked up by mineral waters.

In 1942 a contract was made between the Saratoga Springs Reservation and the U.S. Veterans Administration whereby the Veterans Administration was to use the Roosevelt Bath House No. 2 as a veterans hospital for the treatment of cardiac and rheumatic cases as well as other cases that would benefit by spa therapy.

The Saratoga Spa medical and research departments stood to benefit by this arrangement in that it would make possible continuous twenty-four hour observation of patients under treatment whereas previously these patients were only available for study less than an hour each day. The Veterans Administration agreed to make all clinical data on these patients available to the Spa. It was believed that in this way the known value of mineral water therapy could be demonstrated and confirmed in a medical sense.

In February 1943 the Veterans Hospital at Saratoga Springs was activated for service. Between this date and June 1947 when the unit was temporarily closed, a very interesting study of the effect of the Saratoga mineral baths, together with spa therapy on arthritis and related conditions, was carried on. Approximately four-fifths of the patients treated at the hospital fell in the rheumatic group. The remainder fell into miscellaneous classifications of diseases, mainly cardiovascular. Of the 1,280 patients admitted to the hospital, 993 patients with arthritis or a related condition were included in the study. All patients received general hospital care under supervision of the regular staff physicians. A special program of treatment included use of the naturally carbonated mineral waters in the form of baths and packs. In addition, other forms of spa therapy, such as electric cabinets, whirlpool treatments, massage, etc. were utilized where indicated. The results of treatment were very gratifying with over 92% of those thus treated showing definite improvement.

This pilot program demonstrated the great effectiveness of spa therapy utilizing the carbonated mineral waters in the treatment of rheumatic disorders.

The patients treated at the Veterans Hospital, but not included in the pilot study, also showed improvement on the Spa regime. The final conclusion after evaluating all patients treated at the hospital was that spa therapy such as is available at the Saratoga Spa could contribute greatly to the medical care of chronic disease, a problem facing the Veterans Administration even today.

By special arrangement with the Veterans Administration, the Veterans Hospital at the Spa was reopened in September 1947. It continued to operate until June 30, 1951 when the new Veterans Hospital in Albany opened.

In commenting on the beneficial effect that the mineral waters have on various chronic diseases, Dr. McClellan noted that scientific knowledge of the action of these waters is gradually replacing empirical observations of the past centuries. He referred to the work of Dr. Baudisch, Research Director at the Saratoga Spa, whose work in newer chemical analysis and in studies of radioactivity and spectrum analysis has provided rational explanations of the results obtained with the use of the mineral waters.

During the 1936-1950 era the Saratoga Spa experienced its finest times. The peak was reached in 1946 when the Spa attracted the greatest number of visitors and the number of treatments given at the bath houses exceeded those of every year before or since.

20

Therapy at the Spa

"I firmly believe that if the whole materia medica as now used could be sent to the bottom of the sea, it would be all the better for mankind - and all the worse for the fishes."
—Oliver Wendell Holmes

For many hundreds of years the mineral waters of Saratoga have been used by people with the firm conviction that they have therapeutic value. The Mohawks believed that healing powers had been bestowed on them when the great god Manitou stirred the waters and endowed them with health-giving properties. For this reason early users considered the springs as sacred wells, just as many of the Europeans regarded their springs as holy wells in their early days.

Early inhabitants of the Saratoga area, the Iroquois bathed in the spring water, drank it, and found it effective in healing their ills. The use was entirely empirical. There was no attempt made to explain their beneficial effect, nor was there any reason to. Those benefited were satisfied that the results could be explained by the fact that the waters had been blessed by a deity.

Such an explanation does not satisfy our modern day scientific community. Today we wish to know why and how certain reactions occur. It is understandable, therefore, that only a very few years after the Saratoga mineral waters became known to the early settlers, men of science began to investigate them to determine their chemical composition and mode of action.

The first person to attempt an analysis of the Saratoga mineral waters was Dr. Constable of Schenectady, who in 1770, by very crude analysis determined that the waters of Saratoga and Ballston contained certain minerals including iron and certain salts such as bicarbonates and chlorides. He also discovered

239

that the gas in the water was "fixed air" which had been discovered by Priestley. This "fixed air" is known today as carbon dioxide gas. Further than stating that the waters were "highly medicinal" he left no other observations.

One of the first reports on the therapeutic use of the mineral waters was made by Dr. Samuel Tenney, a regimental surgeon in the Continental Army stationed at Fish Creek near the Saratoga Battlefield during the Revolutionary War. On September 1, 1783, Dr. Tenney wrote to Dr. Joshua Fisher, who was a member of the American Academy of Arts and Sciences in Boston, giving an account of his experience with the Saratoga mineral waters. The letter was published ten years later in 1793 in the *Memoirs of the American Academy of Arts and Sciences*.

In his letter Dr. Tenney described some experiments he had performed on the Saratoga mineral waters in which he determined that they contained iron and a large quantity of calcareous earth suspended in the water by means of "fixed air." He observed that these waters were essentially the same as the waters of Pyrmont, Seltzer and others which have been famous for so long in Europe. He believed that the Saratoga waters were far superior to the European waters because they were so strongly impregnated with "fixed air."

He described in detail his experience with patients he sent to the spring for treatment with the mineral waters as follows:

> The first patients that I sent were about thirty in number. Their disorders were rheumatick, scorbutic complaints, etc., with which old regiments generally abound. They almost all returned perfectly relieved, particularly the rheumatick patients. Indeed, I am disposed to believe, as well from the accounts of the people in the vicinity, as from my own observation, that in the chronic rheumatism, the waters are a very certain cure.
>
> Among these patients was one, whose case deserves more particular description. He was a man of about twenty-four years of age, of a slender habit, and delicate constitution. He had not been fit for duty much above half the time, for his two years he had served in the regiment; and for five or six months, had been troubled with scrophulous and pulmonick complaints; a pain in his breast, cough and sometimes a slight hemoptysis. At this time he had a hectic fever; and I suspect that he had tubercles formed in his lungs, which were about suppurating.
>
> I sent him to the springs in the month of April. By drinking the acidulous waters about a fortnight, his symptoms were so far removed, that he has enjoyed tolerable health, and has done his duty in the corps ever since, except that very lately he has felt some symptoms of his old disorders, which were somewhat removed by a return to the waters.
>
> I had afterwards two patients, whose livers were left greatly tumefied, indurated, and painful, by an obstinate jaundice, on which the common deobstruents had little or no effect. I sent them to the springs for relief, and within a week they returned perfectly

cured.

A girl belonging to Albany, in consequence of a fall on the ice, about two years before, had seven or eight sores broke out on the whole length of her left thigh, which in time became ulcerous. By the advice of Dr. Young, who had very faithfully attended her, she was carried to the springs. On her way she stopped at the garrison, and I saw her. All the muscles of her thigh were useless, and her knee consequently destitute of any voluntary motion. Her leg was drawn backwards, and fixed; her thigh was considerably enlarged, and in places, very hard; the ulcers had a foul and angry appearance; and at times she suffered considerable pain. After she had used the waters for a fortnight, she returned and I saw her again. The swelling and induration were removed, her pains were much abated, her knee was more flexible; and her ulcers had assumed a favorable appearance. It is not supposed that in such a case, any course of internal medicines could effect a cure; but, I believe that so much could not have been done towards it, in the same time, by the best medicines of the shops, though ever so judiciously administered; nor perhaps in a much longer time.

Many people in the vicinity, suppose the waters a cure for intermitting fever and when properly used, I have no doubt but that they may be. For this purpose, after using the acidulous waters a few days, recourse must be had to the tonick virtues of the chalybeate. But for most of the proper directions, I believe that has not been practical. The advantages derived from them, therefore, were the same that are produced by evacuations, and small doses of tartar emetic, by which the fits may very often be broken, and the disorder sometimes removed. I have made trial of them in but one case of this disorder; and that was before I had discovered the properties of the different springs. The patient used the acidulae alone; and was very well prepared by them for the use of the bark.

As a practical proof of the tonick powers of the chalybeate waters, I might mention the case of a woman whom I found at the springs. She complained that the acidulous waters (of which alone she had drank for several weeks) reduced her strength. From a persuasion of the astringency of the chalybeate spring, I advised her to drink a moderate quantity of it, for a day or two, and to repeat it occasionally. I saw her again some time after, when she informed me that she had followed my advice, and always found from it, a remarkable restoration of strength.

These are all the cases, that are worth mentioning, in which the good effects of the waters were evident; though perhaps eighty patients belonging to the regiment may have used them successfully, most of their complaints being of little consequence.

I must not, however, omit one case, in which the success attending the use of the waters answered neither my wishes, nor my expectations. An officer in the regiment, a little past the meridian of life, had been for many years, troubled with a tetterous eruption, on different parts of his body. It gave him no great uneasiness, 'till the summer of the year 1780, when it fixed on one of his ankles. Notwithstanding many topical applications, it daily gained ground; and the latter end of the year 1781, after an active campaign, had possessed the whole leg, and part of the other. The disorder would sometimes alternate with his stomach and bowels, produce severe pain, with a copious discharge of foul matter, and sometimes by stool. The eruption was removed from his legs by a very ingenious surgeon in the American hospital. His stomach was, however, frequently disordered afterwards, and he was on the whole, not much better for the removal of the disorder from the surface. During the last winter, his stomach and bowels were frequently affected; and though his appetite was generally good, yet his digestion was impaired, and few kinds of food would remain on his stomach. Evacuations with the bark and bitters yielded a temporary relief; but pronounced no permanent advantage.

In this situation he resolved, about the middle of April, to try the effect of the springs. From the accounts I had received (for I had not then seen him) I approved of his plan; and he immediately proceeded to execute it. After using the acidulous waters for twelve or fifteen days, he returned to the quarters surprisingly reduced; complaining that "they had torn his stomach all to pieces."

As soon as he had recovered strength enough to ride, he retired from service, and I have not heard from him since. I apprehend that he used the waters imprudently, and that if he had made a judicious use of the two different kinds, he might have found the assistance from them, which he had in vain sought from other medicines. He is fully of this opinion himself; and ascribes their failure to his drinking them in pretty large quantities, when his stomach was too weak to bear them.

I beg leave to subjoin two or three general remarks on the virtues of these waters. From the cases related, I think we may conclude, that the acidulous waters possess considerable aperient or deobstruent powers, and may, therefore, be useful in most kinds of obstructions. That they share the refrigerant and sedative properties of the acids cannot be disputed. By these they are well calculated to remove the inflammatory diathesis, which usually accompanies so many disorders, and embarrasses the physician in his prescription.

Among the rest, do they not promise to be serviceable in removing the obstinate, though sometimes small, inflammation of the lungs, which so often terminates in a phthisis pulmonalis and death? I think their success in the pulmonick case above related some proof of it.

The chalybeate water may, without doubt, be an excellent remedy in all cases of simple relaxation, or where there is the primary disorder; and is always at hand to brace up, and invigorate these patients, who are debilitated by the use of the acidulous.

These are a few of the obvious medicinal virtues of these curious springs. But, perhaps, nothing but a series of accurate observations by ingenious practitioners, can determine all their properties and

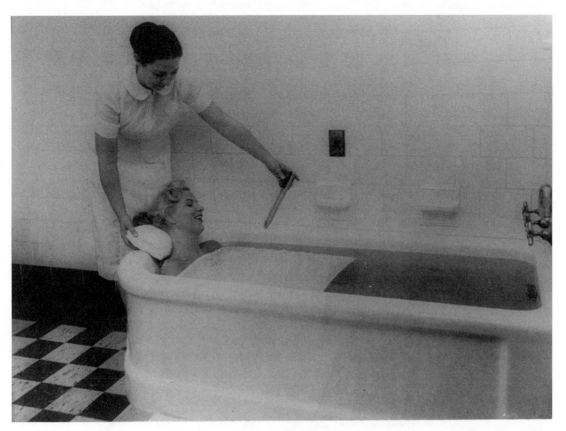

Checking the temperature of mineral water bath

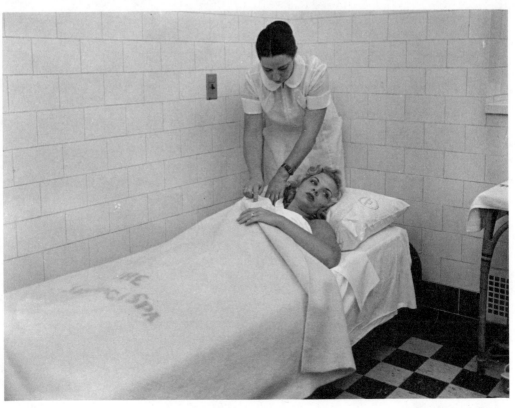

Rest following a relaxing bath

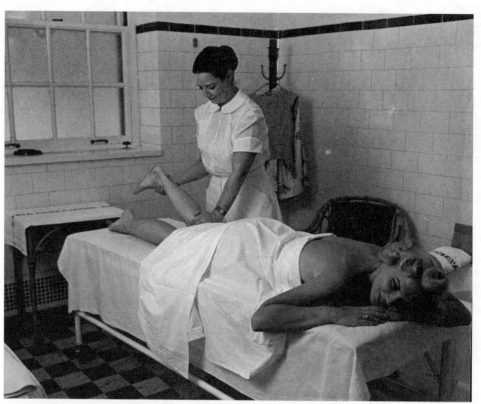

Massage is an important part of spa therapy

Photo by George Burns

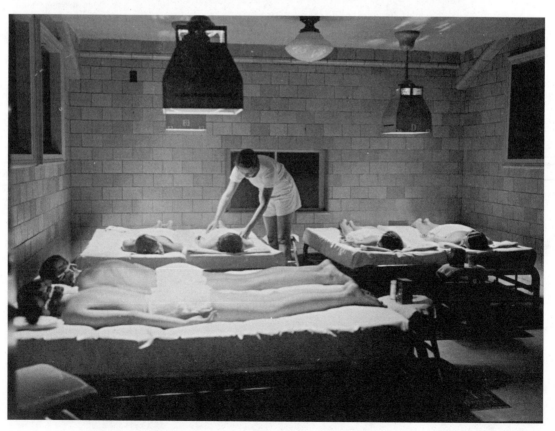

Radiation Therapy.
Both infrared and ultraviolet given at the Spa

Photo by George Burns

Cabinet treatment precedes salt rub

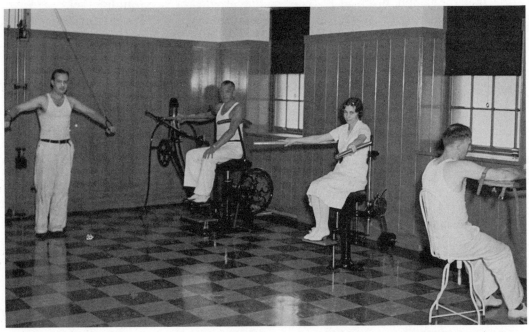

Mechanotherapy takes off pounds

excellencies.

I am, etc.

(signed) Samuel Tenney

Dr. Fisher,

  P.S. Five months after writing the above, I saw the officer whose case is there related. He informed me, that he got home with difficulty, and for some time declined so fast, that he despaired of recovering. At length, however, his constitution, naturally vigorous, prevailed over his disorder; his strength was restored; for several months he had been entirely free from any symptoms of his former complaints; and had enjoyed a better state of health than he had for several years before. As he used little or no medicine after drinking the waters, I think we may justly conclude that the acrimony, which for two years had rendered his life miserable, was eradicated by them alone. The pulmonick patient likewise, whose case is there mentioned, continues in good health.

S. Tenney

Dr. Joshua Fisher, F.A.A.

  Dr. Tenney's enthusiasm for the waters is interesting. We must remember that the people involved in these studies lived over two hundred years ago, long before modern medical science had produced the wonder pharmaceuticals and the sophisticated modalities in use today. In their time patients were largely dependent on the miraculous recuperative power of the human body. Nature, if not interfered with, tends to restore health. Given the right environment and the psychological assurance that health will be restored, the salutary physiological effect of the waters and minerals necessary for rebuilding body tissues will accomplish wonders.

  This concept is basic to spa therapy. The mineral waters are not necessarily specific for any given disease. They contribute to the basic welfare of the person by improving the general health and thereby aiding nature in the natural healing process.

  In 1787 Samuel Latham Mitchell, a young physician recently graduated from the University of Edinburgh, who was later to become famous, visited the springs at Saratoga. He performed some experiments on the waters using animals. He concluded that the gas contained in the water was "fixed air" or carbon dioxide. He described the effects of the waters on the human body as follows: "The effect it produces on the human body is various; the natural operation of it, when taken, is cathartic; in some instances an emetic. As it is drank, it produces an agreeable sensation in passing over the organs of taste; but as soon as it is swallowed, there succeeds an unpleasant tang, and the eructations which take place afterwards, have a pungency very similar to that produced by the use of cyder or beer in a state of fermentation."

His report represents the first report on the nature of the Saratoga waters to appear in print.

The first truly scientifically accurate analysis of the Saratoga mineral waters was made in 1792 by Dr. Valentine Seamon, a New York City physician. From his experiments he concluded that each quart of mineral water contained:

Cretacious acid -	about 40 cubic inches
Mineral alkali -	5.2 grains
Common marine salt -	34.6 grains
Aerated lime -	38.0 grains
Aerated iron -	1.7 grains

On therapeutic use of the waters he admitted that he had had no personal experience. However, he did venture an opinion or two based on the chemical analysis of the water.

His book, published in 1793, drew great attention to the waters with the result that people came from long distances to visit the springs.

The physician who was to introduce vaccination for smallpox into America, Dr. Benjamin Waterhouse, professor of the theory and practice of medicine at Harvard, made a journey to Saratoga in 1794. A complete description of the springs of both Saratoga and Ballston is given in his account which was published some time later. He noted that the waters contain iron, a mineral alkali, common salt and lime, and that they are brisk and sparkling like champagne, a property which they derive from the *spiritus mineralis* which they contain. "This is the same thing which gives activity to yeast and life to malt liquors. It is used in the neighborhood of the springs instead of yeast in making bread, and is found to raise it more speedily and effectively than any other ferment in ordinary use." He suggested that, "since the waters of Saratoga and Ballston resemble the famous chalybeate waters of Pyrmont, Spa and Seltzer, they might well be bottled and circulated through the United States, which would make them lucrative for the entrepreneur and beneficial to the people of the country."

The mineral waters of Ballston were analyzed by Peter Vandervoort, M.D. of New York. The report of the analysis was published in 1795.

In 1807, Robert Livingston of New York had a sample of Ballston water analyzed by a celebrated French chemist. The report of the results was much publicized in this country and served to call attention to Ballston.

John H. Steele, M.D., a resident physician in Saratoga in the first half of the nineteenth century, made an analysis of the mineral springs of Saratoga and Ballston. He published his findings, along with a history of Saratoga and the springs in a volume which was so popular and informative that it went through two editions several years apart.

He wisely cautioned against the indiscriminate use of the mineral waters as follows:

These waters are so generally used, and their effect so seldom injurious, particularly to persons in health, that almost everyone who has ever drunk of them, assumes the prerogative of directing their use to others; and, were these directions always the result of experience and observation, they certainly would be less objectionable; but there are numerous persons that flock about the springs during the drinking season, without any knowledge of the composition of the waters, and little or none of their effects, who continue to dispose of their directions to the ignorant and unwary, with no other effect than to injure the reputation of the water and destroy the prospects of the diseased.

Many persons who resort to the springs for the restoration of health, seem to be governed by the idea that they are to recover in proportion to the amount they drink; and, although many who are in health may, and frequently do, swallow down enormous amounts of the water with apparent impunity, it does not follow that those whose stomachs are enfeebled by disease can take the same quantity with the same effect. Stomachs of this description frequently reject large portions of the water, and thereby protect the system from the disastrous consequences that would otherwise follow. But when it happens to be retained, the result is indeed distressing.

Dr. J.J. Moorman states in his book on the mineral waters: "When Americans shall have acquired more prudence upon the subject, and learned to inquire more carefully into the adaptedness of mineral waters to their diseases, before committing themselves to their use, far more good will be derived by the invalid; our mineral waters will be appreciated, and their character better established in public confidence."

During his twenty-two years as medical director at the Saratoga Spa (1931-1953), Dr. Walter McClellan carried on extensive research on the mineral waters of Saratoga Springs paying special attention to their physiological effect on the human body. His experiments were meticulously performed in a very scientific manner, the result of his thorough training in scientific research at Harvard and Cornell medical schools. His results were published in the most respected medical journals of the day, thus assuring permanence and future access to them by posterity.

One of the first research studies undertaken at the Saratoga Spa was done by Dr. McClellan and his medical assistants in 1932. Studied was the effect of the mineral water baths on the blood pressure of persons with hypertension. The results were gratifying in that they showed that there was a significant drop in blood pressure in patients with hypertension after a series of mineral water baths.

One of the outstanding accomplishments in research at the Saratoga Spa has been the development of the program for cardiovascular diseases which evolved over the years as a result of experience and research.

Cardiovascular disease represents the major cause of death in this country. It produces a great amount of disability in all ages, but particularly in the older age group. For more than a hundred years balneotherapy has been used in the treatment of this group of diseases. This form of cardiac therapy had its origin at Bad Nauheim in Germany in 1859 when Beneke observed that carbon dioxide baths were not only tolerated by patients with heart disease but that their cardiac condition improved markedly during the course of their treatment. Previously it had been considered that carbon dioxide baths were not appropriate for cardiac patients. Most of the treatments given at Bad Nauheim had been for rheumatic ailments. Following this observation on cardiac patients by Beneke, physicians confirmed its validity and developed a program of carbon dioxide baths for cardiac patients. Its reputation for effectiveness spread. In France at Royat, a spa which also has naturally carbonated mineral water, a center for cardiac therapy was established using basically the Nauheim regime.

At Saratoga Springs, shortly after the Reservation had been taken over by the State of New York, Dr. Simon Baruch, a balneologist, who had been engaged as a consultant by the state, developed a program of cardiac therapy based on the Nauheim regime using the Saratoga mineral waters. Previously the Saratoga waters had been used largely for gastrointestinal complaints, rheumatism and related diseases.

Twenty years later when the Spa was put under medical control and a research laboratory was established, studies were done and careful observations made on the effect of the carbon dioxide gas and the waters on the cardiovascular system of patients under many experimental conditions. This careful research has established the fact that the carbon dioxide gas in the mineral water, absorbed through the skin, has a cardiotonic effect on the circulatory system very comparable to that of digitalis. It was noted that cardiac patients, following the program of treatment at the Spa with carbon dioxide waters, showed clinical improvement in their ability to exercise without producing pain, or other evidence of coronary embarrassment. Clinical observations over the years support the conclusion, obtained in similar waters in Europe, that these patients do indeed experience real improvement.

Spa therapy includes a great deal more than the use of mineral waters. Its purpose is to introduce a person to a total life program which will yield the greatest dividends in health and well being. It includes a program for the maintenance of health which is dependent on a mode of living which includes: consideration of diet, patterns of sleep and rest, type and amount of exercise and assurance of adequate and appropriate recreation. All of these factors must be integrated in a manner suitable to the individual with due regard to his physical and mental condition.

On entering a course of spa therapy a person sees a physician, who, after taking his history and doing a complete physical examination, prescribes for him appropriate therapy which may include mineral baths or other modalities such as mineral water packs, electric cabinet or any of the various forms of therapy available at the Spa. He recommends appropriate exercise which may be as light as graded walks or golf on the par 3 golf course, or more strenuous, as golf on the championship course, tennis or swimming. He discusses the patient's life style with him and recommends any modifications which may be indicated in his rest and sleep habits, his diet, and his forms of recreation. Thus following a course of spa therapy a person has to start on a regime for living a healthful life which he would do well to follow after returning home.

The cornerstone of spa therapy is the bath in the naturally carbonated mineral water. This is an experience of true relaxation. The body is comfortably immersed in the mineral water with a barrier rest for the feet and a cork pillow under the head. The water has a buoyancy, because of its mineral content, which supports the body just as sea water does. This gives a sensation comparable to that of the weightlessness experienced by astronauts when they are outside of the earth's gravitational field. The muscles do not have to support the body, and they can, therefore, effectively relax. This process is aided by the temperature of the water, which, though approximately the same as that of the body, is warmer than the atmosphere and, therefore, feels warm on the surface of the body. As the body lies in this very comfortable, relaxed state, the carbon dioxide gas, which was in solution in the water, comes out of solution in the form of tiny bubbles which accumulate on the skin and gently massage it, causing a healthy glow to appear. This reminds one of the "champagne baths" so famous in the twenties. After lying in this comfortable bath for fifteen minutes, one is taken from the tub, covered with a warm sheet and gently patted dry, then covered with a warm dry sheet and allowed to rest. Truly this is nature's tranquilizer. It far surpasses any drug in the pharmacopoeia.

Even for those with no specific disease requiring therapy, the spa experience is very rewarding and one would do well to take advantage of this opportunity for an investment in health afforded by the State of New York at the Saratoga Spa.

21

The Saratoga Spa Since 1950

*"The health of the people is really the foundation
upon which all their happiness and all their powers
as a state depend."*

—Francis Bacon

The 1950's were somewhat of a transition period for the Saratoga Spa, from the old order of growth and development to a new uncertain, difficult era of struggle for survival. There were many changes in personnel during this period with the result that the whole complexion of the Spa seemed to change.

Dr. Oskar Baudisch, Research Director of the Saratoga Spa, was the first person to be taken from the ranks. He died suddenly on March 29, 1950. This brilliant scientist, in a quiet, unobtrusive way had made phenomenal contributions to the field of the chemistry of the mineral waters. He had done a great deal toward explaining scientifically the hidden reasons for the favorable therapeutic effects of the mineral waters. As early as 1926, while at Yale University and later while at the Rockefeller Institute for Medical Research in New York, he had carried on investigations to determine the basic reasons for the therapeutic values in the Saratoga mineral waters. He was the first to coin the phrase "inorganic vitamins" to explain the function of the trace elements in the human body. He developed a theory to explain the actual mechanism of the function of these elements in the cell based mainly on his magneto-chemical research. He came to the Saratogs Spa in 1939 and continued his research until his death. His death was a tragic loss to the field of science as well as to the Saratoga Spa. In 1955, John M. Reiner, PhD. replaced him as Director of Research at the Saratoga Spa.

Another member of the research staff to leave the spa during this period was Dr. Lester Strock, Research Radiographer, who had come to the Spa in 1939. He made a study of trace elements in the mineral waters and devised methods for their detection. He also made many other contributions in the chemistry of the mineral waters and, based on his findings, proposed a theory of the origin of the Saratoga mineral waters. He left the spa in 1952 to take a position in private industry.

Dr. Walter McClellan, who came to the Spa as Medical Director in 1931, retired in 1953 after twenty-two years of service. During this period he conducted much valuable research on the mineral waters, investigating their therapeutic effect on the human body. As a result of this research he became an international authority on mineral waters. His work was recognized all over the world and is still referred to in papers published in many languages. Dr. Frank Reynolds of the World Health Organization replaced him as Medical Director. Dr. Reynolds remained at the Spa only from September 1953 until April 1955.

In October 1953, Pierpont B. Noyes, who had been chairman of the Saratoga Springs Commission since 1930 and president of the Saratoga Springs Authority since its beginning, resigned by letter to Governor Thomas E. Dewey, stating that "while I have enjoyed and still enjoy my work as chairman of the Saratoga Springs Commission, I believe that the time has come to retire in favor of a younger man."

A resolution was unanimously adopted by the Saratoga Springs Commission in recognition of Mr. Noyes' outstanding service to the Spa. It included the following verse:

"All hearts grow warmer in the presence
Of one who, seeking not his own,
Gives freely for the love of giving
Nor reaps, for self, the harvest sown."

The untimely death of Herbert (Doc) Ant in 1954 was a great loss to the Spa. He came to the Spa in 1914 and for forty years served as chemist. During this time he analyzed the waters of all of the mineral springs and periodically checked them and recorded any variation in their composition. Based on his knowledge of the waters, he proposed a theory on the source of the minerals contained in them.

In November 1956, Cyrus B. Elmore retired. He had been associated with the Saratoga Spa since 1915 when he was first engaged as an engineer. In 1932, on the death of Mr. John G. Jones, he was appointed superintendent of the Spa, a post he held until his retirement. In 1933 he visited and made a study of European spas. On his retirement the position of superintendent of the Spa was jointly covered by assistant director Walter R. Moore and Arthur J. Kearney, water sales consultant, until the appointment in 1958 of David Liston, M.D. as director.

Following World War II and the signing of the peace treaty, Germany, by the terms of the treaty, became responsible for the rehabilitation of the survivors of the Holocost. Many of these people had suffered severe injuries from the experiments that were performed on them by German doctors while they were in concentration camps. Many were permanently incapacitated. Following the war a large number of these people came to the United States, and many of them chose to have spa therapy and so came to Saratoga for treatment, all of which was paid for by the German government.

It was a most enlightening experience for the Spa staff to see these people with their scars and deformities caused by cruel treatment at the concentration camps, and to talk to them and learn of the incredible torture and suffering they survived. These people had phenomenal capacity to endure the suffering which seemed, from their description, to have been far beyond the limits of human endurance. One had the feeling, after seeing them, that even the most we could do for them would be far too little to in any way compensate for what they had been through. It was gratifying to see at the end of their treatment how grateful they were for the baths and other treatments they had received at the Spa and how much improved all of them were after their stay in Saratoga. These people, with their European background, appreciated spas. It was all a way of life in Europe and they had great confidence in the ability of the waters to heal. For that reason they were very satisfactory patients and the experience of caring for them was quite rewarding.

There are still, at the present time, a number of these people coming to the Spa. They place great confidence in the ability of the mineral waters to help them, and look forward to their visits.

In 1954, at the convention of the American Congress of Physical Medicine in Washington, D.C., a group of people interested in spas and spa therapy met to form an organization to promote interest in and a greater understanding of the use of the mineral waters of America. The organization was known as the Association of American Spas. The Saratoga Spa was represented at this meeting by Dr. Frank W. Reynolds, the medical director, and Leon Woodworth, information secretary. Standards were set for membership in the organization, the most important being that to be a member of the organization the spa must be under medical direction. Twenty spas became charter members.

The first annual meeting of the Association was held in 1955 at Safety Harbor Spa on Tampa Bay in Florida. Dr. Walter McClellan, former medical director of the Saratoga Spa, attended this meeting and gave a paper. The Association's second meeting was held at the Saratoga Spa and Sharon Springs Spa in September 1956.

Many of the members of this association are still active in the interest of spas as members of the American Society of Medical Hydrology and Climatology which is affiliated with the International Society of Medical Hydrology and Climatology. These societies include in their membership directors and officials of all of the leading spas of the world. The International Society holds a congress every two years. Its thirtieth congress was held in Vittel and Nancy in Lorraine, France in November 1986. Representatives of many countries convened there to report and compare the results of their observations and research carried on at various spas all over the world. The papers presented showed a wealth of achievement in the field of medical hydrology and emphasized the preventive and social value of spa therapy as well as its therapeutic value.

This society, since its organization in 1921, has fulfilled the goal of its founders by assuring the development of scientific hydrology and keeping very much alive the interest in spas and mineral water therapy.

Many physicians, as well as other persons interested in spa therapy, visited the Saratoga Spa over the years. All were impressed with the very fine facilities and the picturesque beauty of the grounds and buildings. All expressed surprise that so many Americans went to European spas for treatments when America had such a fine spa as Saratoga in their own country.

A group of French doctors who visited the Spa were especially impressed by what they saw. This group of about twenty physicians, all directors of spas in France, were on a tour of American spas in the course of which they were entertained at the Saratoga Spa. They were taken on a tour of the Spa buildings and grounds, and each was given a mineral bath and massage, after which all took part in an informal discussion with members of the Spa staff and some of the Spa commissioners. Their surprise at finding such a beautiful, well-equipped and well-run spa in America was interesting to see. They wondered why Europeans did not come to America for spa therapy and expressed the opinion that if Europeans knew of the existence of such a beautiful spa as Saratoga they would certainly avail themselves of it.

From the time of his first association with the Saratoga Spa, Bernard Baruch had insisted that the Spa should be under medical direction and that the patrons should be checked by a physician and have special therapy prescribed before taking the mineral baths or other forms of therapy. This is the procedure that is followed in European spas. Having seen the fine results of spa therapy as it is employed in Europe, he firmly believed that the Saratoga Spa should be administered in the same way. The 1929 Baruch report submitted to the Legislature by Governor Roosevelt requesting appropriation for the "new" Saratoga Spa included specific provisions calling for the Spa to be operated under medical direction. From time to time Mr. Baruch expressed disappointment that his recommendation had not been completely carried out since patrons were allowed to take mineral baths without a doctor's prescription. When, during the 1950's the Spa declined, Mr. Baruch reiterated his belief that the Spa would not have deteriorated to the point that it had if it had been conducted as are European spas.

In the middle of the 1950's the survival of the Spa was threatened when a joint commission on coordination of state activities known as the "Little Hoover" Commission, after investigation, recommended that the Spa be abolished and the property made into a park. At the same time the Legislature cut a large slice of the budget appropriation for the Spa. At about this time the Saratoga Spa Commission decided to follow Mr. Baruch's recommendation and provide greater medical control at the Saratoga Spa.

With the cooperation of the Saratoga County Medical Society, a plan was devised whereby the Society would cooperate with the Spa to provide greater medical coverage. The plan called for a medical screening program, the value of which was to be determined by a pilot program to be set up for a period of three months during which time patients could be screened if they so desired. The screening, to be done by Medical Society members on a voluntary basis, would include a physical examination with indicated laboratory tests and a prescription for appropriate spa therapy. At the end of the course of therapy, another physical examination would be conducted, with a report to be sent to the patient's physician.

The sum of $30,000 was requested for this pilot project. The Republican Legislature, however, cut out the $30,000 which had been included in the budget by Governor Harriman. In addition, many other items were eliminated from the budget resulting in a cut of $111,615 from the Spa appropriation, leaving an amount far short of that necessary to operate the Spa.

The problem of insufficient funds appropriated to operate the Spa had been gradually accelerating for twenty years or more. There was great dissatisfaction among the legislators because the expenses of the Spa exceeded the income from operations. They insisted that the Spa was costing the state $500,000 a year, which was a great exaggeration. It was also claimed that an appropriation of this sum could not be justified because an insufficient number of people were enjoying the Spa, as, for example, compared with Jones Beach where the per capita expenditure was much less than that of the Spa. The Saratoga people and others interested in the Spa believed that the basic problem was the fact that the legislators were not getting enough political patronage value out of the money spent for Saratoga. The Saratoga Springs Commission insisted that, according to law, the Spa was to be a part of the public health policy of the state and was never intended to produce revenue. It was essentially a service for the people of the state just as were many other tax-supported facilities which the Legislature supported with sufficient appropriations without question.

When Nelson Rockefeller became Governor of New York State in 1959, he put the Saratoga Spa on a "pay its own way" basis. In 1960 an appropriation of $400,000 was cut from the state budget. This represented the difference between income and expenditures for the fiscal year beginning in April. The underlying philosophy behind this move was that the spa should be self-supporting. It was suggested that this be accomplished by restricting unprofitable service, charging a higher fee for service, cracking down on passes which were issued to selected individuals such as physicians and state officials and cutting out some of the "fluff." These were suggestions that were included in the report of the "Little Hoover" Commission.

In 1960 Governor Rockefeller signed a bill permitting the Saratoga Springs Authority to sell five parcels of land which they owned in the City of Saratoga Springs. These included the High Rock and Peerless Springs on High Rock

Avenue, the Broadway Drink Hall, the Hathorn #1 Spring and the parking lot on the corner of Putnam and Spring Streets. An agreement was made between the Authority and the City which specified that the City would develop an historic park around the springs on High Rock Avenue, and that the property which included the Hathorn #1 Spring and the parking lot on Putnam Street would be used for park, recreation or playground. The latter two properties were purchased in 1965 for one dollar each and in 1968 the High Rock properties were purchased for the same price. This left only three state-owned properties in the city, namely the Congress and Columbian Springs in Congress Park and the Old Red Spring at Excelsior and High Rock Avenues.

The Conservation Commission, under pressure to make the Spa self-supporting by making it attractive to more people, conceived the idea of constructing a recreation center using 800 acres of undeveloped state-owned land on the Reservation. In 1960, at the request of Conservation Commissioner Harold G. Wilm, a special committee of the State Council of Parks was appointed by Robert Moses, Chairman of the Council. The committee was headed by L. L. Huttleson, Assistant Director of State Parks. It was charged with the task of advising on development of the undeveloped land on the Reservation, with the twofold objective of "first, development to the greatest extent possible of those portions of the Reservation available for broad public recreation; and second, provision of facilities to supplement the present Spa use, which would not only be self-supporting, but would, by broadening the attraction of the Spa, serve to reverse the trend of increasing losses in its operation."

An appropriation of $40,000 was obtained with which to carry out an engineering survey of the Reservation.

On July 5, 1960, the consulting engineering firm of Arnold H. Volmer Associates was retained to prepare a survey and master plan for the development of the Reservation to accommodate these expanded uses. The firm presented a preliminary report to a joint meeting of the State Council of Parks and the Saratoga Springs Authority on July 14, 1960. The recommendations for proposed park facilities included:

• A swimming pool complex capable of serving up to 8,000 persons daily.
• Picnic sites for 1,000 families.
• Group picnicking areas with a total capacity of 3,000 people, designed for use by organizations.
• Expansion of the present 9-hole golf course to 18 holes of championship character.
• Improvement of Hall of Springs as a dignified but popular priced dining and dancing pavilion.
• Modification of other existing structures for park maintenance and operational uses.
• Revamping of the road system to permit better control, and to separate the areas of intensive park use from the Spa itself.

Total cost of these improvements was estimated at $2,700,000 with con-

Picnic Area in Geyser Park

Bridge in Geyser Park

struction to be carried on over a three-year period.

A letter of protest was sent to the committee by the Saratoga Springs Chamber of Commerce. This letter represented the feelings of the citizens of the city and the County of Saratoga as well as the business men and women, and the professional organizations of the community. They expressed the opinion that over the past years there had been a deliberate plan to abolish the Saratoga Spa and to divert its facilities to uses other than those for which they were designed. They viewed this last project as the final blow that would strike the death knell of the Spa.

Letters were also received from other citizens of the state, all of whom were opposed to the "vacation" approach embodied in the 2.7 million dollar plan; believing that it would destroy "the unique value of a wonderful spa." They did not object to the planned recreation area, but they regretted its closeness to the Spa, feeling that it would be a disturbing element to the serenity of the Spa. They expressed the opinion that there were many other areas where such a recreation center could be developed without invading Spa territory.

Bernard Baruch felt very deeply about the plan. In a letter he stated: "The Saratoga Spa was not undertaken as a recreation center, but as a spa in hopes that it would be the greatest in America, if not the world. It was undertaken after an examination by the Academy of Medicine of New York, whose president appointed the Commission. It had been advocated for many years previously by George Foster Peabody and Governors Miller and Smith. Upon recommendation of a committee appointed by the then Governor Roosevelt of which I was chairman, the work on the Spa was commenced, but only after an exhaustive study here and abroad."

In spite of the many protests, the project was undertaken, and so, with its beginning, the Spa was on its way to losing its identity as the finest in America and probably the world, to become another state park. Contrarily, in the words of the Committee of the State Council of Parks, it was to become "the most attractive recreation center in the Northeast." With the completion of the project, the state-owned Spa, in reality became a state-owned recreation center with recreation activities eclipsing Spa activities.

In 1966, a cultural dimension was added to Saratoga Springs with the opening of the Saratoga Performing Arts Center, popularly known as SPAC. The idea of such a center had gradually been taking root. Its concept was compatible with that of a spa. Among the local people who actively supported the idea was Robert McKelvey, who personally raised money for it by soliciting donations from many of the residents of Saratoga Springs. With the support of numerous wealthy and influential people, the idea of such a center finally became a reality. SPAC was established as an autonomous, non-profit organization to build and operate the center. An area in the vicinity of the Vale of Springs on the Reservation was selected as the ideal location for the project. The site preparation work and parking facilities were built by the state, and an amphitheater costing 3.5 million dollars was built by SPAC. It has a seating capacity of 3,500 in the orchestra, 1,600 in the balcony and 7,000 on the sloping lawns.

George Balanchine, with his inimitable New York City Ballet, was induced to take a summer residence in Saratoga Springs and to perform at the Center in the month of July; while Eugene Ormandy and the peerless Philadelphia Orchestra were persuaded to make Saratoga Springs their summer home in August and to give concerts during that month.

SPAC has been a great asset to the community. It has increased in popularity season after season and has come to be identified with Saratoga as much as the Saratoga Spa has.

In July 1970 when several departments of the state were reorganized, operation of the Saratoga Springs Reservation was transferred from the Conservation Department to the newly organized Office of Parks and Recreation in the Executive Department.

In September 1972, under the Parks and Recreation Law (Chapter 36B of the Consolidated Laws of 1972), the Saratoga Springs Commission and the Capital State Parks Commission were merged into a new agency, the Saratoga Capital District State Park and Recreation Commission. From that time on the Saratoga Spa has been administered by the Saratoga Springs Commission which is now a division of this department. The Saratoga Spa Authority came to an end on March 31, 1961 when all of its outstanding obligations were retired by state appropriation.

One of the problems that contributed greatly to the decrease in the number of people visiting the Spa was the shortage of masseurs and masseuses. Most people, when they came to the bath house, requested a mineral bath and a massage. When they were informed that, due to the shortage, they could have the mineral bath but no massage, they stopped coming. When in 1968 a law was passed requiring that all persons operating as masseurs or masseuses be licensed by the New York State Professional Education Division of the State Education Deparmtent, those who had been practicing without a license had to stop. As the problem became more acute, it seemed that the only way to ensure an adequate supply of personnel to administer massages was for the Spa to train their own.

With the cooperation of Saratoga-Warren County Board of Cooperative Education Services (BOCES) and Skidmore College, the Saratoga Spa School of Massage was organized. Using the science laboratories of Skidmore and the physical therapy facilities of the Spa, the first class of twenty students started in January 1970. The course of study was that prescribed by the New York State Department of Education. The curriculum called for 500 hours of instruction consisting of 300 hours of classroom instruction in the basic sciences, including anatomy, physiology, myology, neurology, pathology, hygiene, first aid and massage techniques. An additional 200 hours were devoted to hands-on instruction in massage technique and practice. These requirements were to be increased in 1973 to a total of 1,200 hours, 400 of which would consist of massage practice under supervision.

The first class, which began in January 1970, was graduated in December

1970 and to gain licensure, the graduates took the state board examinations on completion of the course.

A second class was graduated in 1972. Unfortunately this was the last class to be graduated. State funds, which had supported the project, were withdrawn, and the school, which, even in a short two years, had become known as one of the finest in the country, had to be discontinued.

Since the School of Massage was discontinued, the Saratoga Spa has continued to suffer from the lack of masseurs and masseuses. Realizing the importance of having a source of trained licensed personnel, the Saratoga School of Massage is to be opened again in 1988 and operated under the management of BOCES.

The Spa continued to have trouble with the mineral baths due to underfunding. In 1971 funds for operating the Lincoln Bath House were cut completely from the budget. For this reason the Lincoln did not open that season. The large number of people who, over the years, had been coming to the Lincoln Bath House in July and August, felt stranded. With its limited capacity, the Washington Bath House was unable to handle the increased number who were in the habit of going to the Lincoln. The result was total confusion. Crowds of people gathered on the porch and lawn of the Washington Bath House unable to gain admission. They were held back by a park ranger assigned to the job. There was a very long wait to be admitted for a mineral bath and some were never accommodated. Such a situation resulted in great harm to the public image of the Spa and did incalculable harm to its public relations.

In spite of the many abuses, there were people who did not accept the idea that the Spa must die. Support groups were formed from time to time, and attempts were made to create interest in the Spa as a spa. "Save Our Spa" was such a group. However, not having the kind of support that the early Spa had in such men as Spencer Trask, George Foster Peabody and Franklin Roosevelt, adequate political clout was lacking, and they were never able to get support of the Legislature to operate the Spa in an acceptable manner.

In 1978 a group of concerned citizens headed by Mary Ann Lynch, banded together in a desperate effort to save the Spa as a spa. They formed a nonprofit, non-partisan organization which they called "Friends of the Spa" whose purpose was to restore it as a creditably operated spa with well-maintained bath houses.

Letters were sent to the Spa Commission and to selected legislators as follows:

> FRIENDS OF THE SPA is a non-profit, non-partisan organization whose primary goal is to ensure that the Saratoga mineral waters, and in particular the mineral baths and related activities, continue to be made available to the public at large as a public health service and historic tourist attraction.
>
> We believe, as the State of New York has proclaimed in a Spa brochure, that "without the Saratoga waters, there would be no

Saratoga Spa." And we believe, as history has demonstrated, that Saratoga is indeed "The Queen of Spas," and we want her to retain rights to that title.

Unfortunately the last two decades have seen a steady pattern of decline in the staffing, programs and facilities pertaining to the mineral baths. With no attention to maintenance, with virtually no promotion, and with a continuing decrease in services available as well as adequate, well trained staff, the mineral baths, though still "available" to the public, are in fact a far cry from anything that merits the title "Queen of Spas."

Increasingly, emphasis has been placed on the park aspect of the Saratoga Spa. As cross-country ski trails, skating rinks, outdoor activities, the Performing Arts Center and even Artists-in-the-Parks programs have been developed, all of which have required very large outlays of capital, the mineral baths themselves have been all but forgotten. While officials at the Parks level testify to their support for "keeping the baths open," in reality their hands are tied in the absence of monetary appropriations for even a basic maintenance of the mineral bath facilities.

Thus in 1979 we find that at the "Queen of Spas" it is impossible, for instance, for two people to visit the baths together, have a bath and a massage (the basic treatment) and leave at the same time. Since only one masseuse or masseur is available, it follows that only one massage can be given during one time period. Attempts to promote the mineral baths as they are, with the present staff and facilities, probably do more harm than good. Only a year ago a promotion campaign conducted by the Saratoga Springs Chamber of Commerce resulted in overflow crowds who had to be turned away. That was business lost, not gained.

FRIENDS OF THE SPA is not asking for support for a new program. They are asking that the State honor their commitment to keep the mineral baths open as a public health service, and include the bath facilities in their budget.

PARK OPERATIONS "includes all activities related to the planning, operation and maintenance of recreational facilities within the State's 11 park regions." Although the mineral baths are not mentioned as part of the State Park System, they do fall under its jurisdiction. The budget states that "to provide equal opportunity for everyone to enjoy the park system in 1978-79, the Office of Parks and Recreation will develop and implement a plan for the systematic maintenance and replacement of all park equipment." We would like to see bath facilities and equipment included in this plan. At the present time, the Parks have been removing mineral bath fixtures and tubs and converting bath-related spaces to other uses rather than proceeding with a program of "systematic maintenance and replacement."

We would encourage the Departments of Health and Commerce to take a special and active interest in the potential of the Saratoga Spa mineral baths, when restored to an active state, to serve vital needs of the public at large. The waters are a unique natural resource which can bring major economic returns to the Capital District area and to the State as well through tourism and related industries. In addition the Spa, with its vacant and in some cases converted facilities, could once again be a major research center in the use of hydrotherapy for chronic diseases as well as part of a preventive approach to disease. While other states develop health resorts and find them major tourist attractions, New York State allows its unique and world-famous spa to be neglected.

In 1908 New York State saw fit to take possession of the mineral waters to insure that so great a resource would not be lost.

In 1979, after the Golden Years of years gone by, when Saratoga earned its distinction as the "Queen of Spas," and after years of neglect, the pendulum has swung in another direction. If indeed the State does regard the mineral baths as a financial burden and liabiltiy; if they are unwilling to undertake an active effort to formulate a systematic plan for revitalization and restoration of the Spa, then it is doing the public a great disservice to allow the Spa mineral baths to continue in their present state of decline and offer the public no option.

If the State cannot, or will not, take advantage of the enormous economic and social potential of the Spa, then we feel the State should actively seek other sources of funding, support and development in the federal, public and private sector.

But as long as the Saratoga Spa is "owned and operated" by the State of New York, we feel it a prime responsibility that the State once again include the mineral baths in thier budget decisions, and in their plans for expansion of tourism and recreational activities. Towards this end, we feel that the creation of a committee or commission which would address itself towards the Saratoga mineral baths and waters and their potential in economic and social/health terms would be an appropriate starting point.

Citizens have been fighting for the Saratoga Spa for years, and the pleas of past employees and citizens groups seem to have never been heard. The baths have been kept open, but the issue has been larger than simply keeping them open; we believe it is in the best interest of the State and Nation for the Saratoga mineral baths to be rehabilitated, revitalized, properly staffed and promoted. Governor Carey in his recent message to the Legislature stated that his "primary emphasis will continue to be health, education and preventive care." In addition he looks to means to increase tourism. The Spa mineral waters, when fully developed, contribute to each of these areas and could have an impact that has yet to be assessed. We urge Governor Carey and the Commissioners of Parks and Recreation, Commerce and Health to look once again at a unique natural treasure and to consider its potential.

In March 1982 the New York State Office of Parks, Recreation and Historic Preservation (OPRHP), aware of its responsibility to do something about the baths and other facilities at the Spa before further deterioration occurred, commissioned a comprehensive study to evaluate the feasibility of various marketing and programming options for the future use of the Spa facilities, including the mineral baths. The purpose of the study was to explore types of health/recreation facilities which might be developed at the Spa and to investigate the possibility of securing private investment and management for such facilities. In the final analysis the solution would have to attract private investment and at the same time be compatible with the traditional use of the Spa.

The study entitled "A Marketing and Programming Study at the Saratoga Mineral Baths and State Park" was conducted by Jeanne V. Beekhuis, as primary contractor, working in association with four subcontracting firms and two expert consultants. The scope of the study included five analytic components: 1. Evaluation of the resource base in Saratoga Spa State Park and surrounding area; 2. Identification and evaluation of Comparable Programs and Facilities in other places which might be adaptable to the Saratoga situation; 3. Development and preliminary evaluation of alternative development options; 4. Feasibility studies of recommended projects, and 5. Implementation strategy.

From a group of several prototypes for development at the Saratoga Spa State Park, suggested by the contractors after a comprehensive study and thorough analysis of the situation by all members of the contractor groups, the OPRHP chose, for detailed feasibility investigation, three mutually complimentary projects: the Bath/Fitness Center, the Rehabilitation Institute and the Seasonal Bath House. The creation of a total wellness center was envisioned which would reinstate the Saratoga Spa as an outstanding health center and an international spa. The baths and buildings would be saved and the traditional medical direction of the Saratgoa Spa would be revived. The Bath/Fitness Center would be located in the Roosevelt Bath Houses, numbers 1 and 2. At Bath House #1 the traditional mineral bath in carbonated mineral water would be presented to visitors with the idea of reducing stress through relaxation and balneotherapy. At the Roosevelt Bath House #2 a program for reducing stress and improving health would be offered. The Saratoga Rehabilitation Institute, to be located in the Lincoln Baths building, would provide programs for the disabled to improve the quality of life for those who have suffered from cardiac, stroke, arthritis, alcohol and other disabilities by helping them readapt to the activities of daily life.

The Office of Parks, Recreation and Historical Preservation solicited, from interested parties, bids and proposals that would combine recreation-oriented baths and fitness facilites in one financially viable package. The main objectives of the state were to obtain: 1. The best approach to creating a total wellness center in the State Park, one that has potential to achieve regional, even national, status; 2. The best approach to saving the Saratoga baths, a primary goal of the state; 3. Maximum economic utilization of the buildings in question, and minimum new construction; 5. Maximum financial return to the state.

From the bids and proposals received by the OPRHP, one was selected, and a fifteen-year contract with option of a five-year renewal was awarded to the firm of T/W Recreational Services for management of the Gideon Putnam Hotel and the Roosevelt Bath Houses #1 and #2. It was agreed that T/W Recreational Services would invest the sum of 5.2 million dollars to rehabilitate the hotel and the bath houses, making a fine mineral bath center of the Roosevelt #1 bath house and a health-related facility of the Roosevelt #2.

In addition, Governor Cuomo submitted a request to the Legislature for 13.5 million dollars to be used to repair and restore the other buildings of the Spa. The Lincoln Bath House will continue to be operated by the state.

At long last it appears that the Saratoga Spa may be about to experience a renaissance.

22

The Future of the Saratoga Spa

*"Ill health of body or of mind is defeat. Health
alone is victory. Let all men, if they can manage
it, contrive to be healthy."*

—Sir Walter Scott

The time may well come again when the American people will realize what a valuable treatment modality they have in spa therapy as available at the Saratoga Spa; when they will realize the value of the revitalization and sense of well-being that follows a course of spa therapy.

We are living in the atomic age, the age of computers, rockets and fast foods. Today's hurried life style is not conducive to good health. The pressures and competition in our society have a devastating effect on people. They live in an environment of tension, the result of which is the development of hypertension and other degenerative cardiovascular diseases in a large percentage of the population. Many of our most productive citizens die prematurely as a result.

The scientific advances in medicine in our day have been mind-boggling. However, they have proven to be a two-edged sword. We find that we are living in a "push button" age where machines give the diagnosis much faster and more accurately than the instruments used by doctors in the old days. Vaccines, antibiotics and other pharmaceutical products are able to perform miracles, and they have saved millions of lives. For all of these great advances we are truly grateful and we gasp when we contemplate what the future may hold for us. But on the other side of the coin is the fact that our people have come to rely too much on these wonders. We sometimes expect more from them than they are capable of delivering. We have come to the point where we

266

believe that anything that cannot be cured by an antibiotic or a shot, or prevented by immunization, is incurable. We must not forget that our bodies must still perform basic physiological functions. Even the best machinery needs to be maintained properly. It cannot suffer excessive abuse without ill effects. To remain healthy our bodies must be maintained in the best possible physical condition. This is where good physiological living comes in. This is where we see the importance of sensible living which includes proper diet, rest, exercise, relaxation, recreation and, most important of all, a healthy mental attitude. In the rush of modern life these are the very things the average person is likely to neglect. It is all too easy to skip a meal or to "grab" some fast food when we are pushed for time. The same is true of exercise, relaxation and recreation. Too often these important necessities of life are placed on the bottom of our list of "things to do today." Too often do we let ourselves, in stressful situations, become "uptight" because of fatigue and an unhealthy mental attitude. Over a period of time we find that we are on a merry-go-round and we can't get off. It is in just such situations as this that spa therapy is of inestimable value.

In many countries of the world, especially in Europe and Japan, medically supervised spas have long been accepted, by both physicians and laymen, as an important component of health care, not only for the treatment of certain ailments, but also as a form of preventive therapy. This is especially true in the U.S.S.R. where large sums of money are being invested in spas, and a substantial portion of Soviet medical manpower is being committed to spa therapy.

The Soviet Union has 3,500 spas and some 5,000 reconditioning centers, all of which are owned and administered by the health authorities of the State as a public service. Russia has developed the science of health resorts more than any other country. More than a million people are treated every year in spas, usually at the expense of the Soviet Insurance Fund or trade unions. The development of health resorts has been one of the most brilliant achievements of Soviet medicine.

As in Russia, spas in many countries are owned and administered by the state. In Czechoslovakia there are 52 mineral water health spas and more than 1,900 mineral springs. Every year about 220,000 Czech workers and members of their families are granted free spa treatment for three weeks, paid for by the National Health Insurance Service.

In France, Germany, Belgium and many other countries spas have developed a popular appeal and are supported on a scale which ranks them among the major economic and social enterprises of the country. These spas could not exist without trade union, social security or insurance company support. It stands to reason that spa treatments would not continue to be paid for by these agencies unless they received full value for the money spent on them, and patients could not afford to pay the fees to these agencies unless they were rehabilitated sufficiently to enable them to return to their jobs.

In spite of the fact that spa therapy has been proven beneficial over the centuries and has been accepted and officially sanctioned by many countries in the world, the United States has lagged behind in making use of its many fine mineral springs. Employment of mineral waters for health purposes dates back thousands of years as has the use of other physical agents such as water, sun, climate and the like. Physical medicine is the proud offspring of spa therapy.

Today, especially in the United States, more than ever before there exists a growing awareness of the need to maintain good health. People have become health conscious. This is seen in the number of people who are seriously trying to control their diets according to the dictates of health authorities. The health food industry is thriving. Countless people are jogging or exercising in other ways on a regular basis. Many have discovered that medications and drugs are not the answer to their illness or other problems.

Many signs on the horizon portend a brighter future for the Saratoga Spa, not the least of which is the "back to nature" movement where people are rejecting some modern, sophisticated therapies for a more natural way of healing. Certainly, nature's way may take longer, but one can be sure that there will be no deleterious side effects as are occasionally seen with modern drugs and modalities.

At present, the average person in this country knows nothing about the advantages of spa therapy. Hopefully, in the future, visits to spas may become a way of life for our people as it is for people in many countries in the world.

To accomplish this end, it will be necessary to take the message of the spa to the people. Unfortunately this requires money, and lots of it, for publicity. This is the main reason that the Saratoga Spa declined as it has. The advertising budget has dropped to practically zero, so no money has been available for publicity. Another reason for the decline is the fact that the facilities were allowed to deteriorate, and finally, the service staff was reduced. As a result, even some of the most devoted patrons have stopped coming.

Hope for increased use of the spa is afforded by the Urban Cultural Parks program which was initiated by the State of New York in 1982. The object of this program was to select historical areas in the state with special social, natural or cultural significance and to revitalize them in such a way as to emphasize their unique historic characteristics, and to combine all of these areas into a statewide system that would show the development of the state.

Saratoga Springs was one of the thirteen New York State communities chosen as a site for an Urban Cultural Park because of the community's contribution to the development of the state.

In spite of the ups and downs the Saratoga Spa has experienced over recent years, the fact remains that we still have the mineral springs on the Reservation and they are just as therapeutically effective today as they were fifty or a hundred years ago. With the changing times we must find a new place for these valuable springs.

Appendix

INDIAN DEED FOR KAYADEROSSERAS PATENT
October, 6, 1704

Samson Shelton Broughton Esquire

TO ALL CHRISTIAN PEOPLE to whom this present Writing shall come Joseph Hendrick and Cornelius Owners, Proprietors and native Maquas Indians and Sachims in the Behalf of that Nation send Greeting.

KNOW YE that for and in consideration of sixty Pounds current Money of the Province of New York to them in hand paid, at and before the Ensealing and delivery hereof by Samson Shelton Broughton Esquire Attorney General of the said Province in Company, the Receipt whereof is hereby acknowledged, and of and from every Part and Parcel thereof doth fully Clearly and absolutely acquit Exonorate and discharge him the said Samson Shelton Broughton Esquire in Company their Heirs Executors Administrators and Assigns for ever have therefore granted bargained Sold Aliened Released Enfeoffed Conveyed and Confirmed and by these Presents do fully clearly and absolutely grant Bargain sell Alien Release Enfeoffe Convey and confirm unto the said Samson Shelton Broughton Esquire in Company all that Certain Tract or Parcell of Wood Land situate lying and being in the County of Albany in the Province aforesaid Called or known by the name of Kayaderrosres adjoining to the North Bounds of Schoneghtade Patent together with the vacancy that lies between the ael Place [Aalplaats creek] down along the River about one Mile more or Less on the East Side thereof to the West Bounds of Saratogas Patent, on the North Side thereof to Albany River and on the West Side thereof to the Native Indians and Proprietors thereof for their Improvement, the North Bounds running along said River of Albany, To have and to hold the aforesaid Tract or Parcel of Wood Land and all other the Premises thereunto belonging with all and Singular other the Premisses and Appurtenances Unto him the said Samson Shelton Broughton Esquire and the rest in Company their Heirs and Assigns forever in His and their quiet and peacable possession and enjoyment forever In Testimony whereof and said Indian Proprietors have hereunto set their Hands and Seals in Albany the Sixth day of October in the third Year of her Majesty's Reign. Anno Domini 1704 Joseph × his Mark (Ls) Hendrick his × Mark (Ls) Gedeon his × Mark (Ls) Amos × his Mark (Ls)

Signed Seal'd and deliverd in the Presence of us being first interpreted by Millitie Van Olinda Sworn Interpreter Hend, Jansen Justus, Johannes Rosseboome Justus, Johannes Cuyler Justis Johannis Mijingode Justis.

Secretary's office New York 2ᵈ October 1764 The above is a true Copy of the Record in this office in Lib: Lycenses to purchase, Warrants Indian Deeds &c 1692 to 1714 page 125 &c Examᵈ By

Gw. Banyar D Secry

[Indorsed]
6 October 1704

Copy Indian Deed for Kayoderosseras

Assembly Chamber Read October 2ᵈ1764

KAYADEROSSERAS PATENT

Ann by the Grace of God of Great Brittain France and Ireland Queen & Defender of the Faith & to all to whom these presents may come or in any wise concerne sendeth greeting Whereas *** loving subjects Nanning Harmense Johannes Beekman Rip Van Dam Ann Bridges May Bickley Peter Fauconnier Adrian Hoghland Johannes Fisher John Tudor Joris Hoghland John Stevens John Tathem and Sampson Broughton by their petition presented to our right trusty and well beloved couzin Edward Vis*ount Cornbury Capt Generall and Govenour in theise of our province of New York and territories depending thereon in Americia and vice admirall of the same ** ** Councill have prayed our grant and confirmation for all that tract of land Situate lying and being in the County of Albany called Kayadorosses alias Queens Borrough beginning at a place on Schenectady river about three miles distant from the Southwesterly corner of the bounds of Nestigione the said place being the Southwesterly corner of the pattent lately granted to Naning Harmense Peter Fauconnier and others thence along the said Schenectady river westerly to the Southeasterly corner of a pattent lately granted to William Apple thence along the Easterly Northerly and Westerly lines of the said William Apples pattent down to the above said river thence to the Schenectady bounds of the Southeasterly corner of the said pattent on the said river soe along the Easterly Northerly and Westerly bounds thereof down to the said river againe thence along the said river up westerly to the Southeasterly bounds of a tract of land lately granted to Ebenezer Willson and John Abeele and along the said pattent round to the Southwesterly corner thereof on the said Schenectady river to a place or hill called Twectenondo being Five miles distant or thereabouts from the said Southwesterly corner of the said Willsons and Abeele pattent thence Northerly to the Northwestmost head of a creeck called Kayadorosses about Fourteen miles more or less thence eight miles more Northerly thence easterly or Northeasterly to the third falls on Albany River about twenty miles more or less thence along the said river down Southwest to the Northeasterly bounds of Sarachtoga thence along the said Sarachtogas Northerly Westerly and Southerly bounds on the said river thence to the

Northeasterly corner of Anthony Van Scaicks land on the said river soe northerly and westerly along the said Van Scaicks pattent to the Northeast corner of the above said pattent granted to Naning Fauconnier and others thence along the Northerly and westerly bounds thereof down to the above said river of Schonectady being the place were it first begun The which petiion wee being willing to grant KNOW YEA that of our especiall grace certaine knowledge and meer moion wee have given granted ratti-fied and confirmed and by these presents for ourselves our heirs and successors Doe give grant ratifie and confirme unto the said Naning Harmense Johannes Beekman Rip Van Dam Ann Bridges May Bickley Peter Fauconnier Adrian Hoghland Johannis Fisher John Tudor Joris Hoghland John Stevens John Tatham and Sampson Broughton their heires and assigns all the before mentioned tract of land and premises and all and singular the Hereditaments and appurtences thereunto belong-ing within the bounds and limits above in these presents mentioned and expressed together with all woods underwoods trees timber feedings pastures meadows marshes swamps ponds pooles waters water courses rivers rivoletts runns and streams of water fishing fowling hawking hunting mines and mineralls standing growing lyeing and being or to be had used or enjoyed within the bounds and limits above expressed and all other proffitts benefits privileges liberties advantages Hereditaments and appurtences whatsoever unto the said land premises or any part or parcell thereof belonging or in any wise appurteyneing in thirteen parts to be divided (Except and always reserved out of this our present grant all gold and Silver mines) TO HAVE AND TO HOLD one thirteenth part of the tract of land and premises aforesaid with the appurtences hereby granted or meant mentioned or intended to be hereby granted as aforesaid unto the said Naning Harmense his heires and assignes forever to the only proper use and behoofe of the said Naning Harmense his heires and assignes forever one other thirteenth part thereof unto the said Johannes Beekman his heires and assignes forever to the only proper use and behoofe of the said Johannes Beekman his heires and assignes forever one other thirtheenth part thereof unto the said Rip Van Dam his heires and assignes forever to the only proper use and behoofe of the said Rip Van Dam his heires and assignes forever one other thirteenth part thereof unto the said Ann Bridges her heires and assignes forever To the only proper use and behoofe of the said Ann Bridges her heires and assignes forever one other thirteenth part thereof unto the said May Bickley his heires and assignes forever To the only proper use and behoofe of the said May Bickley his heires and assignes forever one other thir-teenth part thereof unto the said Peter Fauconnier his heires and assignes forever to the only proper use and behoofe of the said Peter Fauconnier his heires and assignes forever and one thirteenth part thereof unto the said Adrian Hoghland his heires and assignes forever to the only proper use and behoofe of the said Adrian Hoghland his heires and assignes forever one other thirteenth part thereof unto the said Johannes Fisher his heires and assignes forever to the only proper use and behoofe of the said Johannes Fisher his heires and assignes forever one other thirteenth part thereof unto the said John Tudor his heires and assignes forever to the only proper use and behoofe of the said John Tudor his heires and assignes forever one other thirteenth part thereof unto the said Joris Hoghland his heires and assignes forever to the only proper use and behoofe of the said Joris Hoghland his heires and assignes forever one other thirteenth part thereof unto the said John Stevens his heires and assignes forever to the only proper use and behoofe of the said John Stevens his heires and assignes forever one other thirteenth part thereof unto the said John Tatham his heires and assignes forever to the only proper use and behoofe of the said John Tatham his heires and assignes forever and the other thirteenth part thereof unto the said Sampson Broughton his heires and assignes to the only proper use and behoofe of the said Sampson Broughton his heirs and assignes forever (except before excepted) To be holden of us our heires and Successors Successors in free and common Soccage as of our Mannor of East Greenwich in the County of Kent within our Kingdom of Great Brittaine Yielding Rendring and paying therefore yearly and every year from henceforth unto us our heires and successors at our Custom house at New York to our Collector or receiver generall there for the time being at or upon the feast day of ******* of our ******* Virgin Mary (commonly called Lady day) the rent or same of Four pounds currt money of New York in lieu & stead of all other rents dutyes Services and ****** provided always and these presents are upon that condiion that if noe improvent be already had or made upon the sd tract of land hereby granted and ****** any part of ****** thereof that then and in such case they the said Naning Harmense Johannes Beekman Rip Van Dam Ann Bridges May Bickley Peter Fauconnier Adrian Hoghland Johannes Fisher John Tudor Joris Hoghland John Stevens John Tatham and Sampson Broughton theire heires & assignes some or one of them shall within the time and ****** of seven years now next following from and after the date hereof settle clear and make improvment of or upon some part or parcel thereof IN TESTIMONY WHEREOF wee have caused these our Letters to be made pattente and the Seale of our said province of New York to our said letters pattents to be affixed and the same to be recorded in the Secrys office of our said province WITNESS our right trusty and well beloved Couzin Edward Viscount Cornbury Capt Generall and Governor ****** in and over our said province of New York and territories depending thereon in Americia and Vice Admirall of the same &c in Councill at our Fort this second day of November   in the seventh year of our reigne Anno**Domini 1708

L.S.   Geo. Clarke

(Verbatim translation of the Kayaderosseras Patent including Old English wording. Asterisks designate illegible portions.)

BILL FOR THE SARATOGA RESERVATION

LAWS OF NEW YORK, 1909.

Chap. 569.

AN ACT to authorize the selection, location and appropriation of certain lands in the town of Saratoga Springs, for a state reservation, and to preserve the natural mineral springs therein located, and making an appropriation therefor, and authorizing an issue of bonds to pay such appropriation.

Became a law May 29, 1909, with the approval of the Governor.
Passed by a two-thirds vote.

The People of the State of New York, represented in Senate and Assembly, do enact as follows:

Section 1. Within ten days after the passage of this act, there shall be appointed by the governor, by and with the consent of the senate, three commissioners, each of whom shall be a resident of the state of New York, and such persons thus appointed are hereby constituted a board under the name and style of "The Commissioners of the State Reservation at Saratoga Springs." Each of said commissioners shall hold office for the term of five years from the time of his appointment and until another is appointed in his place. No member of said board shall receive any compensation for his services, but each commissioner shall be entitled to receive his actual disbursements for his expenses in performing the duties of his office. In case of a vacancy in said board, it shall be filled by appointment by the governor, and the person appointed to such vacancy shall hold his office for the term of five years from the time of his appointment, and until another shall be appointed in his place. *[margin: Commissioners of reservation, appointment. Terms. No compensation. Disbursements. Filling vacancies.]*

§ 2. It shall be the duty of said board, and it shall have power, from time to time, to select and locate such lands in the town of Saratoga Springs, in the county of Saratoga, and any rights, easements, or interest upon or in any lands in said town, as it shall deem proper and necessary to be taken for the purpose of preserving the natural mineral springs in said town of Saratoga Springs, and of restoring said springs to their former natural condition, and for that purpose, to acquire any rights, easements, or interest in any property, the whole of which it shall not acquire, for the purpose of protecting the springs or mineral water rights upon any lands it shall acquire. Said commissioners shall, from time to time, cause to be made by the state engineer and surveyor maps of such lands which, or rights and easements in which, it shall determine to take, which maps shall be certified by a majority of such commissioners and filed in the office of the secretary of state and in the Saratoga county clerk's office, and shall specify with respect to *[margin: Board to acquire lands and rights therein to perserve mineral springs. Maps of lands selected.]*

each piece of such land, whether the whole title thereof is to be taken, and if the whole is not to be taken, the rights, easements or interest therein, that is taken. From time of the filing of any such map, the title of the lands, or rights, easements, or interests therein specified, shall become the property of the state of New York, and shall constitute a portion of the reservation herein provided for.

Title, when to vest in State.

§ 3. Said board, by a majority vote of its members, shall have the power at any time within sixty days after the filing of any such map, to fix and determine with each and any of the respective owners of any lands, rights, easements, or interest specified on such map thus filed, upon the fair value of such lands, rights, easements, or interest, and may agree upon a price to be paid therefor by the state, and accepted by said owners, respectively, and the amount thus agreed upon shall be audited by the comptroller and shall be paid therefor by the state treasurer, upon the certificate of said board, and upon the written approval of the governor, out of any funds appropriated for that purpose. In case said board shall not agree with the owner, or owners, of said lands, rights, easements, or interest, within the said sixty days from the filing of such map specifying such property, then such owner, or owners, may recover judgement for the value thereof in the court of claims, as a claim against the state.

Agreement as to value and payment.

Court of Claims to have jurisdiction where no agreement.

§ 4. From and after the acquisition of any piece of land by the board, as hereinbefore provided, the same shall be kept, and remain, and be known, as a part of the state reservation at Saratoga Springs, for the purposes of restoring, and forever preserving, the mineral springs and wells and mineral water, and the natural carbonic acid gas on, and in, and under said lands, and the rights, easements and interest acquired in, or upon, or over, lands, the fee of which shall not be acquired by such board, shall be held for the restoration, and perpetual preservation, of the mineral springs and wells, the mineral water and natural carbonic acid gas on, in or under the lands thus acquired. No part of such lands, rights, easements or interest thus acquired. No part of such lands, rights, easements or interest thus acquired, shall be sold without the express direction of the legislature.

Lands or rights therein acquired to become part of reservation.

To be sold only by direction of Legislature. Board to have control of reservation.

§ 5. Said board shall have the care, custody and control of said reservation, and of all the mineral springs, wells, mineral water and natural carbonic acid gas thereon, therein, or thereunder, and of all the rights, easements, and interests acquired by it; it may prescribe and publish and enforce all proper regulations for the maintanance and care and protection of said properties, and may grant concessions and leases of any portion of the same upon terms to be fixed by it, and may limit and prescribe the terms upon which any excess of mineral water not used on said premises shall be sold and the labels to

May grant concessions.

Sale of excess mineral water.

be attached thereto, or may, itself, sell such excess of water, and any violation of any regulation of said commission may be punished as a misdemeanor; it may hire such employees and *Employees.* do such things as shall be found necessary, from time to time, to restore, preserve and protect said properties, and the expense thereof shall be paid from the revenue derived from sales of water or rentals from leases of said properties. All sums *Sums received to be paid into state treasury.* received by said commission shall be paid into the state treasury, and all the expenses of said commission shall be paid upon the warrant of the comptroller; it shall report in writing each year to the legislature, specifying, in detail, its receipts *Annual report.* and expenditures for such year.

§ 6. The sum of six hundred thousand dollars ($600,000), or *Appropriation.* so much thereof as may be needed, is hereby appropriated for the purchase of such lands, rights, easements and interest by said board, and the payment of any judgments that may be recovered therefor in the court of claims as hereinbefore provided. The state comptroller, upon the written request of such *Bond issue.* board, is hereby authorized and directed to borrow not more than six hundred thousand dollars for the purposes specified in this act, and to issue bonds or certificates of the state therefor payable within ten years from their date, bearing interest at a rate not exceeding five per centum per annum, and which shall not be sold at less than par. The sum hereby appropriated *Sum appropriated, how paid.* shall be payable on the order of such board, and upon the written approval of the governor, by the treasurer on the warrant of the comptroller, only out of the moneys realized from the sale of such bonds or certificates.

§ 7. This act shall take effect immediately.

BROWN-ESMOND BILL
ACT CREATING THE TEMPORARY COMMISSION

LAWS OF NEW YORK, 1929

Chap. 668

AN ACT creating a temporary commission to make a study and survey of the mineral springs at Saratoga with a view to further development for health purposes, and making an appropriation for the expenses of the commission.

Became a law April 16, 1929, with the approval of the Governor.
Passed, three-fifths being present

THE PEOPLE OF THE STATE OF NEW YORK, represented in Senate and Assembly, do enact as follows:

Section 1. A temporary state commission is hereby created, consisting of one senator, to be appointed by the temporary president of the senate, one member of the assembly, to be appointed by the speaker of the assembly, the temporary president of the senate, the speaker of the assembly, and three members to be appointed by the governor, to make a comprehensive study and survey of the mineral springs at Saratoga, the advisability of the further development, for health purposes, of such springs and of facilities for their increased use by the public and the extent and character of the development thereof which may be practicable, and, for the above purposes, to investigate generally the value of mineral springs and of their development for health purposes.

§ 2. Such commission shall elect a chairman and a vice-chairman from its own members and may employ such assistants as may be needed and may fix their compensation within the amount appropriated by this act and available therefor. Such commission may sit anywhere within or without the state, may take testimony, subpoena witnesses and require the production of books, records and papers, and otherwise have all the powers of a legislative committee under the legislative law. Vacancies in the membership of the commission occurring from any cause, shall be filled by the officer authorized to make the original appointment and from the same group.

§ 3. The members of such commission shall receive no compensation for their services, but shall be entitled to their necessary traveling and hotel expenses within and without the state, incurred in the performance of their duties. Such commission shall make a report to the legislature on or before March first, nineteen hundred thirty, with its recommendations, and accompanying such report with such proposed legislative bills as it may deem necessary to carry its recommendations into effect.

§ 4. The sum of fifty thousand dollars ($50,000), or so much thereof as may be needed, is hereby appropriated, payable from the state treasury on the audit and warrant of the comptroller, on the certificate of the chairman of such commission.

§ 5. This act shall take effect immediately.

ACT FOR THE DEVELOPMENT OF THE RESERVATION AS A HEALTH RESORT

LAWS OF NEW YORK, 1930

Chap. 866

AN ACT to provide for the development of the Saratoga Springs reservation as a state health resort, creating for such special purpose a temporary state commission, to be known as the Saratoga Springs commission, providing for its organization and duration, defining its powers and duties and making an appropriation therefor.

Became a law April 28, 1930, with the approval of the Governor.
Passed, three-fifths being present.

The people of the State of New York, represented in Senate and Assembly, do enact as follows:

Section 1. COMMISSION established; organization; purpose. A temporary state commission, to be known as the Saratoga Springs commission, is hereby created, to consist of seven members to be appointed by the governor, with the advice and consent of the senate, for the purpose of ultimately developing the Saratoga Springs reservation as a state health resort and spa for use by the public for balneological, therapeutic and other similar healthful purposes. The development of such reservation for public health purposes is hereby declared a policy of the state in accordance with the recommendations of the commission appointed pursuant to the provisions of chapter six hundred and sixty-eight of the laws of nineteen hundred twenty-nine. The Saratoga Springs commission is hereby constituted a body corporate and, in addition to the powers conferred upon it herein, it shall have, possess, use, exercise and enjoy any and all other powers conferred upon corporations in this state by the general corporation law which are not inconsistent with the provisions of this chapter. The governor shall designate one of such appointees as chairman of the commission and each member thereof shall be appointed for and hold office during the term of seven years from the date when this act takes effect. Any vacancy occurring for any reason in the membership of such commission shall be filled in like manner as is prescribed herein for an original appointment thereto, but a person appointed to fill a vacancy shall be appointed for and hold office during the unexpired portion only of the term of the member whom he succeeds. The members of such commission shall receive no compensation for their services, but shall be entitled to such traveling and other expenses within and without the state as may necessarily be incurred by them in the performance of their duties.

2. Definitions. The following terms, whenever used or referred to in this act, shall have the following meanings unless a different meaning clearly appears from the content:

1. The term "commission" shall mean the Saratoga Springs commission created in and by section one of this act.

2. The term "chairman" shall refer to the chairman of the Saratoga Springs commission.

3. The terms "reservation" or "reservation property" shall mean and include all the lands, properties, property rights, easements, mineral springs, wells and such other things as now constitute the Saratoga Springs reservation and over which, the conservation department through its division of Saratoga Springs reservation possessed and exercised full jurisdiction and control before the enactment of this act and also such other lands, properties, property rights, easements and other adjuncts and projects as may be constructed by or under the direction and supervision of the commission or acquired by it under the provisions of this act.

4. The term "director" shall mean the medical and scientific director of the reservation.

3. Principal office of commission. The commission shall set apart and provide for itself to be used by it as its principal office suitable and adequate offices in or near Saratoga Springs either within or without the reservation property. The commission may, however, meet in Albany or elsewhere within or without the state for the purpose of conducting any hearing, inquiry, study or investigation pertinent to the purpose to be accomplished by it.

4. Assignment and transfer of certain functions; powers and duties to commission. Jurisdiction, supervision, possession and control of all the lands, properties, property rights and easements, mineral springs, wells and all the other adjuncts constituting the Saratoga Springs reservation now possessed and exercised by the conservation

department acting by or through the division of Saratoga Springs reservation are hereby transferred to the commission for the term of seven years from the date when this act takes effect and all the functions, powers and duties of the conservation department pertaining to such reservation and hitherto by the conservation law assigned to, possessed by and imposed upon the division of Saratoga Springs reservation in the conservation department are hereby assigned to and shall hereafter be possessed by and imposed upon the commission for the term herinbefore specified. All the provisions of article fifteen of the conservation law and all other provisions of such law or of any other general, special or local law inconsistent with the provisions of this act are hereby suspended in their operation for the period during which the commission shall be operative and in existence as such and, upon the expiration of such period, the conservation department shall resume jurisdiction, supervision, possession and control of the reservation and shall become revested with all the functions, powers and duties relative to such reservation which the commission shall possess and exercise at that time and such department shall then exercise the same by or through the commission which shall be then continued as a division in the conservation department.

5. General powers and duties of commission. The commission shall have the power and it shall be its duty, subject to the provisions of this act, to conserve, maintain, control and develop each and every part of the reservation property. It shall prescribe and publish such rules and regulations to govern the maintenance, care, protection and preservation of the said property and the proper use of all the lands and waters therein contained and the sale, distribution and use of all waters, minerals and gases, as it may in its discretion adopt. It shall have the power to enforce all such rules and regulations and to impose and collect a fine for any violation thereof. Subject to the approval of the governor and for proper rentals or other payment or consideration and upon other proper terms and conditions, it shall have the power to grant leases or concessions for the use of any portion of the reservation property or of the waters and gases therein, thereon or thereunder, but every such lease and concession shall provide that the lessee or lessees, concessionee or concessionees of any of the property included in the reservation shall be at all times subject to the rules and regulations of the commission and shall reserve to the commission and its duly authorized representatives a reasonable right of inspection and supervision. The commission may prescribe the terms upon which any excess of mineral water and gas not used on said reservation, or used under such leases or concessions, shall be sold or distributed, and shall prescribe the names, labels and advertisements to be affixed to the bottles or other vessels containing such waters, gases or other products, and may itself sell or dispose of the same. The commission and each member thereof is empowered to administer oaths and take such testimony, subpoena such witnesses and require the production of such books, papers, records or other documents as may be necessary or pertinent to the subject of any study, inquiry or investigation to be made by it or conducted under its supervision. The commission may make or cause to be made scientific studies and experiments concerning kinds of illnesses and diseases which lend themselves to the treatment of the mineral waters, products and facilities of the reservation, and shall exercise exclusive control and supervision over the manner and method of the use of the products and facilities of the reservation.

6. Protection of reservation property. The commission is hereby empowered to adopt, compose, invent or devise any and every mark, name and device which it may see fit to use in connection with the sale and use of any of the products of said reserva-

tion and to register and file descriptions thereof as trade marks, or trade names, or otherwise, for the protection thereof, under any of the laws or statutes of the state of New York or the United States of America, or any other state or country in which the sale of such waters or products may be carried on. In its corporate name the commission may institute and prosecute any and all suits, actions and other proceedings to restrain or recover damages or penalties for the unauthorized use of such marks, names or devices by any other person or corporation; may institute and prosecute any and all suits, actions and other proceedings under the laws of the state of New York or of the United States of America, against any person or corporation for the violation of any such law regulating the sale of mineral water or preventing the adulteration thereof and to sue for and recover any penalty which may be imposed for the violation of any such law for the recovery of which the attorney-general of the state shall not bring action which thirty days ofter a written statement of the fact of such violation has been presented to him by the commission. The commission may bring any proper suit or action in equity, or at law, whether within or without the state, to protect and enforce the repute of the reservation, its springs, wells, mineral waters and gases, or to prevent any corruption, pollution, impairment, diversion or depletion thereof, or interference therewith, or to prevent the unauthorized or unfair use of the name of the state or the commission or any publication or use of any label or advertisement in connection with the reservation or with reference to the mineral waters and gases as are or may be distributed or are sought to be distributed or sold as products from the Saratoga Springs reservation.

7. Acquisition of lands and other properties by commission; procedure therefor. For the proper development and protection of the reservation property as a health resort and watering place, the commission shall have the power, from time to time, to select and acquire such lands in or near the reservation, and any rights, easements, or interest upon or in any lands, as it shall deem proper and necessary. The commission shall from time to time cause to be made by the department of public works maps of such lands, which, or rights and easements in which, it shall determine to take, which maps shall be certified by the chairman of such commission and filed in the office of the secretary of state and in the office of the county clerk of the county in which such land is situated and shall specify, with respect to each parcel of such land, whether the whole title thereof is to be taken, and, if the whole is not to be taken, the rights, easements or interest therein that are to be taken. From the time of the filing of any such map, the title of the lands, or rights, easements, or interests therein specified, shall become and be the property of the state of New York, and shall constitute a portion of the reservation property. The commission shall have the power at any time within sixty days after the filing of any such map, to fix and determine with each and any of the respective owners of any lands, rights, easements, or interest specified on such map thus filed, upon the fair value of such lands, rights, easements, or interest, and may agree upon a price to be paid therefor by the state, and accepted by said owners, respectively, and the amount thus agreed upon shall be audited by the comptroller and shall be paid therefor out of the state treasury, upon the certificate of the chairman of the commission and upon the written approval of the governor, out of any funds appropriated for that purpose. In case said lands, rights, easements, or interests, within the said sixty days from the filing of such map specifying such property, then such owner or owners may recover judgment for the value thereof in the court of claims as a claim against the state. From and after the acquisition of any land or interest therein by the commission, as hereinbefore provided, the same shall be

kept, remain and be known as a part of the reservation property, for the purposes of restoring and forever preserving the mineral springs, wells, mineral water, and the natural carbonic acid gas on, in and under said lands, and the rights, easements and interest acquired in, upon or over lands, the fee of which shall not be acquired by such commission, shall also be held for such purposes. No part of any lands of the reservation or rights, easements, or interest therein thus acquired shall be sold or aliened without the consent of the legislature except by lease or concession made, granted and limited as hereinafter provided. The commission may let any and all contracts in behalf of and in the name of the state for the carrying out of the projects and the construction of the buildings hereinafter in this act provided for and for the construction or alteration of such other buildings and the completion of such other projects as may be deemed necessary by the commission for the accomplishment of its purpose.

8. Employees of commission. The commission shall have sole and exclusive power to appoint and at pleasure remove a medical and scientific director who shall, subject to the supervision of the commission, be in full and complete charge of the health activities of the reservation; a superintendent of plant who shall have charge of and the care, custody and control of all the physical properties, appurtenances and appliances connected with or adapted for use in the reservation and who shall supervise the care, maintenance, repair and preservation thereof; a physical director, counsel, physicians, technicians, curators, keepers, laborers, clerks, stenographers, and such other assistants and employees as may be required by the commission. All employees except the medical and scientific director, the superintendent of plant, physical director, counsel, physicians and technicians of the commission shall be in the competitive class of the civil service. It shall fix the compensation of all such employees within the appropriations made available therefor, from time to time.

9. Encouragement of and assistance to private enterprises. The commission shall encourage capital investment in private enterprises and projects in furtherance of its work and may, subject to its regulations, provide for and assist in the construction by private individuals or corporations of sanitariums, hotels and other buildings upon lands of the reservation. It may lease to responsible persons or corporations, for a nominal rental and for a reasonable period, sites within the reservation property and may supply and furnish such persons or corporations, at nominal charge, with products of the reservation and the use of its facilities. The commission shall reserve at all times a reasonable right of inspection of and supervision over the affairs and conduct of such sanitariums and hotels and over the activities of such persons or corporations.

10. Projects to be planned and completed by commission.

1. The commission shall first cause to be made: (a) a scientific survey of the physical properties of the entire reservation, which may include the drilling of any test wells, to the end that accurate knowledge of the extent to which such reservation may be employed for health purposes may be acquired and strict medical control and supervision thereof obtained; and (b) an engineering, architectural, landscape and organization study to enable it more effectually to carry out its purpose.

2. Sites, either within the reservation or closely in proximity thereto, may be selected and acquired by the commission and the commission may erect or cause to be erected thereon, with all reasonable dispatch and as soon as sufficient moneys are made available thereof: (a) an administration building which shall contain, among other things, laboratories for diagnostic research and for systematic technical inquiry into the biological and biochemical nature of and the uses and possibilities of the mineral waters in, on, adjacent to or under the reservation property. Such building

and such other buildings as may be required by the commission shall be so constructed that additions may be made thereto from time to time as the need for them develops; (b) an adequate drink-hall which shall be centrally located on the reservation and which shall have in connection therewith, as necessary adjuncts thereof, promenades, a concert hall, solaria and drinking rooms for the inhalation and internal use of the various mineral waters; (c) a residence or residences for the medical and scientific director and for the physical director who shall be entitled to the use thereof while in the employ of the commission.

3. The commission is hereby authorized and empowered to negotiate with the Saratoga State Waters Corporation for the modification of its present lease, or for the execution of a new lease between such corporation and the state, so that such corporation shall be limited to the use of the springs now set apart for such purposes or which may hereafter be set apart for such purposes by the commission and shall be otherwise subjected to the rules, regulations and supervision of the commission.

4. The commission is hereby authorized and empowered to maintain and conduct the bath houses now on said reservation and such other bath houses as the commission may from time to time cause to be erected; to maintain and conduct the drink-hall or halls on said reservation and such others as may be built under the supervision of the commission; and also to maintain and conduct the bottling plant now on said reservation and is further authorized and empowered to enlarge or rebuild the same or construct a new and more adequate one as, in its discretion, will be most advantageous.

The commission shall have exclusive control of the walks and thoroughfares throughout the reservation and shall prescribe suitable traffic regulations and may close such parts thereof to vehicular traffic as it shall deem necessary. The entire reservation shall be in keeping with the plan and scope of a health spa. All walks in the reservation shall be uniformly and scientifically laid out and interrelated as to length, grade and pavement. Any building or appurtenance thereof now a part of the reservation property and no longer useful or not in keeping with the plan of the commission may be altered, razed or sold in the commission's discretion.

11. Capital fund of commission. The comptroller of the state of New York shall designate a depository or depositories for receiving all moneys appropriated by the legislature for the carrying on of the various business activities of the commission as authorized by this act or for such other purposes as may be provided by law. The commission shall deposit at least once in each week in the depository or depositories designated by the comptroller all moneys received by it for all purposes. Before any such deposit shall be received by any such depository, such depository shall execute and file with the comptroller a bond, in such penal sum, with such sureties and upon such conditions as shall be approved by the comptroller. The commission shall send to the comptroller weekly a statement showing the amount of moneys so received and the dates on which such deposits were made, which statement shall be certified by the proper officer of each depository receiving such deposit and shall also be verified by the oath of the chairman that the sums so deposited included all the moneys received by the commission during such week and up to the time of the last deposit appearing on such statement. The moneys so deposited by the commission shall be subject only to check or draft of the commission. Immediately upon the taking effect of this act, all of the moneys in the capital fund of the division of the Saratoga Springs reservation shall be transferred to the capital fund of the commission as and when created and established.

12. Equipment; how purchased. The commission is authorized, within the appropriations which may be placed at the disposal of the commission or from the capital fund herein provided for, to procure and maintain all necessary equipment, machinery, tools, apparatus or accommodations needful for the purposes of carrying on, protecting and maintaining the sale or disposal of the waters and gases of the reservation or in connection with the furnishing of baths or treatments in connection therewith. All contracts for the purchase of such equipment, machinery or materials shall be made on competitve bids, except when the amount involved does not exceed the sum of one hundred dollars, or the commission deems it to be in the interest of the state to purchase the same in the open market. Whenever proposals for furnishing equipment have been solicited by the commission, the parties responding to such solicitation shall be duly notified of the time and place for opening bids and they may be present, either in person or by attorney, and a record of each bid shall then and there be made. The commission shall furnish bidders, upon demand, with schedules and specifications giving a full description of the equipment, materials or machinery required, the date, manner and place of delivery and all other necessary information. The person or corporation offering to furnish such equipment, materials or machinery upon terms most advantageous to the state and who or which will give satisfactory guaranty and security for the performance thereof in case immediate delivery is not required, shall receive the contract to furnish such equipment, materials or machinery, unless the commission shall deem it to be in the best interest of the state to decline all proposals.

13. The sum of one million dollars ($1,000,000), or so much thereof as may be necessary, is hereby appropriated out of any moneys in the treasury not otherwise appropriated for the expenses and expenditures of the commission in carrying out the provisions of this act and such moneys shall be paid out of the state treasury on the audit and warrant of the comptroller, on vouchers approved by the chairman of the commission.

14. This act shall take effect immediately.

THE PRICES OF THE HOTELS AND BOARDING-HOUSES.

NAME.	Street.	No. of accomm'd'ns.	Per day, transient.	WEEKLY. June.	July and August.	September.	Proprietors.
Addison House	Matilda	75	...	...	...	...	
Albemarle	South Broadway	75	...	...	...	...	
Albion House	Front	35	$2 50	$8—$10	$10—$12	$8—$10	Walter Balfour.
American Hotel	Broadway	450	3 50	17— 21	21 00	17— 21	Bennett & McCaffrey.
Arlington	B'dway, cor. Div	350	3—4	17— 21	21— 25	17— 25	Campbell & Shaw.
Broadway Hall	North Broadway	100	2 50	10 00	10— 14	10 00	J. Howland.
Broadway House	B'dway, cor. Grove	50	2 00	10 00	10— 12	10 00	Wm. Wheelock.
Circular St. House	Circular	50	2—3	12— 15	15— 20	12— 20	J. Palmer.
Coleman House	Broadway	....	...	...	...	...	
Commercial	Church	80	2 00	5— 12	5— 12	5— 12	S. W. Smith.
Continental	Washington	200	3 50	15— 18	21— 23	15— 18	Adams & Mann.
Cottage Home	Broadway	....	...	...	...:...	...	Miss. L. Burbank.
Dr. Strong's	Circular	175	3 50	15— 20	20— 25	18— 25	S. S. & S. E. Strong.
Elmwood Hall	Front	65	2 00	7— 8	10— 12	7— 8	Orrin Ford.
Empire Hotel	Front, cor. Rock	50	2 00	7— 10	10— 15	7— 10	Levi Parris.
Empire House	Front	30	2 00	8— 10	10— 14	8— 10	Moses Breckett.
Franklin House	Church	100	2 00	7— 8	8— 10	7— 8	N. Waterbury.
Green Mount. House	Washington	50	3 00	10— 14	12— 20	10— 14	Mrs. Wooster.
Huestis House	South Broadway	60	2 50	15— 17	15— 18	15— 17	J. L. Huestis.
Kendall House	Railroad Place	20	2 00	5— 10	6— 14	5— 10	C. H. Kendall.
Manor House	South Broadway	50	2 00	8 00	10— 15	10— 15	R. S. Moscrip.
Mansion House	Sp'g av. n. Ex. Sp'g	50	3 00	10— 15	12— 20	10— 15	Mrs. E. G. Chipman.
Mt. Pleasant House	Broadway	50	2 50	12— 14	14— 18	12— 14	C. H. Tefft.
New York Hotel	Lake avenue	....	....	...	...	...	

SARATOGA. 161

NAME.	Street.	No. of accomm'd'ns.	Per day, transient.	WEEKLY. June.	July and August.	September.	Proprietors.
Pitney House	Congress	100	. ..	... ...	...	...	J. Pitney.
Spring St. House	Spring	20	2 00	12— 14	12— 14	12— 14	Wm. P. Carpenter.
Temple Grove	Circular cor. Spring	200	3—4	15— 20	18— 25	18— 25	H. M. Dowd.
Vermont House	Front, cor. Grove	120	2 50	8— 10	10— 15	8— 12	B. W. Dyer.
Wager House	South Broadway	25	2 50	14— 18	14— 18	14— 18	
Washington Hall	North Broadway	100	3 00	12— 15	12— 17	12— 17	A. J. Star.
Waverly House	North Broadway	150	3 00	15— 20	20— 25	15— 20	R. H. & J. E. Stoll.
Western Hotel	Church cor. Law'ce	40	1 50	7— 12	7— 12	7— 12	French & Co.
Wilbur House	Washington	100	3 00	10— 14	14— 18	14— 18	Mrs. Wilbur.
Andrews. Mrs. H	Franklin	50	$3 00	$10—$14	$14—$18	$10—$14	
Badgley, Mrs. B. S.	Div., near Square	15	2 00	8— 10	10— 14	8— 10	
Balch, Mrs. W. S.	B'way n. Town hall	25	3 50	17— 25			
Bennett, Mrs. C. F.	Regent cor. Un. av.	25	....				
Carpenter, Mrs. E.	North Broadway	20	...	10— 12	10— 12	10— 12	Prices vary
Chase, Mrs.	Division	15	2 50	12 00	14 00	12 00	
Cole, Mrs. E. W.	Phila., cor. Putnam	18	2 00	7— 12	10— 14	11— 14	
Cogswell, Mrs. R.	Phila., cor. Henry	20	2 50	10— 12	12— 15	10— 12	
Dyer, B. V.	Grove, cor. Front	120	2 00	8— 10	8— 15	8— 10	
Hart, Rev. J. S.	Circular	25	2 00	8— 10	10— 15	8— 10	
Hawley, A. B.	West Circular	20	....	5 00	5 00	5 00	according to
Kelley, G. M.	Beekman	8	....	6— 10	6— 10	6— 10	
Lebarron, H.	Front, cor. York	20	1 50	5— 6	8— 10	5— 6	
Morey, N. D	Franklin	75	3 50	15 00	17— 20	15 00	
Morse, E. G.	26 Spring	15	2 00	6— 10	10— 15	6— 10	
Pond, W. J.	Philadelphia	15	2 00	10— 12	10— 15	10— 12	
Reed.	Church, cor. R. R.			12— 20	12— 20	12— 20	rooms occupied.
Smith, Mrs. E. P.	Spring and Henry	25	2 50	12— 20	12— 20		
Smith, Mrs. T. I.	Church, cor. R. R.	20	....	7 00	7— 8	7 00	
Taylor, Dr. E. A.	Vandam, cor. Front	35	2 00	6— 8	8— 12	6— 8	
Thompson, Rev. J.	Wash., cor. Frank.	20	2 00	10— 12	12— 14	8— 10	
Thorn, Mrs. S. B.	Circular	35					

Entered according to act of Congress, by R. F. Dearborn, in the Office of the Librarian of Congress.

SARATOGA. 162

Prices of Saratoga Hotels and Boarding Houses.
Published in Dearborn: Saratoga Illustrated, *1873*

ANALYSES OF THE WATERS OF THE SARATOGA SPA

Hypothetical combination	Geyser	Coesa	Hathorn No. 2	Hathorn No. 3	Hathorn No. 1	Lincoln	Hayes	Karista	Old Red	State Seal
Ammonium chlorid	48.25	45.25	59.10	49.56	31.29	11.45	38.24	60.94	7.63	Trace
Lithium chlorid	21.07	20.52	64.49	75.85	21.69	24.54	24.07	39.16	6.94	None
Potassium chlorid	361.91	307.27	789.54	759.42	437.86	371.41	465.40	303.46	72.33	3.43
Sodium chlorid	2,010.48	6,370.30	8,594.84	7,454.05	3,578.81	3,099.78	5,941.82	2,941.04	869.04	0.12
Potassium bromid	9.23	2.00	160.00	97.60	13.33	20.00	30.00	8.56	12.50	None
Potassium iodid	1.10	1.60	4.80	3.78	1.14	Trace	1.25	1.00	.50	None
Sodium sulphate	None	None	None	None	None	None	None	None	Trace	6.35
Magnesium sulphate	None	None	None	None	None	None	None	None	None	18.10
Sodium metaborate	Trace	Trace	Trace	Trace	Trace	Trace	Trace	Trace	Trace	None
Sodium nitrate	Trace	Trace	Trace	Trace	Trace	Trace	Trace	Trace	Trace	Trace
Sodium nitrite	Trace	Trace	Trace	Trace	Trace	Trace	Trace	Trace	Trace	Trace
Sodium bicarbonate	2,213.78	1,617.08	424.71	547.72	942.89	1,346.85	712.76	1,384.51	295.46	None
Calcium bicarbonate	1,829.14	2,819.86	3,380.84	3,178.56	2,170.09	2,020.67	2,849.13	1,797.32	1,100.94	61.66
Barium bicarbonate	16.67	34.93	25.65	35.55	37.22	14.73	30.88	37.22	10.04	None
Strontium bicarbonate	Trace	Trace	Trace	Trace	Trace	Trace	Trace	Trace	Trace	Trace
Ferrous bicarbonate	9.94	19.59	40.07	12.48	18.85	78.04	10.82	31.33	22.29	Trace
Magnesium bicarbonate	735.89	1,650.54	2,244.88	1,918.61	1,166.96	1,264.20	1,626.90	1,119.66	436.30	14.95
Alumina	7.14	10.79	4.98	41.80	14.74	3.97	.74	21.13	1.99	Trace
Silica	19.40	13.20	14.40	11.00	20.00	40.60	10.80	21.80	38.00	5.60
Total solids	7,284.00	12,912.93	15,808.30	14,185.98	8,454.87	8,296.24	11,742.81	7,767.13	2,873.96	110.21

All of the above waters, except State Seal, are highly effervescent as they flow from the springs, containing from two to four liters of carbon dioxide per liter of mineral water.

These are the latest analyses available at the time of this printing.

Bibliography

Allen, Richard L., M.D. *An Analysis of the Principal Mineral Fountains at Saratoga Springs, together with General Directions for their Use*. New York: W.H. Graham, 1844.

_____. *Handbook of Saratoga and Stranger's Guide*. New York: W.H. Arthur, 1859.

Alsopp, Bruno. *A History of Classical Architecture*. London: Sir Isaac Putnam and Sons, Ltd.

Althaus, Julius, M.D. *The Spas of Europe*. London: Turner and Co., 1862.

The American Heritage Book of Indians. New York: American Heritage Publishing Co., 1861.

Amory, Cleveland. *The Last Resorts*. New York: Harper and Bros., 1952.

Anderson, G.B. *Our Country and its People. A Descriptive Biographical Record of Saratoga County, N.Y.* Prepared and published under the auspices of *The Saratogian*. The Boston History Co., Publishers, 1899.

Ant, H. and McClellan, Walter S., M.D. "The Physical Equipment for Administration of Health Resort Treatment." *Journal of the American Medical Association*, 1943.

Bacon, James G., M.D. *On the Medicinal Character of Hathorn Spring Water*. Albany: Van Benthuysen Printing House, 1879.

Bachelder, John B. *Popular Resorts and How to Reach Them*. Philadelphia: John B. Bachelder, Publisher, 1875.

285

Baird, J. E. "American Spa Therapy in the Treatment of Rheumatoid Diseases." *The Journal of Missouri State Medical Association*, July 1909.

Barnes, I., Irwin, W. R. and White, D. E. "Global Distribution of Carbon Dioxide Discharge and Major Zones of Seismicity." *United States Geological Survey Open File Report*, WRI, 1978.

Bates, G. H. *The Use and Value of Congress, Empire and Columbian Waters*. New York: Hotchkiss, 1866.

Baruch, Simon. *The Principles and Practice of Hydrotherapy*. New York: Wm. Wood and Co., 1897.

————. "Natural and Artificial CO_2 Waters in Cardiac Diseases." April 3, 1919.

————. "Discussion of Dr. Danzer's Paper: 'The Restorative Action of Baths on the Fatigued.'" May 1916.

————. "Carbon Dioxide Baths, Observations on their Action." *New York Medical Journal*, May 13, 1916.

————. "The Giving of Nauheim Baths in this Country." *Medical Record*, June 13, 1915.

————. "Nauheim Baths of Saratoga." Correspondence, *Medical Record*, June 10, 1916.

————. "The Nauheim Method." *Medical Record*, June 17, 1917, New York: Wm. Wood and Co., 1916.

"Report of Simon Baruch, M.D., on European Spas." *Report of the Commission of the State Reservation at Saratoga Springs*, Albany: J. B. Lyon Co., Printers, 1914.

————. "Saratoga as a Health and Recreation Resort." *Medical Times*, October 1913.

————. "The Therapeutic Resources of the Saratoga Springs." *New York Medical Journal*, June 10, 1916.

————. "Saratoga's Chance." *New York Times*, March 10, 1916.

Baudisch, Oskar, Ph.D., "Biological Function of Minor Elements." *Soil Science*, August 1945.

————. "Chemical Clues to the Origin of the Saratoga Mineral Waters." *Science*, Vol. 86, no. 224, December 10, 1937.

————. "Geochemistry of The Saratoga Basin: The Radioactivity of Saratoga Spring Waters and Rocks." *American Journal of Science*, Vol. 237, November 1939.

————, and George Heggen, "Qualitative Colorimetric Determination of the Iron in Biological Material." *Archives of Biochemistry,* Vol. 1, no. 2, 1942.

————. *"Magic and Science of Natural Healing Waters." Journal of Chemistry Education*, September 1939.

————. "Significance of Magneto-Chemistry in Studies of Trace Metals (1). Linkage of Nitric Oxide to Copper." *Archives of Biochemistry*, July 1945.

Baudisch, Oskar, Ph.D., *Biological Function of Trace Elements and Natural Mineral Water Research*, Le Congress International des Bains 1947 en Tchecoslovaquie, Marianske Lazne-Plestany., Compte Rendu, 1948.

Beazell, W.P., "The Spas of the Eastern United States." *Report of the Saratoga Springs Commission to the Legislature*, Legislative Document No. 70. Albany: J.B. Lyon Co., 1930.

Behrend, H.J., M.D., "The Role of Hydrotheraphy in Rehabilitation." *New York State Journal of Medicine*, October 15, 1944.

Bell, John, M.D., *A Treatise on Baths*. Philadelphia: Barrington and Haswell, 1850.

_____. *Baths and Mineral Waters*. Philadelphia: Literary Rooms, 1831.

_____. *The Mineral and Thermal Springs of the United States and Canada*. Philadelphia: Parry and McMillan, 1855.

Boas, Franz, "Romantic Folklore among Indians." *Romanic Review*, XVI, 1925.

Boethius, Axel, Ward et al., *Etruscan and Roman Architecture*. Penguin Books, 1970.

Bradley, Hugh, *Such Was Saratoga*. New York: Doubleday, Doran and Company, 1940.

Brewer, A. Keith and Baudisch, Oskar, "The Isotopes of Potassium and Lithium in Saratoga Mineral Waters and Cryptozoan." *Journal of the American Chemistry Society*, 1939.

Brandow, John Henry, *The Story of Old Saratoga*. Albany: Brandow Printing Co., 1919.

Brant, Marion, "Bottles." *The Antique Journal*, February 1971.

Britten, Evelyn Barrett, *Chronicles of Saratoga*. Brooklyn: Gerald K. Rickard, 1959.

Brown, Clayton H., *Greenfield Glimpses*. Greenfield Town Board, 1976.

Brun, A., *Recherches sur L'exhalaison Volcanique*. Geneva, 1911.

Bullard, Edward F., General, *History of Saratoga: An Address delivered at Schuylerville, July 4, 1867*. Ballston Spa: Waterbury and Inman, 1876.

Burchard, Thomas H., M.D., *Nature's Therapeutics, The Saratoga Waters*. New York, 1888.

Butler, Benjamin Clapp, *From New York to Montreal*. New York: American News Co., 1873.

Butler, Capt. J.P. *The Secrets of the Medicinal Waters of Saratoga Springs, The True Story of their Origins and Source of Supply*. Albany: Weed Parsons, 1888.

Callahan, E.T., "Convalescent Care at the Saratoga Spa." *New York Journal of Medicine*, Vol. 41, no. 6, March 15, 1941.

Chamberlin, R.T., *The Gases in Rocks*. Carnegie Institution, 1908.

Chandler, Charles F., "Account of Remains of Prehistoric Fire, High Rock Spring." *American Chemist*, December 1871.

Chandler, Charles F., "A Lecture on Waters - Mineral Waters." *American Chemist*, December 1871.

_____. *Report on the Seltzer Spring*. New York: Wynkoop and Hallenbeck, Printers, 1867.

Clayton, R.N. et al., "The Origin of Saline Formation Water, Isotopic Composition." *Journal of Geophysics Research*, Vol. 71, no. 16, 1966.

Coan, Titus Mundon, "Home Uses of Mineral Water." *Harper's New Monthly Magazine*, 1888.

Colden, Cadwallader, *The History of the Five Indian Nations*. Great Seal Books, Division Cornell University Press, reprint of the 1927 edition, 1958.

Colony, R.J., "Report on a Restudy of the Geology of the Saratoga Area and the Problem of the Mineral Waters." *Report of the Saratoga Springs Commission to the Legislature*, Legislative Document No. 70. Albany: J.B. Lyon Co., 1930.

Comfort, Alex, D.Sc., "Balneotherapy, Crenotherapy and Naaman, the Syrian's Law." *Medical Opinion*, August 1971.

Comstock, C.R., M.D., *Convalescence in Coronary Disease with* "Special Reference to Saratoga Spa Therapy." *Bulletin of the New York Academy of Medicine*, October 1940.

_____. "The Place of Spa Therapy in the Treatment of Cardiovascular Conditions." *Archives of Physical Medicine*, September 1945.

Craig, Harmon, "Isotopic Variations in Meteoric Waters." *Science*, Vol. 133, no. 3465, 1961.

Cronheim, George, "The Catalytic Action of Natural Mineral Waters." *Journal of Physics and Chemistry*, December 1943.

_____, and Wink, William, "Determination of Divalent Iron." *Industrial and Engineering Chemistry*, May 15, 1942.

_____. "Natural Mineral Waters as Catalysts in Biological Oxidations." *Archives of Biochemistry*.

Crook, James K., *The Mineral Waters of the United States and their Therapeutic Uses*. New York: Leo Bros., 1899.

Cushing, H.P. and Ruedemann, R., "Geology of Saratoga Springs and Vicinity." *New York State Museum Bulletin*, No. 169, February 1, 1914.

Darden, Genevieve (ed.), "A Visit to Saratoga, 1826." *New York History*, July 1961.

Dake, Percy W., "The Saga of Glass Factory Mountain." unpublished paper.

Dana, Hames Freeman, "Analysis of the Waters of the Congress Spring, Saratoga, New York." *The New York Medical and Physical Journal*, 1827.

Davison, Gideon Minor, *The Fashionable Tour or a Trip to the Springs in the Summer of 1821*. Saratoga Springs: G.M. Davison, 1822.

Davison, Gideon Minor, *The Visitor's Guide and Directory of Saratoga Springs for 1862*. Saratoga Springs: G. M. Davison, 1862.

Dawson, C. C., *The Eureka White Sulfur Spring Bathing Pavilion and Park*. Saratoga Springs: Saratoga Press, 1897.

_____. *Saratoga, Its Mineral Waters and their Uses in Preventing and Eradicating Disease and as a Refreshing Beverage*. New York: Russell Bros., 1874.

Dearborn, R. F., M.D. *Saratoga and How to See it, Containing a Description of the Watering Place with a Treatise on its Mineral Springs*. Albany: Weed Parsons and Co., Printers, 1873.

Deines, P., Langmuir, A. and Harmon, R. S., "Stable Carbon Isotope ratios and the existence of a gas phase in the evaluation of Carbonate Ground Waters." *Geochem, et Cosmoch, Acta*, Vol. 38, 1974.

Delamater, J. J., "Thesis on the Use and Abuse of the Saratoga Waters." *New York Journal of Medicine*, July 1844.

DeVeaux, S., *The Traveler's Own Book to Saratoga Springs, Niagara Falls and Canada*. Buffalo: Paxon and Reid, 1841.

Disturnell, J., *The Northern Traveler: Containing the Hudson River Guide and Tour of the Springs, Lake George and Canada*. New York: J. Disturnell, 1844.

Dorrance, S. and McClellan, W. S., "Effect of Natural Carbonated Baths on Rate and Amplitude of Pulse and Blood Pressure." *Archives of Physical Therapy*, Vol. XXI, March 1940.

Dorsey, Leslis, *Fare Thee Well: A Backward Look at Two Historic Centuries of Historic American Hostelries, Fashionable Spas and Seaside Resorts*. New York: Crown Publishing, 1964.

Dunn, Violet (ed.), *Saratoga County Heritage*. Syracuse: Salina Press, Inc., 1974.

Durkee, Cornelius E., *Reminiscences of Saratoga*. unpublished manuscript, Saratoga Springs: 1929.

Eager, M. A., *Pageant of Saratoga - Congress Park, Saratoga Springs*. New York: August 1912.

Emmons, E. E., M.D., *Empire Spring, Its Composition and Medical Uses*. Albany: Van Benthuysen, Printer, 1849.

Ferber, Edna, *Saratoga Trunk*. New York: Doubleday and Co., 1941.

Fish, Charles F., "The Mineral Springs of Saratoga." *Popular Science Monthly*, Vol. 19, 1881.

Fisher, Donald W. and Hanson, George F., "Revisions in the Geology of Saratoga Springs, N.Y. and Vicinity." *American Journal of Science*, November 1951.

Flexner, James Thomas, *Mohawk Baronet, Sir William Johnson of New York*. New York: Harper Bros., 1959.

Gibbon, Edward, *The History of the Decline and Fall of the Roman Empire*. New York: Heritage Press.

Gilpin, Henry Dilworth, *A Northern Tour, Being a guide to Saratoga*. Philadelphia: H.C. Carey and Lea, 1825.

Goldberger, Jacques, M.D., "Physiologic Fundamentals for Spa Therapy." *Archives of Physical Medicine*, September 1945.

Goldring, Winifred, "Algae Barrier Reefs in the Lower Ozarkian of New York." *New York State Museum Bulletin*, No. 315, 1938.

_____. "On the Origin of the Saratoga Mineral Waters - Cryptozoan Plant Nature and Distribution." *New York State Museum and Science*. Service Bulletin, Vol. 86, no. 2241, December 10, 1937.

Gordon, Lawrence S., *General Geologic History of Saratoga County and an Evaluation of Related Resources*. Report for the Saratoga County Planning Board, April 1975.

Granville, M.D., F.R.S., *The Spas of England*. London: Henry Colburn, Publisher, 1841.

_____. *The Spas of Germany*. London: Henry Colburn, Publisher, 1839.

Heggen, George, "A Quantitative Determination of Boron in Saratoga Mineral Waters." *American Journal of Science*, October 1944.

Herrara, y Tordesilla, *Historia General de los Hechos de los Castellanos en las Indias*. Book IX, Chapter XII, Vol. III. Madrid.

Howe, Louis McHenry, "Saratoga Springs." *New England Magazine*, 1905.

Howe, Timothy, *A History of the Medicinal Springs at Saratoga and Ballston*. Brattleboro, Vermont, 1801.

Howell, B.F., et al, "Correlation of the Cambrian Formations of North America." *Geological Society of America Bulletin*, Vol. 55, 1944.

Hunt, T. Sherry, M.D., "Chemistry of Natural Waters." *American Journal of Science and Arts*, 1865.

Irwin, J.A., *Hydrotherapy at Saratoga, A Treatise on Natural Mineral Waters*. New York: Cassell Publishing Co., 1892.

Isachsen, Y.W., "Possible Evidence for Contemporary Doming of the Adirondack Mountains, New York, and Suggested Implications for Regional Tectonics and Seismicity." *Tectonophysics*, Vol. 29, 1975.

Ishezu, R., *The Mineral Springs of Japan*. Karsha, Tokyo: Sankyo Kabushi, Publisher, 1915.

James, W.L., "The Geology of Saratoga Springs and Vicinity." unpublished paper, Saratoga Springs, 1921.

Jung, Frederick T. and McClellan, W.S., M.D., "Climate and American Health Resorts." *Journal of the American Medical Association*.

Kemp, J.F., "The Mineral Springs of Saratoga." *New York State Museum Bulletin*, No. 159, 1912.

Kemp, J.F., "Physiography of the Adirondacks." *Popular Science Monthly*, March 1906.

_____. "Physiography of Eastern Adirondack Region in the Cambrian and Ordovician Periods." *Geological Society of America Bulletin*, 1897.

_____, and Hill, B.F., "Report on the Precambrian Formations in parts of Warren, Saratoga, Fulton and Montgomery Counties." Albany: *New York State Geological Report*, 1901.

Kersley, George D., *Bath Water, the Effect of the Waters on the History of Bath and of Medicine*. Bath, Somerset: Lonsdale University Printing, Ltd., 1979.

Keyes, Fenton, "The Springs, Glass Houses and Bottles of Saratoga Springs, N.Y." *New York History*, April 1957.

Knapp, Clarence, "Saratoga Springs." *Holiday Magazine*, 1947.

Karacs, Richard, M.D., "Spa Treatment of Rheumatic Diseases in the United States. II Representative Spas." *Archives of Physical Medicine*, October 1945.

Lasher, Bruno, "The Wand of Manitou, The Development of a Great Health Resort by Public Enterprise." *Survey*, Vol. 44, June 5, 1920.

Lavery, Albert A., *A Geography of Saratoga County, State of New York*. Ballston Spa: Journal Print, 1905.

Marshall, C.A., *Saratoga Springs: An Illustrated Descriptive Story of this Resort, Historical Points of Interest and of the State Reservation*. Saratoga Springs, 1917.

McClellan, Walter S., M.D., "American Spas." *Archives of Physical Medicine*, August 1948.

_____. "The Clinical Use of Mineral Waters." *Medical Digest*, Vol. 17, no. 6, June 1949.

_____, Joslin, E., Maguire, G.M., "The Influence of Natural Carbonated Mineral Water Baths on Blood Pressure and Pulse Rates." *New York State Journal of Medicine*, Vol. 34, no. 3, February 1, 1934.

_____. "Nature of Therapeutic Agents used at Health Resorts, I Mineral Waters, II Peloids." *Journal of the American Medical Association*, February 12, 1944.

_____. "Physical Therapy in a Health Resort." *New York State Journal of Medicine*, Vol. 34, no. 14, July 1934.

_____. "Physical Medicine in the Treatment of the Aged." *Journal of the American Medical Association*, May 8, 1943.

_____. "Rehabilitation of the Arthritic Patient." *Transactions of the American Clinical and Climatological Association*, 1947.

_____. "Spa Therapy." *Intern 12*, October 1946.

_____. "Spa Therapy for Patients with Arthritis and Related Disorders." *Transactions of the International Congress on Rheumatic Diseases*.

McClellan, Walter S., M.D., "Spa Therapy for Patients with Chronic Disease." *New York State Journal of Medicine*. Vol. 53, no. 4, February 15, 1953.

_____. "Spa Treatment in Rehabilitation after Accidents and War Injuries." *Archives of Medical Hydrology*, April 1948.

_____. "Treatment of the Cardiovascular Patient in Spas." *Publication of the Saratoga Spa*, No. 20, 1953.

_____. "The Treatment Program of the Saratoga Spa." special issue of *Health News*, July 28, 1947.

McGuier, Henry, *A Concise History of High Rock Spring*. Albany: House of G. Van Benthuysen and Sons, 1867.

McKearin, George S. and Helen, *American Glass*. New York: Crown Publishers, 1948.

McKearin, Helen A., "Saratoga County Glass and its Personality, Oscar Granger." *Antiquarian*, Vol. XIV, no. 1, March 1930.

McLaren, Daniel, *The Saratoga Pavilion Fountain*. New York: Thompson and Hart, 1842.

MacGregor, Jean, "Founder's Kin Describes Glass Factory Origin." *The Saratogian*, June 27, 1947.

Martin, Alfred, M.D., "On Bathing." *Ciba Symposia*, Vol. 1, no. 5, Summit, N.J., August 1939.

Mather, William W., *Natural History of New York, Part IV, Geology*. Albany: Carroll and Cook, 1843.

Mazzulo, S.J., Agostino, P., Seitz, J.N., Fisher, D.W., "Stratigraphy and Depositional Environments of the Upper Cambrian Lower Ordovician Sequence, Saratoga Springs, N.Y." *Journal of Sedimentary Petrology*, Vol. 48, no. 1, 1978.

Meade, William, *An Experimental Enquiry into the Chemical Properties and Medicinal Qualities of the Principal Mineral Waters of Ballston and Saratoga in the State of New York*. Philadelphia: Harrison Hall, 1817.

Milas, William J., "The Adirondack Mountains." *New York State Museum Bulletin*, No. 193, January 1, 1917.

Miller, William J., "Geology of the Broadalbin Quadrangle, Fulton, Saratoga Counties, New York." *New York State Museum Bulletin*, No. 153, 1911.

_____. "The Geological History of New York State." *New York State Museum Bulletin*, No. 168, 1914.

Mitchell, S.L. "Medicinal Springs of Saratoga, Report on Experiments, Description of High Rock Spring." *The Rural Magazine* or *Vermont Repository*, Vol. 1, September 1795.

Monaghan, Nance, "High Rock Area, Buildings, Springs." unpublished paper, Skidmore College, 1975.

Moorman, J.J., M.D., *Mineral Springs of North America, How to Reach and How to Use Them*. Philadelphia: J.B. Lippincott and Co., 1873.

Moriarta, Douglas C., *The Natural Mineral Waters of Saratoga Springs, Some Suggestions as to their Use*. Saratgoa Springs: Brunner, 1898.

_____. "Practical Side of Saratoga Springs as a Health Resort." *Albany Medical College Annals*, October 1920.

Morse, Jedidiah, *The American Universal Geograph*. 5th edition, Part 1. London: 1805.

_____. "The Natural History of Medicinal Springs at Saratoga." *The Rural Magazine* or *Vermont Repository*, September 1795.

Nammuck, "Political Fraud and the Dispossession of the Indians." *The Kayaderosseras Grant*, Chap. IV.

Neuman, Karl, "Do Drink the Waters." *Travel Magazine*, October 1974.

New York State Conservation Commission, *Annual Reports*, 1916-1930.

_____. *Booklets of the Saratoga Reservation*, 1917-1928.

New York State Department of Health, *Report of Water Quality of Mineral Springs of Saratoga Springs, New York*. February 1973.

New York State, Saratoga Capital District, State Park and Reservation Committee, *Annual Report*. 1971-72, 1973-74.

New York State, Saratoga Springs Commission, *Report to the Legislature*. Legislative Document no. 70, Albany: J.B. Lyon Co., 1930.

North, M.L., M.D., *American Mineral Springs, Containing Analyses and Directions to Invalids*. Philadelphia: Lillis P. Hazard, 1852.

_____. *The Use and Value of Congress, Empire and Columbian Water of Saratoga Springs in the Treatment of Various Diseases and as a Refreshing Beverage*. New York: Hotchkiss's Sons, 1866.

_____. *Saratoga Waters or the Invalid at Saratoga*. New York: Saxton and Miles, 1843.

O'Callaghan, E.B., *The Documentary History of the State of New York*. Vol. I. Albany: Van Benthuysen, 1819.

Olsehki, Leonardo, "Ponce de Leon's Fountain of Youth: History of a Geographical Myth." *Hispanic American Historical Review*, Vol. XXI, no. 3, August 1941.

Peck, Charles E. and William B., *Peck's Tourist Companion to Niagara Falls, Saratoga Springs*. Buffalo: 1845.

Peterson, Phila, *An Indian Tale of Frontier Life - Saratoga, The Famous Springs*. 1787.

Pratt, George D., "New York State's Policy in Saratoga Springs." address given before the Saratoga Springs Medical Society, May 25, 1916. Albany: J.B. Lyon Co., Printers, 1916.

Preston, D.R., *The Wonders of Creation*. Vol I. Boston: John M. Dunham, 1807.

Prosser, C.S., "Notes on Stratigraphy of the Mohawk Valley and Saratoga County." *New York Museum Bulletin*, No. 34, 1900.

Richards, Thomas Addison, *Miller's Guide to Saratoga Springs and Vicinity*. New York: James Miller, 1873.

Ritchie, William A., "Introduction to Hudson Valley Prehistory." *New York State Museum and Science Service Bulletin*, No. 367, 1958.

Roberts, H.M., "The Therapeutic Value of the Spas and Health Resorts of America." *Medical Record*, March 1, 1919. New York: Wm. Wood and Co., 1919.

Robertson, D.S., *A Handbook of Greek and Roman Architecture*. Cambridge University Press, 1954.

Rowles, Catherine Bryant, *Tomahawks to Hatpins*. Lakemount, New York: North Country Books, 1974.

Ruedemann, Rudolph, "Different Views Held on the Origin of the Saratoga Mineral Waters." *Science*, Vol. 86, no. 224, December 10, 1937.

"Saratoga Glass is Now Antique." *The Saratogian*, July 6, 1935.

Saratoga Illustrated: The American Guide of Saratoga Springs, New York. New York: American Guide Book and Directory Co., 1912.

Saratoga Illustrated: The Visitor's Guide to Saratoga Springs with a Brief History of the Springs and the Village. New York: Tainter Bros., Publishers, 1887.

Saratoga, The Queen of Spas, Springs, Drives, Walks, etc. Saratoga Springs: Cozzens and Waterbury, 1891.

"Saratoga: The Waters." *Fortune*, August, 1935.

Saratoga Springs: A Look at Saratoga Springs, New York in Yesteryears. Saratoga Springs: Historical Society of Saratoga Springs, 1973.

Saunders, William, *A Treatise on the Chemical History and Medicinal Powers of the Most Celebrated Mineral Waters*, 1800.

Seaman, Valentine, *A Dissertation on the Mineral Waters of Saratoga*. New York: Samuel Campbell, 1793.

————. *A Dissertation on the Mineral Waters of Saratoga including an Account of the Waters of Ballston*. 2nd ed. New York: Collins and Perkins, 1809.

Sears, Reuben, *A Poem on the Mineral Waters of Ballston and Saratoga*. Ballston Spa: J. Comstock, 1819.

Shepherd, Daniel, *Saratoga: A Story of 1787*. New York: W.F. Fetridge and Co., 1856.

Shepherd, Edward, *An Address Delivered at a Commemoration of the Establishment of the State Reservation*. June 3, 1911.

Sheppard, Nathan, *Saratoga Chips and Carlsbad Wafers*. New York: Funk and Wagnalls, 1888.

Sigerist, Henry E., "American Spas in Historical Perspective." *Bulletin of the History of Medicine*, Vol. XI, no. 2, February 1942.

_____. "Collections on the History of Balneology in Saratoga Springs, N.Y." *Bulletin of the History of Medicine*, Vol. XX, no. 57, November 1946.

_____. "The Early Medicinal History of Saratoga Springs." *Bulletin of the History of Medicine*, Vol. XVIII, no. 5, May 1943.

_____. "Health Resorts." *Ciba Symposia*, Vol. XIII, nos. 1 and 2, April and May 1946.

Steele, John H., *An Analysis of the Congress Spring with Remarks on its Medicinal Properties*. revised by J. Perry, Saratoga Springs: G.M. Davison, 1861.

_____. *An Analysis of the Mineral Waters of Saratoga and Ballston together with a History of these Watering Places*. Saratoga Springs: G.M. Davison, 1831.

_____. *A Report on the Geological Structure of the County of Saratoga in the State of New York*. Saratoga Springs: G.M. Davison, 1823.

_____. "Description of High Rock Spring at Saratoga Springs." *American Journal of Science and Arts*, Vol. XVI, no. 2, July 1829.

_____. "Iodine in the Mineral Waters of Saratoga." *American Journal of Science and Arts*, Vol. XVI, no. 2, July 1829.

Stillman, William O., *A Guide to the Use of the Saratoga Mineral Waters*. New York: Tainter Bros., Merrill and Co., 1881.

Stoller, James H., "Glacial Geology of the Saratoga Quadrangle." *New York State Museum Bulletin*, No. 183, Albany: 1916.

_____. *Geological Excursions: A Guide to Locations in the Region of Schenectady and the Mohawk Valley and the Vicinity of Saratoga Springs*. Schenectady: Union Book Co., 1932.

Stone, William L., *Life and Times of Sir William Johnson*. Albany: J. Munsell, 1865.

_____. *Saratoga Springs, being a Complete Guide*. New York: T. Nelson and Sons, 1867.

"A Story of Society's Favorite Summer Resorts, Saratoga Springs, Ballston Spa and Lake George." *American Journal of Commerce*, New York: 1900.

Strock, L.W., "Geochemical Data on Saratoga Mineral Waters - Applied in Deducing a New Theory of their Origin." *American Journal of Science*, Vol. 239, no. 12, 1941.

_____, and Drexler, S., "Geochemical Study of Saratoga Mineral Waters by a Spectrochemical Analysis of their Trace Elements." *Journal of the Optical Society of America*, 1941.

Sullivan, James (ed.), *History of New York State*. Vol. I. Series Historical Publishing Co., 1927.

Sylvester, Nathaniel B., *Indian Legends of Saratoga and of the Upper Hudson Valley*. Troy: N.B. Sylvester and Co., 1884.

————. *History of Saratoga County, New York*. Philadelphia: Evarts and Ensign, 1878.

Syrcher, E.V., "The Meaning of Spa Therapy." *Bulletin of the Association of American Spas*, December 1955.

Taintor, Charles Newhall, *The Hudson River Route, New York to West Point, Catskill Mountains, Albany, Saratoga Springs*. New York: Taintor Bros., 1883.

Temple, George, *The American Tourists' Pocket Companion, or a Guide to the Springs, also a Poetical Address to the Nymphs of Saratoga Mineral Springs*. New York: D. Longworth, 1812.

Tenney, Samuel, "An Account of a Number of Medicinal Springs at Saratoga in the State of New York." *Memoirs of the American Academy of Arts and Sciences*, 2, part 1, 1793.

Therapeutic Saratoga. Souvenir of the American Medical Association meeting in Saratoga Springs, June 1902.

Thomson, William, A.B., M.D., *Spas That Heal*. London: Adam and Chas. Black, Publishers, 1978.

Thorndike, Lynn, *History of Magic and Experimental Science during the First Thirteen Centuries of Our Era*. New York: 1923.

Toole, Bob and Chris, *A Look at Saratoga: New Complete Illustrated Guide*. Ballston Spa: Journal Press, 1975.

Turner, G., "Description of the Chalybeate Springs near Saratoga with Perspective View of the Main Spring taken on the spot." *The Columbian Magazine*, Vol. I. Philadelphia: March 1787.

Wadely, George, "Bottles, Bottles Everywhere." *Adirondack Life*, Winter 1973.

Waite, Marjorie Peabody, *Seeing Saratoga*. Saratoga Springs Business and Professional Women's Club, 1935.

Wakeley, Philip S., *Saratoga in a Nutshell*. Glens Falls: Star Publishing Co., 1893.

Waller, George, *Saratoga, Saga of an Impious Era*. Englewood Cliffs, N.J.: Prentice Hall, Inc. 1966.

Walton, George E., *The Mineral Springs of the United States and Canada*. New York: Appleton and Co., 1873.

Weiss, Harry B. and Kemble, Howard R., *The Great American Watercure Craze, A History of Hydrotherapy in the United States*. Trenton, N.J.: Post Times Press, 1967.

————. *They Took to the Springs*. Trenton, N.J.: The Post Times Press, 1962.

Wheeler, R.R., "Cambrian-Ordovician Boundary in the Adirondack Border Region." *American Journal of Science*, Vol. 240, 1942.

White, D.E., "Magmatic, Connate and Metamorphic Waters." *Geological Society of America Bulletin*, Vol. 68, 1957.

White, Harry Hall, "New York State Glass Houses - Mt. Pleasant." *Antiques*, Vol. VIII, no. 1, July 1930.

_____. "New York State Glass Houses - Mt. Pleasant." *Antiques*, Vol. XVIII, no. 3, September 1930.

Whitnall, Harold O., *A Story in Stone of the Time when the Earth was Young - Petrified Gardens*. Hamilton, N.Y.: Colgate University Press.

Index

298